A Theology of the Jewish-Christian Reality

PART II
A CHRISTIAN THEOLOGY
OF THE PEOPLE ISRAEL

A Theology of the Jewish-Christian Reality

PART II
A CHRISTIAN THEOLOGY
OF THE PEOPLE ISRAEL

Paul M. van Buren

1817

HARPER & ROW, PUBLISHERS, SAN FRANCISCO

Cambridge, Hagerstown, New York, Philadelphia, Washington
London, Mexico City, São Paulo, Singapore, Sydney

FIRST HARPER & ROW PAPERBACK EDITION PUBLISHED IN 1987.

Library of Congress Cataloging-in-Publication Data

Van Buren, Paul Matthews.
  A theology of the Jewish Christian reality.

  Includes bibliographical references and indexes.
  Contents: pt. 1. Discerning the way — pt. 2. A Christian theology of the people Israel.
  1. Theology, Doctrinal   2. Judaism (Christian theology) I. Title.
BT78.V28   1987   231.7′6   83-4734
  ISBN 0-06-068823-8 (pbk.: v. 1)
  ISBN 0-06-254751-8 (pbk.: v. 2)

---

87 88 89 90 91 MPC 10 9 8 7 6 5 4 3 2 1

To David and the Fellows of
the Shalom Hartman Institute
for Advanced Judaic Studies
Jerusalem

Contents

Foreword

Having metaphorically found my way back into the task of theology, and being greatly encouraged by the reviews and responses to *Discerning the Way*, I now feel free to drop the metaphor and adopt a title more descriptive and recognizable by the discipline of theology. *Discerning the Way* constituted the prolegomenon, that which had to be said first, of a Theology of the Jewish-Christian Reality. I would hope that this second volume can be read with profit by one who has not read the first, but what needed to be said first is, of course, the foundation for what is to be said here.

In keeping with the more disciplined title, I have begun each chapter with a thesis, explicating it in the course of the chapter. This second Part is nearly twice as long as the first, and I apologize to my readers for the resulting extra cost, but not for the length itself: the subject matter fully merits careful attention.

I would alert my readers to the fact that the task undertaken here had to be performed on a tightrope: the subject is the teaching of Judaism, but the author is doing Christian theology. In writing this book a Christian theologian has been listening to, learning from, and incorporating the witness of Israel into Christian theological reflection. This is a work of Christian theology as I believe it needs to be done once the church has confessed the continuing validity of the covenant between God and the Jewish people. I am not sure that I have always kept my balance on the rope, and I feel acutely the lack of teachers in this enterprise, but I have been sustained by the thought that if I have made mistakes, I shall at least have provided others with a point of departure from which they may do the same work better in the future.

I presume that this volume will have Jewish readers, as the Prolegomenon has (indeed, the fullest, most penetrating, and to my mind fairest review of the latter that I have seen was by Rabbi Shamai Kanter in *Conservative Judaism*). I trust, however, that Jewish readers will remember that this book was not written for them, and be tolerant of a Gentile who came to this task too late in life to acquire familiarity with the wealth of Jewish tradition and learning. They must wait for a new generation of Christian theologians, trained in the language and methods of study for firsthand access to the sources of Judaism. It will be obvious to any Jewish scholar that I am an outsider using secondhand material. I can only do what I am able, and hope that others will build more soundly on this crude beginning.

I owe special thanks to Dr. David Hartman and the Fellows of the Shalom Hartman Institute for Advanced Judaic Studies in Jerusalem, a community of halakhically trained and oriented Israeli scholars, philosophically sophisticated, and committed to the renewal of Judaism in the political and social reality of the modern Jewish state. Throughout an incredibly stimulating month, they wrestled with me over an earlier draft of this book, chapter by chapter. The opportunity for a Christian theologian to submit his work to the sympathetic but critical analysis of such a group may be a "first" in the history of the Jewish-Christian reality; it was in any case a far cry from the medieval disputations. This book and its author gained much from the experience. I learned from them, not least, that to every page there will be some Jews who will assert that they cannot recognize themselves in what I say of them, but that others will insist that my interpretation is fair. Let the Christian reader therefore be aware that what follows is what *one* Christian has heard and learned from out of the wealth and diversity of

Judaism. Other Christians can surely learn more and otherwise from other Jews.

I wish to express my thanks to the National Endowment for the Humanities for a Fellowship that provided me an uninterrupted year in which to complete this book.

ABBREVIATIONS

B.C.E. Before the Common Era
C.D. Church Dogmatics, English translation of *K.D.*
C.E. The Common Era, counting from the traditional year of Jesus' birth
E.J. Encyclopedia Judaica, 16 vols. and supplements, Jerusalem, 1972 ff
H.T.R. Harvard Theological Review
J.E.S. Journal of Ecumenical Studies
K.D. Die Kirchliche Dogmatik, by Karl Barth, 1932-1967
NAB The New American Bible
NEB The New English Bible
O.E.D. The Oxford English Dictionary
RSV The Holy Bible, Revised Standard Version
Th.W.z.N.T. Theologisches Wörterbuch zum Neuen Testament, 1933-1979

CHAPTER ONE

Introduction

A Christian theology of the people Israel, as an integral part of the church's self-critical reflection, asks about the church's duty and ability to hear the testimony of the Jewish people to God. Its necessity lies in Israel's election and the consequent dependence of the church's testimony upon that of Israel to the God and Father of Jesus Christ as Creator and Redeemer. Its foundations are the Scriptures of Judaism as confirmed both by the Apostolic Writings and the life of the Christian church, and also by the Rabbinic Writings and life of the Jewish people, including their rejection of the church with its faith in Jesus Christ. Its goal is the definition of Israel's contribution to the church's service to God and, as a part of this, its service to Israel.

1. THE PROBLEM OF A CHRISTIAN THEOLOGY OF ISRAEL

i. The task and the criterion of theology

The opening sentence of the thesis of this chapter proposes a preliminary definition of the subject of this second volume of a systematic *Theology of the Jewish-Christian Reality*. As an "integral part of the church's self-critical reflection," our subject here is "the church's duty and ability to hear the testimony of the Jewish people to God." Before developing and testing the adequacy of this definition, however, we should face up to the difficulties of the task before us. This can be done properly only in the context of an understanding of the task of theology.

The nature and necessity of theology have been addressed in

the prolegomenon, *Discerning the Way*. Since the church claims to have a Lord and to exist because it has been called to God's service through that Lord, it may not say or do anything it wants. It is responsible — answerable — to God for its words and life, for it has been set on a way through history with him and his people Israel. But being not only human and creaturely, but also fallible and sinful, the church can wander, and has all too often wandered, from the path into which God has called it. The church needs constantly to ask itself, therefore, about how it is walking, where it is going, whether it is sufficiently attentive to the directions of the Lord of its journey. This self-critical undertaking is what I mean by theology.

What I have described is sometimes called "systematic theology," with special reference to the coherence demanded by any serious reflection and which is urgently required when the focus is the God who is one. Sometimes it is called "dogmatic theology," with special reference to the major signposts which early walkers have erected along the way. In either case we should be aware of dangers. When "system" rules in theology, another Lord has taken control of critical reflection; when "dogma" rules, the church's reflection is in danger of ceasing to be self-critical.

Theology is a task of reflection, not prophecy. In theology one does not assert, "Thus says the LORD," but one asks, "Is this not what the LORD says?" And one *does* say, "In that case, thus ought we to say and do in response."

As I argued in the prolegomenon, this critical reflection is carried out in an attempt to be faithful to the One who has called us into the Way, as we have tried to understand him through the witness of Israel, given in its Scriptures, and of those who first set out upon the Way for Gentiles, given in the Apostolic Writings. These documents cannot have the last word, but they must always have the first word, and any additional word has to be forged in strenuous conversation with them. We cannot avoid the responsibility of having to say the momentarily last word ourselves, in response to the One whose word we believe we have heard in those documents. In presenting the matter thus, I aimed to do justice to the conviction of the sixteenth-century Reformers of the church, that the Bible not only ought to have but in fact *had* — not least in their own time — the power to exercise a decisive freedom over the church from time to time. The Jewish tradition of taking responsibility for what is made of sacred texts in the present, forced me to recognize that there is no way to the Scriptures or the Apostolic Writings except by way of the interpretation of those, ourselves included, who have come after.

The proximate criterion for the critical work of theology, then, is not simply the Bible, for we never have the Bible pure and simple, *sola scriptura*, but always and only the interpreted Bible. There is no way round our own interpretation to hearing the One who is the ultimate criterion for theology, the God of Israel whom the church has come to know through Jesus Christ. In acknowledging the Bible as its Canon, its rule or norm, the church agrees to go on wrestling with this collection of texts in its effort to understand the One who alone has the last word over the rightness or wrongness of its journey with him through history.

No responsible work of Christian theology today should ignore the powerful argument of Karl Barth's *Church Dogmatics* that the sole criterion of theological work is and can only be the Word of God as attested in the Bible. The word of God is God himself in his self-revelation, and this is, according to the biblical witness, so Barth argued, identical with Jesus Christ. That witness, of course, includes the Hebrew Scriptures, but these too are to be read as witnesses to Jesus Christ, since that is how they were understood by the authors of the Apostolic Writings (the "New Testament"). That apostolic interpretation of the Scriptures was binding, Barth argued, because it was made under the impact of the Word of the God of Scriptures, made flesh in Jesus Christ. In practical effect, then, the working criterion of theology becomes the whole Bible, from Genesis to the Revelation of John, understood as a multiple witness to Jesus Christ.

The merits of this proposal should be noted. (1) It is consistent with the church's initial acknowledgment of the Scriptures of Israel, as well as of the Writings of the Apostles (or apostolic communities), as its Canon. The Marcionite alternative of rejecting those Scriptures would have made nonsense of the Apostolic Writings. (2) It is consistent with the Apostolic Writings' use of those Scriptures as witnesses to Christ. The authors of the Synoptics, of John, Paul, and the authors of the other letters and writings which make up the collection, were all one in this use of Scripture. (3) It is consistent with the centrality of Christ as Lord of the church that has been confessed throughout the history of the church. Barth's definition of the criterion of theology can therefore hardly be considered eccentric.

Theology, as defined and carried out by Barth, is the church's self-critical task of measuring the church's proclamation, its talk of God, by the criterion of the whole Bible, understood as the witness to Jesus Christ as God himself in his self-revelation. Barth's whole theological achievement was built on this foundation. Implied in the foundation as its premise is the conviction that the primary task of the church is proclamation, epitomized in preaching. The church — e.g. in the person of the preacher — takes up in its own words the witness of the biblical authors. Insofar as the church's witness conforms to that of the Bible, and insofar as the witness of the biblical authors is true to the reality of God's self-revelation, then it *can* come about, always and only by the free grace of God (*ubi et quando visum est Deo*), that the preaching of the church *becomes* the Word of God, God himself in self-revelation in the human words of the fallible church. The foundation of Barth's proposal about the criterion of theology, then, rests on the premises that (1) the primary God-given task of the church is to preach the Word of God, and (2) the central and controlling content of the Bible is God's self-revelation.

I am aware that in *Discerning the Way* I departed somewhat from Barth, and I am also aware that, for Barth, there could be no such thing as a small departure on this matter of the criterion of theology. I had and have no interest in taking the paths of either Vatican I Roman Catholicism or Protestant Modernism, as Barth defined them. Each in its own way incorporated the criterion of theology and the church into the church itself. Roman Catholicism, as Barth defined it out of its own teaching and theologians, placed the final criterion in the infallible teaching office of the church itself, whereas Protestant

Modernism located it in the piety and religious insight of the individual believer. Either way, the church ceases to acknowledge that it is a company under orders, that it has a Lord to whom it is answerable as a slave to its master. These do not seem acceptable alternatives and I do not wish to criticize Barth from either of these external — and, as he labled them accurately, heretical — positions. Rather, I want to raise some questions of internal criticism from a position that appeals, along with Barth, to his own criterion: The Bible. My questions are addressed to the basic premises of his proposal concerning the criterion of theology.

1. Is it the case, according to the Bible, that the single primary commission of either God's people or God's church is proclamation? Israel's commission to be a kingdom of priests, a holy nation, a light for the nations, and to do justly, love mercy, and walk humbly with its God, and the church's calling to be a witness to Jesus Christ and the body of Christ, and to live in Christ and be conformed to him, both attested to in the Bible, will surely include talk of God and also something like preaching as a form of proclamation. But proclamation in whatever form is not obviously prior to talk *to* God in prayer and worship, according to the Bible. Worship, praise, prayer, adoration, and confession of sin seem more central to the glad task of Israel and the church, according to the Psalms. According to the Scriptures, Israel's central commission is to do all the commandments and ordinances of Torah. *Halakhah*, walking in the Way, is Israel's commission. According to the Apostolic Writings, "follow me," the life of discipleship, is the primary commission of the church. According to the special Johannine testimony, the "new commandment" — which is not new at all — is "that you love one another." For both Israel and the church, the first and overriding commission is to love God with all that they have and are, and then, in the light and context of that commission, to love the neighbor. Within and as a part of this great commission, proclamation will surely find its place, but the self-critical reflection which the church needs must consider the whole life of the church, not just its scripturally based preaching. It needs to ask of course whether the preaching of the church is faithful to the scriptural word, but it must also ask, among other things, how it has come to pass that the church has ignored and felt it could live without acknowledging its relationship to Israel, and whether it is obeying a commission from God in

doing so. Because we see the commission of Israel and the church more broadly than Barth, we cannot so narrowly conceive the Bible itself as the Word of God, but must see it also as Torah, as instruction, as pointers to the Way into which God has called Israel and the church to walk with him through history.

The Bible is of course also a witness to God's revelation, but it witnesses above all (and this Barth knew) to him who is the living God, and so to One who asks whether we hear his voice today, a voice which we must believe to be the same one heard by prophets and apostles, but one which may yet have a new thing to say to us now. I am not proposing that God has a different thing to say, but that he may have a different way for us to understand what he has told us before. The church has ever again to return to, read, and ponder the Bible in order to hear not only what its authors had to say, but also, through attention to them, to attune its ear to the voice its authors claimed to have heard. The church of God has no more pressing business than to attend to that voice, since it is the voice of its Lord. It needs constantly to ask itself what that voice asks: whether it will choose the life that has been chosen for it. The criterion for this self-critical work will be Israel's and the church's Lord himself, no other than the One to whom the Bible bears witness, but also not other than as the Bible testifies of him, as Lord of his creation and of his Way for them through history.

2. Is it the case, according to the Bible, that revelation — in Barth's phrase, "what the Bible calls revelation" — is essentially God's *self-*revelation? We can begin by noting that the word "revelation" occurs only in the Apostolic Writings and never in the Scriptures. The verb *galah*, to uncover and so to reveal, does occur in the Scriptures in reference to God's uncovering what is hidden, but in only eighteen verses, seven of them in the book of Daniel. "Revelation" is therefore primarily a theological term, a term of interpretation of the Bible, and if it should become a central term for theology, as it did for Barth, then it would be more accurate for us to speak of "what Barth called revelation." "Revelation" *is* an apostolic concept, occuring thirty-eight times (plus two synoptic parallels), but since twenty-one of these are in the undisputedly genuine Pauline letters, it would be more accurate to call it a Pauline concept.

Is it the case, though, that when the concept does occur in the Bible, the reference is to divine *self*-revelation? Only one passage of Scripture bears this meaning, where we are told that God revealed himself to Samuel (1 Sam. 3:21). Ordinarily, God reveals his will, a command, a secret, Jesus Christ at the Last Day. Revelation, according to the Bible, then, is scarcely ever divine *self*-revelation. That is far too narrow an interpretation of the biblical *Deus dixit*. The Bible does witness to God's unveiling of himself as the veiled and hiding One, but it does so as a small element of its witness to God as the Definer and Provider of the Way, of his will and purpose for his people and his church, in their service to the divine purpose of creation. Revelation therefore takes the form primarily of Torah as the path for Israel, a path of prayer, praise, justice and mercy, and just plain obedience to the commandments, and of Jesus as the maker of a Way of righteousness, prayer, praise, and self-giving for the Gentile church.

The issue is no small matter, for it should be recalled that out of an analysis of the proposition "God reveals himself," Barth developed the fundamental first step in his highly original doctrine of the Trinity. His analysis of the concept of self-revelation, which he took to be central to the biblical witness, led him to say that in revelation God posited himself a second time, revealing thereby a distinction in himself, two ways of God's being himself, to be designated Father and Son. Self-revelation, Barth thought, meant that God was himself a second time: he was himself in a way that reduplicated himself.

Barth's conclusion, however, is no more valid than his analysis. We ask, then, is this a reasonable analysis of the concept of "self-revelation?" I think not. If you reveal yourself to me, you allow me to come to know you more fully than I might otherwise, but you do not posit yourself a second time. You are not yourself in a "second way of being yourself" (*Seinsweise* was Barth's term). You do not establish or reveal a distinction in yourself, as one who reveals yourself, on the one hand, and as the self that you reveal on the other. Humpty-Dumpty may talk this way but not fastidious users of English (or German, for that matter. It is interesting that Barth's contemporary, Franz Rosenzweig, made almost the identical mistake in his analysis of revelation. Cf. *Der Stern der Erlösung* (1976), 177, E.T. 158f). Barth's tortured analysis of the concept of revelation refers to God, of course, not to you and me, but we have no other words to use when we speak of God than those we use of ourselves. The inadequacy of all our language when pressed into the service of speaking of our Creator should be kept in mind, but if we risk the attempt, following the Bible's lead, then we have no choice but to use the only language we have. Our analysis of it, therefore, can only be one that serves to clarify it in this as in any other use — or misuse.

In the light of these questions to Barth, we conclude that we were not wrong in developing the Prolegomenon to our *Theology of the Jewish-Christian Reality* around the concept of the Way, rather than that of the Word of God, or revelation, and that we had no alternative but to develop the doctrine of the Trinity within it as a testimony to the action of the God of Israel, and therefore to the God who so acted as to call the Gentiles into his service, alongside Israel, by his Spirit, through Jesus Christ. The result may be called a historical-functional doctrine of the Trinity, but it made room for a doctrine of the essential Trinity, not constructed out of a strained analysis of a theological concept, but as testimony to the conviction that God was truly himself in doing this strange new thing of producing, alongside his people Israel, also his Gentile church.

This discussion, I must add, reflects the experience of wrestling with Barth's *Church Dogmatics* on these matters, an exercise that has proved to me once more that no one has yet produced a systematic theology for the church which is more worthwhile to ponder, not least because Barth took the trouble to explore every conceivable issue. As he was the first to admit, his theology like every other was addressed to the church of a particular time and place. The service he did the church of German-speaking Protestantism of the 1930s to 1960s has still much to teach us. He saw far too dimly, however, something which has become today much clearer: the reality of postbiblical Israel, and especially Israel today in its land and in the Diaspora. To see this reality and to take the Jewish people seriously onto the agenda for Christian reflection leads to more departures from Barth's thought than a revision of his understanding of the criterion and task of theology. Nevertheless, we shall do well to keep on listening to and arguing with Karl Barth. He still has questions to put to us that the church would do well to answer.

The question remaining from the above discussion is whether we have made clear our criterion for making theological judgments. The honest answer, detectable in the thesis of this chapter, is that ours is not as clear as Barth's. We cannot honestly point to the Bible and say, there is our norm. Our norm includes and is even centered on the Bible, but it is the Bible as it has been carried and interpreted, not only by the church, but also by the Jewish people. This means that we are more in danger than Barth of letting the church be, at least to a degree, its own norm and so become its own Lord. Our intent is surely otherwise. Our intent is to discern the finger and voice of the LORD God of Israel in the postbiblical history of both Israel and the church, as well as in the Scriptures and the Apostolic Writings. We shall let this later history have a word in our reflection on the way in which the apostolic authors interpreted the Scriptures, and we shall listen to Israel's reading of those Scriptures alongside that of the church, because we see so clearly what Barth saw but dimly: living Israel as a reality which witnesses to God and the divine purpose for creation. We can only be glad in departing from him that we have had Barth in our midst and have him still in his books. He reminds us of the risks we are running in widening the norm of criterion for the self-critical task of God's Gentile church.

The risk of theology is the risk of faith: it has to be carried out in fear and trembling, as well as with joy, because it is a movement which we trust (but can never know for sure) to be part of the response that God asks of his church here and now. In this risk, then, we ask about a Christian theology of Israel. We ask *coram Deo* and as his Gentile church whether we should say something among ourselves about his people Israel whom we know as our Jewish neighbors in this world. There are weighty reasons for answering, No. Before turning to yet weightier reasons for saying, Yes, we should consider the following difficulties.

ii. Our anti-Judaic tradition

A major difficulty for the attempt to speak positively among ourselves of the Jewish people is that there are almost no precedents in our conversation over the past eighteen centuries for doing so. Some of us are discovering a fresh way in which to listen to the apostolic authors, especially Paul, which enables us to find there the beginnings of a positive and respectful (as well as critical) way in which to speak of *post-Christum* Israel, but this is a new discovery. Whether we be right or wrong in this new reading of Paul today, from the second until well into the twentieth century, our talk about the Jewish people has been almost entirely negative.

In his *Israel und die Kirche* (1980), the German theologian B. Klappert has summed up the alternatives from the past, still alive in the writings of recent or contemporary German theologians. He lists five different views of Israel, and they all lead to the conclusion that Israel has lost its special character as the elect people of God: (1) it is simply replaced by the church; (2) the remnant of Israel has been integrated (by conversion) into the church; (3) Israel is only the type of the church; (4) Israel is the exemplary negative foil of the church; and (5) Israel has no special character since Christ, being only part of the mass of humanity standing in need of justification.

Klappert then develops what he calls a "dependent-participatory model" which would assure for Christian theology, he argues, a proper affirmation of Israel's continuing election: gentile Christians are dependent on the election of Israel and on the fulfillment of the election of all Israel in Jesus Christ: through Christ they participate in the election of and promises to Israel. So defined, however, the model loses touch with historical reality. This can be seen when we recall, for example, that the election of Israel became historical in the covenant, and that life in the covenant means faithfulness to Torah. We may then ask, is this Torah-living something in which Christians are also to participate or has Israel's election been abstracted from Torah in Klappert's model, because Torah has been fulfilled in Christ? Or we may recall that the center of Israel's covenant contains the promise of the land. Are Gentile Christians heirs to that promise too? How? If Klappert's proposal sounds abstract, it should be remembered that it must be difficult to think concretely about the Jewish people when one has no Jewish colleagues or students and precious few as neighbors. The more serious difficulty concerning the concept of fulfillment I shall address later in this chapter.

A severe handicap to the development of a positive Christian theology of the Jewish people is that we have never had one, that our evaluation of the Jews has been consistently negative, and that consequently we would have to proceed without any guidelines from the past. We could receive no help from the Fathers of the church, its great medieval theologians or its Reformers of the sixteenth century. Indeed we shall hear no voices to help us along until we come to the few who are working on the problem today.

iii. *The problematic of a theology about others*

The second difficulty standing in the way is the proper hesitation we may have about developing theologies about other people. Theology is basically an activity of and for the church. In Christian theology, Christians have addressed themselves, by and large, to themselves, concerning their own apprehension of how God has dealt with them, what he is doing for and with them, and how they should respond to him. Are Christians in any position to be telling others what their significance is in the sight of God? If this is a general problem, in the case of the Jews it becomes acute, for over the centuries a large part of their difficulties has arisen from the fact that the church *did* have a theology of Israel, namely as the Israel that had refused to accept its Messiah and therefore had been rejected by God. In the course of that history, Jews have suffered much from having been made into negative figures in the church's theology. Would it not then be best to listen sensitively to the voices of Jews who ask that we leave them out of our theology and simply treat them as we at least claim we ought to treat all others: as human beings made in the image of God? Why need there by any special Christian theology of the Jews? Why should there be, in this particular case, a theology of and about these particular others?

iv. *Actual Israel and the Jewish negation*

We come finally to the greatest obstacle in the path before us. If in spite of the objections considered we are to pursue a positive theology of the people Israel, we would have to take seriously Israel as it is. This poses problems. In the first place, the majority of Jews do not believe in their own election as God's Israel. They do not see themselves as we would have to consider them if we were to develop a *theology* of Israel. Would not such a theology, then, be dealing in abstractions, speaking of an Israel that does not exist, or exists only quite partially, as the people of God? How can a Christian theology of Israel as the Israel of God not end up as a theology of an Israel that is not identical with the actual Jewish people? Would it not then be one further extention of the church's long tradition of talking about the Jews on the basis of the Bible, while ignoring the living Jews of whom it pretended to be speaking?

Serious as is this problem, it is as nothing compared to the other hazard which confronts a Christian theology of Israel that intends to have in focus the living Jewish people. If we have actual, historical, living Israel in view, then we are confronted by the fact that throughout their long history since the first century of the Common Era, the Jews have insisted that the church is wrong in its central judgment concerning Jesus of Nazareth. Judaism has not lived from this negation, it must be pointed out. On the contrary, it has lived from its faithfulness to Torah and Torah's giver. Nevertheless, as a part of that faithfulness, it has felt obliged to give an unambiguously negative judgment on the faith of the Christian church. It has denied that Jesus is the Messiah of Israel, the Son of God, and it has had at best the gravest doubts that with our doctrine of the Trinity we were still speaking of the one God. In a word, Israel has said an unyielding and continuing No to the Christian church and its Jesus Christ. How then can there possibly be a positive theology of Israel, one that takes them seriously and therefore takes this No seriously? Is it possible, either logically or psychologically, for the church to deal positively with this negation of its own fundamental convictions? This difficulty lies at the very heart of the task before us.

The difficulty is illustrated sharply in a Jewish response to the document "Toward the Renewal of the Relationship of Christians and Jews," adopted by the Rhineland Synod of the Evangelical Church in Germany on January 11, 1980, perhaps the most positive official church statement on the subject to have appeared up to that date, and written in the form of a classical Protestant Confession of Faith by the largest *Landeskirche* of that church. At the heart of this document it says, "we confess Jesus Christ the Jew, who as the Messiah of Israel is the Savior of the world and binds the peoples of the world to the people of God." To this Pinchas Lapide, a Jewish theologian, has remarked: "There is no [other] example in the history of the world's religions of one faith-community trying to prescribe for another what role a person — even a bringer of salvation — has to play in the sacred history of that other" (B. Klappert and H. Starck, eds., *Umkehr und Erneuerung*, 1980, 241). What are we to say when, to the Christian assertion that Jesus is the Messiah of Israel, Israel says that we are simply wrong? If our reply is that Israel is wrong, how can there then be a positive Christian theology of Israel? If on the other hand we accept Israel's witness on this point, then could a resulting theology of Israel still be Christian?

2. DEFINITION OF A CHRISTIAN THEOLOGY OF ISRAEL

i. Not a report on Jewish teaching

In the face of these difficulties, the definition of a Christian theology of Israel that would be both Christian and also about the real, living Jewish people requires painstaking precision. As an aid to this, it will be useful to make clear what such a theology will not be.

First of all, it will not consist of a report on Jewish theology, although the importance of such reports for a Christian theology of Israel cannot be overestimated. I have in mind such a work as George Foot Moore's ground-breaking and now classic *Judaism in the First Centuries of the Christian Era*, first published in 1927 and 1930 (hereinafter referred to as *Judaism*). Next to this should be placed the recent work of E.P. Sanders, misleadingly entitled *Paul and Palestinian Judaism* (1977), which fully supports Moore's report. Sanders in fact improves on Moore by refuting explicitly those Christian scholars whose views of Judaism were not based on Jewish sources, not only those who wrote before Moore showed them how to do their neglected homework, but also the mass of so-called scholars since Moore's time who have missed his simple point that if you want to learn about early Judaism, the material is fully available in the Jewish writings of the period. Moore and Sanders have made accessible what Judaism in its early development taught about God, humanity, sin, redemption, and the conduct of life. They have presented that teaching as it was developed by the Rabbis who guided Judaism into its great renaissance of the early centuries of the Common Era. Because that relatively early teaching is important for Judaism today, these works are indispensable to the development of, but they do not themselves constitute, a Christian theology of Israel, since they have not attempted to incorporate this knowledge into, and as an integral part of, the church's self-critical reflection.

Because of its title, Clemens Thoma's recently translated *A Christian Theology of Judaism* (1980) should be mentioned here. In the sense sketched in the thesis of and to be defined further in this chapter, his book is not in fact a theology of Judaism (or Israel), but rather another example of the absolutely essential historical studies necessary to the execution of that task. Such works help to dispel the absurd myth that Judaism ever was or is a "religion of works-righteousness," as if the Pharisees, their rabbinic successors, or later Jewish philosophers and theologians, had ever taught or believed the idea, so utterly blasphemous from a Jewish perspective, that anyone, Jew or Gentile, would or could be justified in the sight of the God of Israel by "works of the law" or any other works, rather than solely by the utterly free mercy and love of God. Thoma's book has the advantage over the others mentioned of surveying also medieval and modern Jewish sources, but it does not yet constitute what its title promises.

Although not a theology of Judaism, the book does propose conditions for that task. At the point (28,ET) where these stipulations are given with any degree of systematic order, however, they leave much to be desired. His demands of a Christian theology of Judaism are that it:

1. interpret Judaism with radical seriousness as the origin, contradiction and partner of the Christian church;

2. criticize the church for its ignorance of Judaism;

3. develop the consequences of the Jewishness of Jesus and his disciples;

4. decipher the existence of Judaism in a Christological sense;

5. be without antisemitism; and

6. test the Christian message in relation to the Jewish tradition.

These stipulations call for comment. Setting aside the first point for the moment, the second is quite in order and the book contributes material for accomplishing what is here demanded. The third point is particularly relevant for scholars of the Apostolic Writings, and the fifth applies to all aspects of Christian theology, having no special relevance to the task before us. More interesting are the fourth and sixth points, the one calling for a Christological interpretation of Judaism, the other presumably (it is too vague as it stands to be a useful guide) asking that Christology, *inter alia*, be judged by Jewish theology. But can one have this both ways? Is it important that they are listed in this order? Does the order mean that we are first to run Jewish teaching through our Christological screen before applying the residue as a test of the Christian message? The tenor of the book does not suggest this, but one is left wondering what the significance of the order might be.

We come then to the first point. As formulated, this stipulation would apply as well or better to a history of the rise of Christianity as it might be described in a history of world religions, which is another but different way of considering the relationship between the church and the Jewish people. In the approach appropriate to the history of religions, no account other than descriptive need be taken of the conviction that at issue is the will of the LORD God of Israel, nor of Torah as God's gracious gift to his eternally elect people, nor need the author know him- or herself as a Gentile miraculously called by the God of Israel into his service alongside of his people Israel. If "radical seriousness" is to be applied to a *theology* of Judaism, however, then the terms will surely be other than those which Thoma has proposed. Would it not be necessary to start from the beginning by speaking of God, and then deal with Israel and the church with reference to him and his election? Only so, as I see the matter, could we be "radically serious" about Judaism for Christian theology.

Evidence of the inadequacy of these stipulations may be found in the way in which the author speaks of the familiar theme of "the profound and essential asymmetry between Judaism and Christianity." This asymmetry, Thoma says, "partly stems from the fact that Judaism ('the root') reaches deeply into Christian identity, while Christianity adds little or nothing at all to Jewish self-understanding" (29, ET). Descriptively (i.e. on the level of the history of religions), the remark is unexceptional and has been made by many. Theologically considered, however, if the existence of the Gentile church is due to the intention of the God of Israel, this can hardly be a matter of indifference to Israel. In which case, the much-mentioned asymmetry cannot be dealt with so lightly; it may even turn out to have no value for theology. The failure to consider this alternative suggests that the task of developing a Christian theology of Judaism or Israel has not yet been addressed but only prepared for in this book. It is another contribution to the necessary preparation for such a theology.

A penetrating substantive critique of Thoma's book, and also of F. Mussner's *Tractat über die Juden* (1979), has been made by Peter von der Osten-Sacken, *Grundzüge einer Theologie im christlich-jüdischen Gespräch* (1982), pp. 12-20. I have confined myself to matters of form, since at this point I am primarily concerned to clarify what I intend by a Christian theology of the people Israel. Von der Osten-Sacken's analysis, however, is well worth reading.

ii. Not a Jewish theology

If a Christian theology of Israel will be more and other than a report on the faith and theology of living Judaism, it most certainly will not be a Jewish theology. Given the conception of theology with which we began, it follows that, as Christian theology can only be the work of Christians on behalf of the church, so Jewish theology could only be carried out by Jews on behalf of the Jewish people. For Jewish theology to be a *self-critical reflection on the life and thought of the Jewish people, testing and proposing Jewish understandings of Jewish life and how Jews ought to understand their present relationship to God, it could only be carried out by Jews. I do not mean to define theology for Jewish theologians, but some of them are in fact engaged in just this work. Not all call themselves theologians, as Franz Rosenzweig did, but (to give only a few examples) Irving Greenberg, David Hartman, and Michael Wyschogrod are surely engaged in critical analyses of Jewish thought and life designed to guide future Jewish thought and action. Whether this be called Jewish thought or Jewish philosophy, it is functionally theology in the sense defined above. Being a self-critical task, it cannot possibly be carried out by other than Jews. A Christian theology of Israel, therefore, cannot be considered Jewish theology. I leave to Jewish theologians the question whether they should undertake a Jewish theology of the Christian church.

iii. Definition of the task

Before turning to a definition of a Christian theology of the people Israel, two preliminary points must be made clear. First, by "Israel" I mean the one people of God, from Abraham through Moses, including all of the Israel of which we read in the Scriptures, but also and explicitly Israel since biblical times, throughout its history up to our own day. I mean primarily present, living Israel, both in the Land and in the Diaspora. I mean, in short, the Jews.

Second, I pointed out in *Discerning the Way* that a number of ecclesiastical statements reversing traditional Christian anti-Judaism claimed that the Holocaust and the existence of the state of Israel have together made the church aware of the need for this reversal (as well as for appropriate theological reflection). I want to say as clearly as possible, however, that neither the Holocaust nor the state of Israel have, now for the first time, made necessary either that reversal or the development of a theology of Israel. Rather, these recent events have opened the eyes of some of us to see a task that should have been undertaken long ago, indeed from the beginning of the assumption of the church's theological work. What is needed is therefore not a "Holocaust theology," whatever that might be, but, I shall argue, a Christian theology of the people Israel.

The preliminary definition in the thesis which opens this chapter reads, "A Christian theology of the people Israel . . . asks about the church's duty and ability to hear the testimony of the Jewish people to God." This statement must now be developed and clarified.

A Christian theology of Israel *asks*. In this undertaking the church puts questions to itself. Specifically, the Christian theologian engaged in this part of the theological enterprise can only aim, as a member of the church, to help the church ask itself certain questions about the Jewish people, inviting the rest of the church into this part of its continuing self-critical reflection. The presupposition of these questions, to which we shall turn soon, is that Israel has something to say which the church needs to hear. The church has always believed that Israel *had* something to say worth hearing, namely, what Israel said in the Scriptures which make up our Old Testament. Here, however, we shall be raising the further question, whether living, postbiblical Israel has something more to say, either in its way of interpreting its Scriptures, or in its further reflections arising out of its continuing history in the covenant with God. In raising this question, we ask on behalf and for the sake of the church, whether Israel continues to this day to be what it was for us in its beginnings: the original and normative effect of God's involvement in and closeness to his creation, both in mercy and judgment.

In a Christian theology of Israel, we ask about *hearing the Jewish testimony* to God. Would it be better to place the emphasis on the God whom we may or may not hear in that testimony? Were it not a matter of hearing and understanding the God of Israel, the God and Father of Jesus Christ, there would of course be no duty lying on the church to attend to the testimony of the Jews. If, however, that testimony is to this God and no other, as the Jewish people have maintained throughout their history, then their voices are just what we have to hear in order to learn with them of the One of whom they speak. Hearing this one God of Israel is the whole purpose of attending to Israel's witness, but we judge it wiser for the church at this point in its history to ask primarily about the testimony itself. The church has turned a deaf ear to Jewish voices for so long, that unless it learns to listen explicitly to living Israel, it may be tempted to try to hear Israel's God apart from his chosen witness Israel. Not hearing him as he elected to be heard means not hearing him as he is. Hearing him as he means to be heard through his witnesses, therefore, calls for the church to be attentive to the voice and life of his witnesses, alive and present to the church in the Jewish presence among us in this world. For the sake of hearing the word of this God, we need to ask about hearing Israel's testimony.

In a Christian theology of Israel, we ask about the *duty* and *ability* of the church to hear. The question of duty precedes that of ability, on the assumption that living Israel's testimony is willed by God to be heard by the church. This assumption rests in turn on the conviction that the God and Father of our Lord Jesus Christ is the God who has made an eternal covenant with his people Israel. If that conviction is well founded, then we must ask how it could be possible to draw near to this God without drawing near to this people.

One part of this question concerns our Canon of Scripture, for this is also and first of all Israel's Canon. What bearing does or should it have on our reading of that Canon that it is also read and cherished by Israel? If Israel's Scriptures are still Israel's Canon, ought we not to attend to Israel's reading of them when we read them in the church?

If the church proves to have a duty, an obligation imposed by God, to listen to the witness of Israel, we shall then have to consider how it can be possible that the church listen to Jews. The question is serious because of the history of the church's stubborn refusal for nineteen centuries to listen to anything that has come from the mouth of Jews.

For some rare exceptions, see B. Smalley, *The Study of the Bible in the Middle Ages* (1952), where we hear of at least a few Christian biblical scholars of the Middle Ages who turned to local rabbis in order to learn Hebrew, but who stayed to learn some lessons in Jewish exegesis. These men were exceptions in their day (and even more in the long history of the church's relationship to the Jewish people) in being willing and able to learn Israel's interpretation of its Scriptures from Jews. The steadfast refusal of the church to hear Israel's testimony and to respect Israel's witness is an important reason why there has been so little mention of either testimony or witness in Judaism. Israel's witness of "sanctifying the Name" has had too regularly to take the form of martyrdom. It has been my experience that when a Christian begins to listen with attention and respect to the Jewish witness, Jews can come to a renewed understanding of their mission in the world.

If the church does acquire the ability to listen to the testimony of the Jewish people, this will surely be by the grace of God, as he works in our day to fulfill at least in part his promise that Israel will be a light to the Gentiles. As the church reflects on its ability to attend to Israel's witness, it will find prayer essential, prayer that Israel become for it what God has promised: a kingdom of priests of the most high God, a light in our darkness, a blessing for all peoples, ourselves included. In the power of God, we must believe, but not without the cooperative effort which God asks of his church, that can happen. If it does, then the miracle of Israel's election and purpose will be enacted anew to the benefit of the church.

We are asking about *Israel's* testimony, not ours. That means in part to ask about the Scriptures as Israel's Scriptures, not primarily as our Old Testament; or rather, it is to ask about what can be our Old Testament only as and because it is first of all Israel's Scriptures. A Christian theology of Israel, therefore, will have to listen to Israel's *Halakhah* and *Aggadah* as Israel's exegesis of and commentary on covenant existence. It will need to listen to Jewish Rabbis, philosophers, and poets as to those who expounded God's will for this people, that they might become what he had made them: a light for the Gentiles and so for the Gentiles' church, as well as ultimately for the whole world. Israel's hope, as expressed by Jews, will have to be listened to as the hope of the world and therefore as our Christian hope. Finally, we shall have to ponder the voices of contemporary Jews who claim to have detected in recent Jewish history a shift in the terms of God's covenant with Israel. Whether we share this insight, we must at least be aware of it, for we are asking about Israel's witness.

These elaborations of the definition of a Christian theology of Israel lead to perhaps the most fundamental problem for such a theology and for the church: our traditional understanding of how the New Testament is related to the Old. If the church has a duty to listen to Israel, and if from the Assignor of this duty it graciously receives the ability to hear, it will have to reconsider its traditional view of the relationship between its New and Old Testaments. The pattern of "promise and fulfillment," its primary interpretative model, will need to come under the closest scrutiny. To evade this critical examination would undercut the development of a Christian theology of Israel.

3. THE NECESSITY OF A CHRISTIAN THEOLOGY OF ISRAEL

i. *Israel's election*

We have defined the task before us as an inquiry into that which God has to say to the church through the testimony and life of the Jewish people. This task only makes sense if Israel is indeed commissioned by God to be his witness before the world, and therefore also before the church, in its life as well as in its words. A theology of Israel would then not only make sense; it would become a necessity for the church, for the same reason that a theology of Jesus Christ is necessary. In both cases, the church would be asking about its faithfulness in listening to and obeying the word of the LORD God of Israel. If this God, the church's God, has set Israel in the world as his witness, then a Christian theology of Israel is no more optional for the church than its Christology.

Israel's election to be a kingdom of priests, a holy nation, to be as Abraham's seed a blessing for all the nations, is clearly central to the Scriptures of Israel which the church from the beginning acknowledged as its Canon, but it has not been interpreted by the church as eternal. Rather, the church, in flat contradiction to other parts of its Canon—the assertion of the apostle to the Gentiles that "the gifts and call of God are irrevocable" (Rom. 11:29), and again, "you do not support the root but the root supports you" (11:18)—has read the story of Israel's election as a tale come to an end. It reads its "Old Testament" as a story that had passed away, having been taken up, renewed and ultimately superseded by its "New Testament." Israel's election, on this reading, valid enough in what was to be called an "old dispensation," had been transferred to the church in a "new dispensation." Indeed, the church had become Israel!

This reading of Israel's Scripture and our Apostolic Writings, however, has become a matter of debate in recent decades. Paul's words are being heard in the church for the first time in its history. Reversing eighteen centuries of its teaching, the church is now asserting officially that if Israel was once elected, its election endures. God's covenant with Israel, it is being argued, is eternal, for this is surely the message of Israel's (and the church's!) Scriptures. That is certainly what Israel has heard from those writings throughout its history. Now the church is beginning to hear this same word. If it does, then it has no choice but to acknowledge God's election of the present, living Jewish people. In that case, a Christian theology of Israel becomes a necessary part of the church's theological task.

If Israel's election is unquestionable from God's side, it is, by the testimony of Israel's Scriptures, equally unassailable from Israel's side, for unfaithful Israel remains God's elect people. Whether Israel accepts its election and is obedient to the covenant or not, it remains Israel. In a Christian theology of Israel, care will have to be taken not to idealize the Jewish people. As any Christian should know who is at all knowledgeable about the Jewish people, just as all is not well with the household of

Jesus Christ, so all is not well with the household of Jacob. It appears to be the case that the great majority of Jews today do not accept their divine election. They may have only a sense that Jews are Jews—i.e. different—but they do not think of themselves as a people elected by God. At most, they may think of themselves as the descendents of those who once thought they were God's chosen people. Moreover, the majority of Jews in the world today do not accept the privilege of living according to Torah. At most they acknowledge a Jewish ethical tradition, more or less definite in content, often reduced to utterly vague "Jewish values," to which they give at least some allegiance. Trust in God and his covenant, however, and faithfulness to Torah, have always been problematical in Israel. There is no charge of this sort that cannot be found in Israel's own prophets and reiterated, or at least accepted, in the writings of its Rabbis. As Israel itself preserved and retells its own story (in Exodus 32), the people set up and worshiped a Golden Calf even as the covenant was being sealed by the gift of Torah. Israel is just this problematic people, only sometimes and in part faithful to its covenant, but nevertheless the people whose life and history is marked forever by its election and God's covenant with it. This is the all-too-human face of revelation, apart from which human beings would never have had any communion with the God of Israel. Israel, faithful and also unfaithful, is where they have to look if they are to see God's participation in his creation and learn who this God is and what he wills to happen in and to his creation.

In the prolegomenon (*Discerning the Way*, Step 8), I developed the concept of revelation as a form of knowledge or understanding. That is certainly part of what is involved in revelation, but only a part. We shall hear from Israel's testimony in this volume that that model of revelation needs to be qualified. Revelation means also, perhaps primarily, involvement or participation, not information and communication. Revelation is the event of men and women being drawn into a drama of which they and God become the co-authors and coprotagonists. That is what happened to Israel at Sinai, and to certain Gentiles in the Easter-Pentecost event. The result of revelation is not first of all knowledge, but community.

Israel's election which became flesh in the establishment of the covenant of Sinai, is the presupposition of the history and mission of Jesus of Nazareth, of Paul and the other apostles, and of all the authors of the Apostolic Writings. They saw themselves in that context and in its light. The story which they had to tell was, so they believed, more of that same story which was Israel's. It was Israel's own story come to a climax.

> In many and various ways God spoke of old to our fathers by the prophets, but in these last days he has spoken to us by a Son, whom he appointed heir of all things, through whom he created the world (Hebr. 1:1-2).

> Paul, a servant of Jesus Christ, called to be an apostle, set apart for the gospel of God which he promised beforehand through his prophets in the Holy Scripture, the gospel concerning his Son, who was descended from David . . . (Rom. 1:1-3).

> My soul magnifies the LORD and my spirit rejoices in God my savior . . . He has helped his servant Israel in remembrance of his mercy, as he spoke to our fathers, Abraham and his posterity for ever (Lk. 1:46-55).

> Blessed be the LORD God of Israel, for he has visited and redeemed his people, and has raised up a horn of salvation for us in the house of his servant David, as he spoke by the mouth of the holy prophets from of old, that we should be saved from our enemies and from the hand of all who hate us; to perform the mercy promised to our fathers, and to remember his holy covenant, the oath which he swore to our father Abraham (Lk. 1:68-73).

This brief selection of passages makes unambiguously clear the dependence of the church's story on that of Israel's election.

At the same time, it confirms Karl Barth's point that Marcion's proposal to dispense with the "Old Testament" could never have worked, for if the "Old Testament" were to go, the "New" would have to follow. The passages drawn from Marcion's favorite Gospel, Luke, show that it would have to be rejected were the church to reject Israel, Israel's prophets, Israel's King David, Israel's covenant, and Israel's father, Abraham. Everything that matters to the Christian church stands or falls with the election of Israel. This dependence is the first reason for the necessity of a Christian theology of Israel.

In the light of this conclusion, it is painful to hear Marcionite echoes from certain quarters of the churches of the so-called Third World. From the churches of South America, the old anti-Judaic note sounds not only in attacks on the Jewish state in the Land, but also in a painfully familiar tendency to read Israel's Scriptures typologically in a way that seems to ignore the historicity of actual Israel, past and also present. In India, if I am correctly informed, there are those who wish to ignore the Scriptures, claiming that the Gospel can stand as well or better on the "cultural traditions" of India as on those of ancient Israel. As if the Jewish tradition were our western Gentile "cultural tradition!" As if "cultural tradition" were the issue, rather than the canonical status of the Scriptures! One cannot help suspecting that the motive behind this is a justifiable desire to break with the colonial past, but that a serious confusion has been made between "the West" and Israel. Does it need to be pointed out that Israel is not "the West" and that "the West" is not by any stretch of the imagination identical with the Jewish people? Ask any Jew! By all means let the churches of the Third World find their own way to articulate and live the gospel. Like us in the "First World," they too are Gentiles. We were just as alien as Indian Christians from the commonwealth of Israel. Christians of every land and culture, Gentiles all, need to ask themselves on what they can stand and to whom they can pray, if they do not recognize the election for all time of Israel by the One whom Jesus called Father. Given that recognition, let them then by all means learn from Israel's Scriptures, and from Israel's further history, to identify the craftsmanship of Israel's God, so as to be able to detect his hand at work in the history of their own people.

ii. Israel's Scriptures as the Canon of the church

The concrete expression of the church's dependence on the people Israel is the presence of Israel's Scriptures in the Canon of the church. The church's Bible begins and has always begun with Israel's Torah. It is historically false to say that the church adopted Israel's Scriptures, as if there had been a time when there was a church apart from those Scriptures. In fact, the church was born and grew up on the basis of the Scriptures of Israel, for they were the only Scriptures there were for Jesus, Paul, and the rest of the apostles. The early church had to make decisions about which apostolic writings should be part of its Canon; it never had to make that decision about the Scriptures of Israel.

In acknowledging Israel's Scriptures as its Canon, however, the church failed to consider the implications of the fact that Israel, without respect to the church, continued to read, preserve, interpret, and live from those Scriptures. The failure may be understandable, in the light of the church's preoccupation with other problems of its own developing life, doctrine, and structure. Its failure to ponder Israel's continuing life with its Scriptures, however, had disastrous consequences. For the Jewish people, it resulted in centuries of persecution. For the church, it produced ears deaf to the witness of God's people and a consequent misunderstanding of God's Torah, leading to a theological misconstruction of "Law" and "Gospel," a polarity of the church's invention.

Not attending to Israel's continuity, the church failed completely to see that the Jewish people under the leadership of the Tannaim (the great rabbis of the first and second centuries of the Common Era) were developing a pattern of fidelity to Torah never before realized in Israel's history. We have of course no records to tell us to what extent the Rabbis were able to inculcate in the common life of the Jewish people the faithfulness which they taught in the Mishnah, just as we have no records to tell us to what extent the bishops and Fathers of the church of the period were able to instill in the members of the church the mind of Christ as presented in their writings. In both cases we have only the records of the leaders, and we may assume that, then as now, many of both communities assimilated to the common culture. To the extent that the Fathers speak for the church of those early centuries, however, the Rabbis speak for a remarkable attempt at putting the covenant between Israel and God into practice in the totality of daily individual and communal life.

Called by the God of Israel to his service, the Gentile church has lived and lives from the promises of that God as testified in Israel's Scriptures. At the same time, however, the people Israel has lived and lives from those same Scriptures. What was the church's first and is still the largest part of its Canon, was and is also the Canon of the Synagogue. The God of whom Jews speak and to whom they pray is no other than the God whom the church knows through Jesus Christ, the Creator of heaven and earth, who called Abraham, who led Israel out of Egypt, and who spoke to Moses at Sinai "face to face, as a man speaks to his friend" (Exod. 33:11). Has the church ever known any other God? No, and that is why it confesses that "salvation is from the Jews" (Jn. 4:22), and that is also why a Christian theology of Israel is not optional for the church.

iii. The confirmation of the Scriptures in the church's witness

A Christian theology of Israel is necessary because in the witness of the church the Scriptures of Israel are confirmed. The church does not intend to witness to any other God than that of Abraham, Isaac, and Jacob. It does not bear witness to the God of the philosophers, in Pascal's phrase, not because it has anything against philosophy, but only in order to testify clearly to the God of Israel. The church has meant to point to the One to whom Moses and the prophets pointed. Its witness is meant to confirm the witness of the Scriptures.

To confirm is to make firm, to corroborate, to ratify. It means to say Yes. When the church, in its Apostolic Writings and in its witness through the centuries, confirmed and confirms Israel's Scriptures, it says Yes to their witness. It says *Amen*, so be it.

It cannot then intend to replace that witness with its own. Rather, it adds its witness to that of Israel's, with the intent of confirming Israel's witness. It does so because it believes, with the Apostle to the Gentiles, that "all of the promises of God find their Yes in [Jesus Christ]" (2 Cor. 1:20). That is why, Paul continued, we "utter the *Amen* through [Jesus Christ] to the glory of God." Because Jesus called none other Father than the one God of Israel attested to in the Scriptures of his people, so the church can only wish with its witness to confirm that of those Scriptures.

From its early days, the church has said that Christ stands to the Scriptures of Israel as fulfillment stands to prophecy. From this it has developed the model of "promise and fulfillment" for understanding the relationship between the Scriptures and the Apostolic Writings, or — and here we may say it bluntly — the Old and New Testaments. The point of departure for this development would be the recurring Matthean "this took place in order to fulfil what was said by the prophet," or the Lukan story of Jesus reading a messianic passage from the scroll of Isaiah and concluding, "Today this scripture has been fulfilled in your hearing" (Lk. 4:16–21). Its classic expression is the comment of the author of the so-called Epistle to the Hebrews on the promise of a new (or renewed) covenant written on the heart, from Jeremiah 31:31–34: "In speaking of a new covenant, [Jeremiah] treats the first as obsolete. And what is becoming obsolete and growing old is ready to vanish away" (Hebr. 8:10–13). The Old Covenant or Testament contains the promises; the New Covenant or Testament testifies to their fulfillment. The emphasis in "fulfillment" is on the "full." All the promises of God to Israel are now fulfilled in Christ.

An interesting and subtle variation on this model was developed by Karl Barth in his *Church Dogmatics* I/2, Section 14, within the framework of his contention that both the Scriptures and the Apostolic Writings witness to the one revelation of God which is identical with Jesus Christ. The Scriptures witness in the form of expectation, the Apostolic Writings in the form of recollection, of the one revelation.

Within this difference, however, a dialectic is at work in both Testaments (80ff, 103ff, E. T.). The object of Scripture's witness is not only coming, not just expected, but also present (94ff). A gift of presence is there even as it points ahead to what is coming. The object of the Apostolic Writings' witness has come and is present as a gift given, and yet that presence also points ahead to a coming (113ff). Both have as their object the one mysterious, hiding God of Israel as he unveils his hiddenness in self-revelation.

Barth's variation, however, is finally only just that, for he clearly thought that that which the Scriptures expect is identical with that which the Apostolic Writings recollect, that the New Testament remembers what the Old Testament expects. Barth failed to take into account the extent to which the Apostolic Writings recollect what was *not* expected by the authors of the Scriptures — e.g. a Messiah who brought no messianic age and no restoration for Israel. And he ignored the extent to which the Apostolic Writings do *not* recollect what the Scriptures surely expect — e.g. nations beating their swords into plowshares and their spears into pruning hooks. Barth's modification of the traditional model of promise and fulfillment is itself in need of modification. Expectation modified by presence, and recollection of presence modified by further expectation, miss the point that the mode of presence is not the same in the two Testaments. Both speak of the presence of the one God of Israel, but he is present to his people in one way (in Torah, Temple, Land, the people themselves), and present to his church in another (in Jesus Christ, the Spirit, the Eucharist, the community of believers). Further, the expectations of the coming of God are shaped to the lives and forms of the two different communities. There is certainly a common focus, since it is never any other than the God of Abraham, Isaac, and Jacob who is recollected, sensed, and expected, yet this same hiding One unveils himself in two different ways for his two communities. In a word, God unveils his love for Israel in Torah and his love for his church in Jesus Christ. The strength of the model of "promise and fulfillment" lies in underscoring this common object of witness; its disqualifying weakness, in however modified a form, lies in its blindness to the different ways in which their object is remembered by, present to and future for the two communities. We therefore judge it an inadequate model for expressing the genuine novelty-within-continuity to which the Apostolic Writings bear witness.

As a confirmation of the Scriptures, the Apostolic Writings testify to Jesus Christ as God's Yes to all his promises. To confirm a promise, however, is not the same as to fulfill it. God's promises to Israel include, for example, possession of the Land. In Jesus Christ, if we are to believe the apostle Paul, God said Yes also to that promise. The church of Jesus Christ, therefore, cannot coherently do other than confirm and support the promise of the Land to the Jewish people. It cannot twist this promise to the Jews into a spiritualized promise to the church, for to do so would be to witness to Jesus Christ as God's No to this particular and by no means peripheral promise of his. Coherence requires that the church be at the least much more cautious with its use of the word "fulfillment" than it has been in the past. Instead of struggling with weaker expressions, such as "partial fulfillment," or "fulfillment in principle," the church will be better served if a Christian theology of Israel proposes a better model. We therefore propose and will use an alternative model: that of *promise and confirmation*. We do so because it seems to us to be clear that God's church cannot be itself without confirming his choice of, covenant with, and promises to his people Israel.

I propose "promise and confirmation" as a model for the church's thinking. To Jewish ears this will sound odd, since for Israel the key term is not "promise," but *mitzvot*, the commandments. In Israel's terms, the model might be "covenant and confirmation," but that would be to presuppose that Israel felt free to affirm God's movement toward the Gentiles in Jesus Christ. In any case, the church is called to find its own models of thought, and in this matter it has the lead provided by the Apostolic Writings.

iv. *The confirmation of the Scriptures in Israel's witness*

A Christian theology of Israel is necessary, further, because Israel lives and by that living confirms its Scriptures. To put this in Israel's terms, Israel lives by Torah. Israel lives by Torah as the church lives by the faithfulness of God in Christ. Not every Jew seeks to live by Torah, and not every baptized member of the church seeks to live by Jesus Christ; we take each community by its own deepest commitments. So conceived, the existence of God's Israel is meant to be nothing but faithfulness to Torah, conformation to God's revealed covenant and so a lived confirmation of the Scripture which bear witness to that covenant.

A Christian theology of Israel will help the church to see Israel in its own terms, not in ours. Israel is not a church, and "Judaism" is no exact parallel to "Christianity." It is not another "religion." The Jews, by their own self-understanding, are a *people*, a nation, not a church or a religion. Their relationship to their Scriptures, therefore, is not like ours to those same Scriptures. For us the relationship is primarily one of hearing; for Israel it is one of participation. True hearing, of course, involves paricipation, and there can be no participation without hearing; the distinction is not absolute. There is nevertheless a relative difference in the way in which the two traditions have understood their relationship to the same text. All Israel shares in a common life of participation in the covenant by means of participation in the life of Torah.

On this matter the Rabbis may speak for Israel, for all Jews: "When Moses summoned the people before God, he said: 'Not with you alone do I make this covenant' (Deut. 39:14). All souls [of future generations of Israel] were present then, although their bodies were not yet created." (*Tanh. B.*, Nizzabim, VIII, 25b, cited from C. Montefiore and H. Loewe, *A Rabbinic Anthology*—hereafter to be referred to as M&L—108.) Israel's participation in and being conformed to Torah is well expressed in another rabbinic saying: "God gave the Israelites two Laws, the Written Law and the Oral Law. He gave them the Written Law with its 613 ordinances, to fill them with commandments, and to cause them to become virtuous, as it is said, 'The Lord was pleased for his righteousness' sake to increase the Law and make it glorious.' And he gave them the Oral Law to make them distinguished from the other nations." (*Num. R.*, Naso, XIV, 10. M&L, 159.) Being "filled with commandments," Israel therefore shared in the eternity of Torah: "Was Israel created for the sake of Torah, or Torah for the sake of Israel? Surely Torah for the sake of Israel. Now if Torah that was created for the sake of Israel will endure forever, how much more Israel that was created by the merit of Torah." (*Eccles. R.*I, #4, I,f.2b. M&L, 39.)

Enduring Israel bears witness by participation in the covenant. Further, every Jew who accepts his or her Jewishness participates in Israel's covenant witness, for the Jew who insists on being a Jew stands in the world as something which, from the world's point of view, just does not make sense. The reason for this, from Israel's perspective, is that Israel's relationship to its Scriptures consists not just in halakhic faithfulness, but in the life of the Jewish people itself.

"So what if some have been unfaithful?" Paul's question (Rom. 3:3) had been that of Isaiah before him and was that of the Rabbis after him. "Will their unfaithfulness make ineffective the faithfulness of God? Of course not!" That was Paul's answer. Faithful and unfaithful, Israel remains God's Israel, and it is just this people, the Jewish people, that a Christian theology of Israel will have in view. Nevertheless, of the unidealized Jewish people we shall say that they are God's Israel not by what they do or do not do, but solely by the grace of divine election. Christians are no more authorized to take Jewish unbelief seriously than they are their own. As Christian theology can only take the church seriously as called of God (and so taking it sometimes more seriously than it takes itself), so it has no choice but to take the Jewish people seriously as the Israel of God. It does so in the one case in the hope that, by the power of the Spirit, the church will again be renewed to be the church, and in the other case in the hope that Israel will again be renewed to return to its God and his covenant and so become what it is, the Israel of God.

When I speak of Israel and its relationship to Torah, I do not have in mind just rabbinic Judaism up to Moses Mendelssohn, the Haskalah (the Enlightenment in its Jewish manifestation) and the rise of Reform Judaism, when more and more Jews began to embrace modernity.

As I believe in *ecclesiam semper reformandam* (or at least in need of being reformed), so I believe in Judaism's need of reformation. But surely *not* as it was initiated and carried through a century and a half ago in Germany. That was too largely a Jewish mimicry of a Protestantism that had lost its way, and a culture-Judaism is no more help to an endangered world than a culture-Protestantism. Neither the church nor the Jewish people can serve the world as God has called it to do by presenting itself as one more variation — and a religious one at that — on how to be modern, or by misunderstanding its calling as the task of realizing a possibility latent in all human beings, be it in a Christian form as piety or in a Jewish form as morality.

v. The Jewish rejection of the church's Jesus Christ

A Christian theology of Israel is necessary, finally and ultimately, not only because Israel lives, but because living Israel stands before the church and its universal message and says No. It says that the address of the church's message does not and cannot include Israel. It rejects the church's "imperialism," or, to say it more objectively, it rejects the church's missionary efforts when they are directed at or conceived to include Jews. It rejects the church's "Old Testament" as a misunderstanding of *Tanakh*, Israel's Scriptures. It rejects the church's claim that all God's promises to Israel have been fulfilled in Christ. It rejects, finally, the church's claim that Jesus of Nazareth was and is the Messiah promised to Israel.

A Christian theology of Israel is essential because Israel's rejection of the church's faith is in no way comparable to that of anyone else's. Atheists, agnostics, and secularists have their own reasons for rejecting the church, but they do so on grounds that the church *coram Deo* dare not take seriously; Israel rejects the church on grounds that the church *coram Deo* dare not ignore: it rejects the church in the name of the One whom the church confesses as the God and Father of Jesus Christ. It rejects the church's claim in the name of the church's God. Its No is an act of fidelity to the One God and his covenant with Israel. Its No therefore takes the form of fidelity to Torah.

The first thing the church must be clear about concerning this No is that it does not refer to a supposed response of the Jewish people, in or about the year 30 C.E., to the so-called historical Jesus of Nazareth. Our evidence on that is far too limited and of such a nature as to make the matter speculative. What evidence we have from the Apostolic Writings suggests that of the tiny fraction of all the Jews in the Roman empire who may even have heard of Jesus, much less having actually heard or seen him, a large number responded positively. Indeed it seems probable that for some fifty years after Easter, the Synagogue tolerated Jews in its membership who, ever faithful to Torah, believed that Jesus was Israel's Messiah whom God had exalted. The split would appear to have developed not because of Jesus, nor even because of Easter; the issue turned on Jewish fidelity to Torah: when Gentile Christians began telling Jews who believed in Jesus that Torah was no more to be followed by them, then all faithful Jews had to say No.

The fundamental meaning of the Jewish No, which the church should understand therefore, is that it was from the beginning and continues to be an act of fidelity to Torah and Torah's God. The Gospel met Gentiles as a demand to abandon their pagan ways and the service of gods that are not God. The Gospel met the Jews, as the church after Paul's time preached it, as the demand to abandon the express commands and covenant of the very God whom the church proclaimed! Here is a profound incoherence that has arisen because of the lack of a proper Christian theology of Israel. The theological reality which such a theology must address, then, is that Israel said No to Jesus Christ out of faithfulness to his Father, the God of Israel.

The one positive lead from the Apostolic Writings for understanding this No in a positive way is to be found in Paul's letter to the Romans: "through their 'trespass' [their No] salvation has come to the gentiles" (11:11); "their 'trespass' [their No] means riches for the world, . . . for the gentiles" (11:12); "their rejection [of the Gospel, and it was God himself who had "hardened" them and given them "eyes that should not see and ears that should not hear" (11:7,8)] means the "reconciliation of the world" (11:15). In sum, "with respect to the Gospel [that is, Paul's Gospel that *now* was the moment of the inclusion of the Gentiles in God's plan of redemption] they [the Jewish people] are enemies of God *for your sake*, but with respect to election, they are beloved for the sake of their forefathers" (11:29).

What shall we say to that? The Jewish No to Jesus Christ, Paul was saying, was according to the will of God for our sake, and therefore it was a faithful service to the purposes of the Father of Jesus Christ. Surely the Gentile church should owe them thanks, as well as thanks to God through Jesus Christ, that they so responded. But that is only one side — and the lesser side — of our debt to Israel. The church is even more indebted to Israel for its Yes, in the context of which alone the No became possible. But for Israel's Yes to God at Sinai, reaffirmed in each Jewish generation through Torah faithfulness, there would have been no continuing Israel, no Scriptures, and so no church at all. Theologically as well as historically, the church is absolutely dependent on Israel's Yes. Theologically as well as historically, the Gentile church is also dependent on the Jewish No that has followed from and reiterated that Yes. The church, then, is Israel's debtor for both its primary Yes and its secondary No. A Christian theology of Israel will be open to both and so help the church to thank God for the dual service he has carried out and continues to carry out through the service of his people Israel. It should also encourage the church to bless the Jewish people for what they have to teach it through their fundamental Yes and their consequent No.

A Christian theology of Israel may also help the Gentile church to give special thanks to God for having placed in its midst a few members in Christ who were born of Israel. Having said their fundamental Yes where the rest of Israel says its derivative No, and their derivative (and sometimes qualified) No where Israel says its fundamental Yes, they may be seen in the singularity of their position as God's concrete reminder to the church of its utter dependence on the people Israel.

It was, after all, one in their position who wrote, "remember it is not you [Gentile Christians] that support the root [the people Israel], but the root that supports [present tense, a full generation after Easter!] you" (Rom. 11:18). Christians of Jewish background are therefore a concrete sign in the church of its debt to the Jewish people.

The task of a Christian theology of Israel is to help the church hear and learn from Israel's Yes and No, its denial of the church's Jesus Christ for the sake of faithfulness to the church's God and the Father of Jesus Christ. Fundamentally, therefore, a Christian theology of Israel will be Christological in ways that may be surprising for traditional Christian theology. If we succeed in hearing the Jewish No positively, indeed explicitly as God's word to his church, and therefore as a word through Jesus Christ (for that is how God has chosen to address his church in bringing it from death into life), it will come to us as Christ's word to his church, delivered through the mouths of his brothers and sisters, the Jewish people. We may learn from him, through them, remedies for our schizophrenic invention of "redemption in principle" with which we have displaced hope in the redemption of God's good creation, and cures for the illnesses we have brought upon ourselves and others through our invented dichotomies of Law and Gospel, faith and works, and theology and ethics. We may learn of him through them of our perpetual flight from the incarnation, from that act of the Creator's intimacy with his creatures which was sealed for Israel at Sinai, and for the church in Jesus Christ. This schooling may even encourage the Gentile church to find what would be for it an authentic—i.e., Gentile, or extra-Jewish—way in which to confess Jesus Christ as Lord. Specifically, that would mean to find some more adequate means than the Jewish concept of "Messiah" with which to define the relationship between Jesus and the Israel of God. Whatever that term may have meant in the first century, its meaning in the long history of Jewish tradition falls hopelessly short of defining the indissoluble connection between Jesus and God's elect people that is essential to the faith and the very existence of the Christian church to this day. A part of the task of a Christian theology of the Jewish-Christian reality is to point out that the term "Messiah" has never been central to the church's confession of Jesus Christ, not to speak of such a neologism as "Jesus as the Christ," and that in the terms "Son," "Word," and "Lord" it has long since developed concepts that can do the job far more adequately. Much of this task will find its proper place in the third volume of this *Theology of the Jewish-Christian Reality*, but we can lay the foundations for doing it only by accepting the necessity of a Christian theology of the people Israel.

4. THE GOAL OF A CHRISTIAN THEOLOGY OF ISRAEL

i. *Israel's contribution to the church's service: the fear of the* LORD

Theology is not an end in itself and so neither is that part of it in which we are here engaged, a Christian theology of Israel. It is an activity of critical reflection carried out within and on behalf of the church, aiming to help the church serve God more faithfully. As an integral part of that activity, a Christian theology of Israel will try to help the church understand, appreciate, and *respond* to Israel's contribution to the church's service to God, on the one hand, and on the other, understand, accept and *carry out* its own service to Israel as a part of its service to God. Whether this comes about in fact is not going to be settled by theology, for the goal which the theological task serves (but can never bring about) is that "responding" and "carrying out" which is the church's service to God. The goal theology longs for but cannot produce depends, humanly speaking, on the fear of the LORD that is the beginning of wisdom.

The word "fear" seems conspicuous by its absence from the vocabulary of contemporary faith and theology, important as it is in the Bible and throughout most of the history of both the church and the Jewish people. On the part of the church, this absence may be due to our current hesitation about the way in which we think our forebears talked of God's power. It seems to many today that the concept of power in our past conversation was shaped too much by images of domination, and too little by thoughts of humility and suffering. Such is clearly the case in the common usage of the world of which we are all a part. But this sort of power seems to be just what God either does not have or else is not exercising in the world, whatever may have been the case in the past. Uncertain of what to say about God's power, we find that we have difficulty seeing how the fear of God could be praised as the beginning of wisdom.

If, however, the church means what it says about the revelation of God in the cross of Christ, and if it means what it says about Easter as God's confirmation of that revelation and not its contradiction, then God's power must be that of suffering and humility, not of dominion. In which case, fear of *this* Lord cannot mean trembling before a magnified version of what we human beings, especially male human beings, prize as power. The issue goes beyond sexual stereotypes, however. Hosea presented the power of God as the suffering love of a betrayed husband whose love would not cease when slapped in the face. Is not this what Paul called the power of the gospel of the crucified, of which he was not ashamed?

As we must ever again listen and learn from God the difference between divine and human power, so we must learn what it is to fear him. It cannot be to tremble before a potentate if God has refused to be a potentate. It is not what Rosenzweig called "the terror of God, which could not muster the courage to become the fear of God" (*The Star of Redemption*, E.T., 37). It would have to be the far deeper trembling that comes from standing in the presence of a love that suffers for and with us and thereby stands in judgment on our usual conceptions of power and fear. It is the fear that can come upon us as we look into the dull eyes of the death camp survivors in those terrifying photographs taken by the camp liberators. Revulsion may be a more "natural" reaction, or maybe shame. It is really not at all as "natural" to be unashamed of the cross as we pretend in the church, and our pretense is revealed by our unwillingness to see the suffering of the starving and oppressed of this world. Not wanting to look into the face of the starved and the oppressed, we miss the suffering of God which could teach us anew what it is to fear him.

The church has fastened too simplistically on the word that love casts out fear (1 Jn. 4:18). God's love indeed leaves no room for fear of a despot, but it opens us for the first time to another fear. Face to face with the long, painful, and stormy love affair between God and the Jewish people, involving so much mutual suffering, the church may learn something of the fear of the LORD that is the beginning of wisdom.

I do not want to leave the impression that suffering is all that the Jewish people have to show us. It is only one of their treasures. Of possibly greater value is their joy. Jewish joy in Torah living, Jewish joy in Shabbat, can also lead us to fear and trembling before the closeness of this people to their God and ours, and of his closeness to them. A God so lovingly and fearfully incarnate is to be loved and feared before all else.

ii. God's, Israel's, and the church's mission

Because the fear of the LORD is the beginning of wisdom, then insofar as the church comes to see the face of this LORD in the suffering and joy of the Jewish people, it may come to a new understanding of the mission or purpose of this God who is the church's Lord as well as Israel's. It would be a new understanding for the church, because it would acknowledge that God's mission has kept Israel's mission in its service, and has then added the role of the Gentile church as a servant to its mission.

Traditionally, and especially in the modern period, when the church has spoken of mission, it has tended to think and speak first of all of the church's mission, of "our mission." If the church is the church *of* God, that cannot be correct. The church's mission can only be a reflection of and response to God's mission. God's mission to his whole creation surely comes first. In second place, however, comes Israel's mission, from Abraham through the patriarchs and Moses, to the prophets, sages, and Rabbis, and on to the government of the state of Israel and other forms of leadership of the Jewish people in our own day. Israel, God's elect people to be a light to the nations, takes second place when we speak theologically and historically of mission. Then and only then, in third place, it is in order to speak of the mission of the church, which, because it is a function of God's mission to the whole world already initiated in Israel's mission, must be in some way reflexive of and coordinated to Israel's historically and theologically prior mission. The church of Jesus Christ cannot wish to assert more, for it walks under the words of him who said, "whoever exalts himself shall be humbled" (Matt. 23:12), words the truth of which it has learned from painful experience but seems ever needing to learn again.

God's mission or purpose comes first. At issue is not simply the church, and not even the church and Israel together. At issue is creation and its future. At issue is therefore whether the church will confirm the testimony of Israel's Scriptures that the Creator will be the Redeemer, indeed the Redeemer of just that which he created. God's creation "in the beginning" was good, but, as we shall learn from Israel, it was good as a beginning. The biblical story of this beginning tells us that it came close to being a total failure, and that only by God's mercy, and only by the promise and covenant of God as given to Noah, are there grounds for any hope that it will not end in failure. The first eleven chapters of the First Book of Moses, which is Israel's creation story, portrays a threatened creation, one sorely in need of a blessing, of redemption, a creation that needed that which was to begin with the calling of Abraham. It was and remains a creation whose Creator must become its Redeemer if it is to succeed. But this Creator has revealed to Israel at Sinai, and to the church in Jesus Christ, that he wills not to be that Redeemer without the participation, first of Israel, and then also of the church.

The coming Redeemer is therefore the focus of hope of both Israel's Scriptures and the church's Apostolic Writings. Torah and the prophets, and Jesus Christ and the apostles, bear witness that he will come to fulfill his promise. In Abraham, first Israel and then the church, the Jew first, and then the Gentile in Christ, are set into the history of creation to point to and serve God's redemptive mission to his endangered creation. Their message and their life have no other goal than to show that because the Creator is the Redeemer, God cares for his creation and calls us to cooperative action for the sake of its preservation. Israel's witness is a reminder to the church that a hope which does not drive us to obey God could not be hope in a Redeemer who is the Creator.

iii. *The church's mission to serve Israel*

According to the testimony of the Scriptures and the Apostolic Writings (e.g., Isa. 2:24, 42:1-4; Ps. 97:1-9, 98; Lk. 1:51-55, 2:29-32; Rom. 11:25-26), the redemption of creation, God's primary and ultimate mission, will accompany his redemption of Israel. This can be said either way: the redemption of the world entails Israel's redemption, but also, Israel's redemption entails the redemption of the world. The second way of putting the single affirmation elucidates the universal element in the frequent and only seemingly narrow Jewish question, asked of any event, "Is it good for the Jews?" Israel's supreme good is also creation's, for their redemption go together. So Jews have come to look to their own experience as the best immediate indication of how it goes with the world.

The Rabbis could therefore say not only that creation is for the sake of Israel—which in this context we may interpret as meaning that the redemption of Israel includes and brings with it the redemption of crea-tion (see Moore, *Judaism*, I, 383, 449 for sources on this)—but also that Israel exists for the sake of creation, or at least of the Gentiles: "If sand is not put into the lime, the lime will not last. But for Joseph, the Egyptians would have died of hunger; but for Daniel, the wise men of Babylon would have perished . . ." (*Pes.R.*, 45b, cited M&L, 39).

With the coming of Jesus Christ and the Gentiles bound to him, something new has now been added: a Gentile church with its own commissioned witness to the world. However that mission is to be further defined (and this will be addressed in my third and fourth volumes), its ultimate context could not coherently be other than God's mission of the redemption of his creation. Since God's mission has taken Israel into its service, however, the mission of the church can only have the mission of Israel as its guide and immediate context. Service to the one entails service to the other; service of the God of Israel entails service to the Israel of God. The church, then, will serve Israel for the sake of the redemption of creation and serve creation's redemption by serving Israel. Living as the miraculous exception to its Lord's mission of being "sent only to the lost sheep of the house of Israel" (Matt. 15:24), the church will recognize, as a central part of its mission to the world, its mission of supportive service to Israel.

The church's mission, coherently conceived, would serve, and therefore never seek to hinder, Israel's own mission. Its mission to the Jewish people, therefore, would be to help Israel to be itself and carry out its role in God's plan for the redemption of creation. A Christian theology of Israel has as a goal (in its minor role as theology) to criticize, correct, and clarify the church's understanding, *coram Deo*, of the service its owes to the Jewish people.

CHAPTER TWO

Israel's Testimony to Creation

Israel's testimony begins with the affirmation of God as Creator, and so of the distinct reality of creation. Because this testimony is grounded in God's investment of himself in his covenant with Israel, Israel's witness to the Creator takes the form of faithfulness to Torah, reminding the church that its faithfulness to Jesus Christ is the form of its concordant witness to the Creator.

1. GENESIS 1:1 AS CONFESSION, TORAH, AND GOSPEL

Israel's Scriptures open with the words, "In the beginning, God created the heavens and the earth" (Gen. 1:1). This is not the first word that living Israel has to say, but these are the opening words of the Torah from which Israel lives. The church has no independent doctrine of Creation. What it has to say on this subject arises from its listening to Israel.

We may, with Nahum Sarna (*Understanding Genesis*, 1966, 1) and others, also translate: "When God began to create the heaven and the earth, . . ."

God is our Creator. This is Israel's confession of faith, the opening words of its praise of, and thanksgiving to, the God who called into being things that were not (Rom. 4:17), by calling Israel into existence as his people from the nothingness of slavery in Egypt. It will therefore come as no surprise when we hear the first word of this confession clearly echoed in that of the church, in the openings of what some reckon to be the church's earliest and latest Gospels: "The beginning of the Gospel of Jesus Christ. . . ." (Mk. 1:1); "In the beginning was the word. . . ." (Jn. 1:1).

The focus of Israel's trust is God the Creator, the Creator of Israel and also of heaven and earth. Certainly heaven and earth are there too, and Israel's testimony is also about creation, but first of all, Israel speaks of God. This God to which Israel testifies is utterly distinct from everything else, for everything else is his. He made it all and he is therefore Lord of all. Israel's testimony is not so much a story of origins as it is a narrative confession of reality, beginning with God creating, an act which we shall refer to as Creation (with a capital C), and then telling of all he created, which is everything there is other than God (creation, lower-case). This is Israel's confession, a particular narrative of reality told by this particular people, an act of thanksgiving for its deliverance and election. With these words Israel's Torah begins, its divine instructions given by the hand of Moses, according to tradition. This is therefore also Israel's good news of its Lord, who delivered and made his covenant with this people. The task before us is to hear this confession, instruction, and good news from Israel, as Israel understands it, as an integral, indeed the foundational, part of our conversation within the church.

i. Trust in the Creator — and in creation

Hearing these words from Israel, we cannot overemphasize that we are dealing with the opening words of "the Torah of Moses," which Ezra brought to Jerusalem after the Exile and read before all the people (Neh. 8:1ff). However we describe the long and complicated history of the writing, assembling, and editing of these writings, we have them now more or less as Ezra read them to a people who had not heard much if any of them before. The scroll(s) he read was "the Torah of Moses which the

LORD has given to Israel" (Neh. 8:1), and which from then on became increasingly the heart of the Canon of Israel's Scriptures, its "Canon within the Canon," so to speak, its rule of life and its sacred core. The rest of its Scriptures were regarded by the Rabbis, as indeed Israel's whole existence was conceived, as a commentary on Torah.

It is essential, more particularly, to realize that this is the Torah of *Moses*. It was read by Ezra and has been read by Israel ever since as the revelation from Sinai. Israel has received every word of it as springing from that awesome revelation which followed upon the Exodus from Egypt, given by the hand of that greatest of all prophets, with whom alone God "spoke face to face, as a man speaks with a friend" (Ex. 33:11). If we forget or ignore the fact that we are listening to the words of the Torah of Moses, we shall never understand what Israel means in giving the testimony that opens with the words, "In the beginning God created the heavens and the earth."

Those opening words, and all that follow, are Israel's testimony *that* God is Lord and *how* he is Lord. *That* God is Lord could have no clear meaning for us if we did not know *how* he is Lord. We have all sorts of models of lordship before us, from eastern potentates to imperial presidents; and since most of the world's literature and its religions have been interpreted by males, we need particularly to beware of the common concept of male lordship. What are its credentials and record, after all? We shall go astray in listening to Israel if we do not notice and keep reminding ourselves that we are not just being told *that* God is the Lord. We are being told primarily *how* he is Lord. When Israel tells the world that God is Creator, it tells more than that God is utterly different from everything that has been created. Israel is telling all who will listen *how*, in what way, God is different from all that he has created.

Where else could Israel have learned the nature of this difference and therefore the meaning of God's lordship, but from its own rescue from slavery? When Israel heard and hears, "I am the LORD your God, who brought you forth from the land of Egypt," it heard and hears from the dependent clause, recalling its own creation, the meaning of the main clause. This is the way in which the LORD is God. This text (from the opening of the Decalogue, Deut. 5:6), unlike the opening verse of Torah, makes use of the divine name. Because Israel never utters that holy name but always replaces it with *adonai*, the LORD, this text makes the point which I am stressing about lordship as one about divinity. Whatever other people in other circumstances may mean by "God" or by lordship, for Israel they mean the One who set his heart on Israel in its nothingness and brought it into existence as his own possession in love. That is the difference between the God of Israel and everything else in the heavens and on the earth. That difference is the heart of Israel's testimony about Creation. Creation-faith, trust in God the Creator, is also revelation-faith, trust in the revelation of the God of Torah, and also redemption-faith, trust in the specific distinctiveness of God as the One who alone rescued Israel from slavery and who will therefore rescue Israel and his whole creation from dissolution and death.

It is consequently a total misunderstanding of the opening words of Torah to take them as a report about events which no one but God could have seen, or as a theory or hypothesis about the origin of the world. That the Creation confession of Genesis 1, or Genesis 2, or both together, could be conceived of as an alternative hypothesis about the origin of the earth and of human life, to those put forward in the growth and development of the natural sciences in the modern period, is a sign not simply of a positivistic misunderstanding of sound scientific reasoning. It is evidence far more of a collapse of sound theological reasoning. The questions and answers of modern science concerning the origins of human life, the earth, or even the universe, were never in the minds of the authors, collectors, or editors of the Genesis text, for these questions and answers are the product of the quite recent development of the natural sciences. The authors of Genesis had other questions in mind. It does them a disservice to ignore their questions and answers in favor of those arising on the basis of presuppositions so foreign to them.

Because Israel trusts that God's lordship is redemptive and covenantal, determining his relationship to everything else, it can also trust in the loved and redeemable reality of all that he has created. The God of the Exodus and Sinai, Israel's God, evidently wills an *other*, distinct from but related to himself. He wills his creature. Israel, therefore, can rely on the reality and solidity of the creature. This is Israel's glad understanding, derived exclusively from the gift of covenant, of the world. The world, either in its most immediate sense of the earth and sky as the enviroment of Israel's gifted life, or in the widest sense of everything there is other than God, things visible and invisible, be they angels or devils, atoms or subatomic particles, stars or thus-far-undetected galaxies, the world has a Lord whose lordship has the character which Israel confesses. Whether in the nearer or farther sense, the world belongs to God as his creation, Israel testifies. Therefore it is real.

The reality of the world, however, is not a part of the reality of God. It is not in any sense an emanation from or an expression of God. It is not some aspect of God. All the more is it true that God is not some aspect of the world, such as its soul or its creative principle. Because God is Lord, the world is creation, having its reality as a gift from him. This is Israel's testimony as we hear it in the opening verse of the First Book of the Torah of Moses. The world is real, Israel tells all who will listen; it has its own independent reality as that which God has created in and for his love.

Israel testifies, consequently, that the relationship between God and the world is personal. The analogy of the potter making a pot seemed appropriate to some of its prophets (Jer. 18:6; Isa. 64:8). As the human potter conceives and then shapes the pot, so God conceived and shaped his creation, which is then his personal creation and possession. Israel seems never to have thought of the relationship as being either logical or biological. God's relationship to the world was not expressed by such a logical relationship as that between myself and my body nor by the biological relationship between my life and my body. God created the world as a human being creates pots, as a person may make his or her personal possessions. And, as we shall see in due course, the relationship becomes personal also from the side of creation, for in and as a part of creation, as its penultimate crown (the ultimate crown, as we shall see, is not humanity but *Shabbat*!), there are human persons, made in the image and likeness of God, there to praise and serve God. Since Israel's testimony to the relationship between the Creator and creation is grounded in and arises out of its experience of Exodus and Sinai, we could hardly expect it to be presented as other than personal.

The personal reality of creation and its relationship to its Creator is therefore defined ultimately in Israel's witness by prayer and praise: as Israel understands itself to have been created for the praise of God, so it understands all creation to have been called into existence for this same personal activity. Israel's fundamental model for expressing the relationship of the world to God, therefore, is not that of the pot and the potter, but Israel itself in the Temple of the LORD, singing praises to its Redeemer who will redeem his whole creation. Looking ahead as well as back, then, Israel in the midst of and as a part of creation plays its divinely appointed role of calling all creation to join with it in praise of its creation.

The Psalms constitute a central part of Israel's testimony to God as Creator and to creation as his possession, owing him, along with Israel, praise and thanksgiving. So Israel can call on heaven and earth to praise God (Ps. 69:34), as well as everything that has breath (150:6). Not only all nations and peoples are to praise God (117:1), but also the angels and all God's host (148:2), sun, moon, and stars (v. 3), highest heaven and the waters above the heavens (4), sea monsters and the watery deep (7), fire, hail, and snow (8), mountains, hills, and trees (9), and beast, cattle, bugs, and birds (10). The whole cosmic order is not called by Israel to this activity as to a work foreign to it; it is already engaged in praise as God's grateful creation: "All your works give thanks to you" (145:10). One of the grandest expressions of this testimony is preserved for us in the *Benedicite* from the Greek Version (the *Septuaginta*) of Daniel.

Israel's response to Creation, however, also takes the form of obedience to the will of the Creator. Observance of God's commandments is for many Jews the way in which they believe God should be praised. With the destruction of the Temple, halakhah, as we shall see, became the central form of Israel's life with God.

ii. *"How things really are"*

We have noted in passing that Israel's confession of trust in God as Creator cannot be reduced to a scientific hypothesis or theory about the origin of the earth or human life. To do so would be worse than bad science; it would be blasphemous theology. Science aims to construct theories about the workings of this world, which will account for all the observable evidence in the simplest possible way, and then account for and predict all future experience. Its ideal expression will be mathematical. The biblical testimony to creation, by contrast, aims to confess the personal relationship between God and his creation, as an extension of Israel's confession of its relationship to the God of Exodus and Sinai. Its actual and necessary expression is narrative. Israel's testimony to Creation, therefore, is grounded in and itself a part of Israel's remembering and retelling its story.

This story, says Israel to any who will listen to it, is nevertheless a narrative of reality. When Israel tells of Creation, and when the church joins its confirming voice to that of Israel, they are saying implicitly, "and this is how things really are." The breadth and inclusiveness of this claim, its style as well as its boldness, should alert us to its difference from any scientific theory. Indeed, the inclusion of that utterly nonscientific word "really" is the unmistakable sign that this claim lies logically in a realm quite other than that of the natural sciences—namely, that of metaphysics. The natural sciences, when conducted according to their own methods and practices, will never make claims that could be construed properly as metaphysical. Were they to do so, they would violate their own methods by ignoring their own self-imposed limitation to statements that are empirically testable. Israel, on the other hand, cannot evade the fact, with all its attendant risks, that its claim is also metaphysical.

Israel's story of Creation entails a claim concerning the facts, all the facts there are, have been, or ever will be. It says of all the facts that they stand in reality and in truth in a certain relationship to God and therefore to each other. Being about *all* the facts, the claim is not itself based on particular factual evidence, nor is it subject to conclusive factual refutation. These are the features of every metaphysics, since each metaphysics constitutes a proposal to see everything that we are already looking at in a certain way, indeed to define what we will count as a fact and what we will count as a proof. If our metaphysics does not succeed in accounting for our experience of reality, we shall need and want to correct it, so that we can continue to see reality as, with its aid, we have believed it to be. Israel's story of reality is threatened by every event or development that challenges it, but Israel has shown that it has, in common with proponents of other conceptions of reality of the same logical type, great ability to adjust to new experiences and to fit them into its pattern, or, because its "pattern" is a narrative, to tell the story as one that changes with Israel's historical experience.

Israel's claim as to how things are has always had to make its way in a world of competing claims about reality. In the face of other views, Israel cannot prove that it has seen the truth. Metaphysical claims cannot finally be proved. They can always be discussed and there is always room for argument, but metaphysical disputes are difficult to settle because the common grounds for reaching a settlement are not present, the foundations themselves being the issue in question. Israel can therefore only confess and live by its conviction that all things are as its story portrays them.

Essential to Israel's testimony to the personal character of reality is its form as a story. Israel's is a narrative metaphysics. Reality for Israel, and for the church that has learned from and confirms Israel's testimony, can only rightly be presented in narrative form. Properly speaking, Israel does not have a *picture* of reality; it has a *story* of reality. As Israel tells it, all of reality other than God has come to be as the result of that One's personal intention and act, and therefore it belongs to him and owes him thanks and praise for its very existence. "How things really are" must be told as a tale because it is grounded in the reality of the person who is God. The world is God's and it stands to him in the relationship of the creature to its Creator, as Israel unfolds this in its story of Creation. The relationship, therefore, is not that of the relative to the absolute, or of the many to the one, but of creation to its Creator. It is the relationship with which Israel was confronted in the events of the Exodus and which was explained and made clear in the revelation from Sinai. Israel understands Creation, consequently, as its own personal story: "This is the word of the LORD, the word of your Creator, O Jacob, of him who fashioned you, O Israel: Have no fear, for I have paid your ransom: I have called you by name and you are mine" (Isa. 43:1).

What has this relationship to do, except by a reductionist move, with the absolute and the relative, or the one and the many? The uniqueness of this God consists entirely in the fact that he is the one who created and rescued Israel. His lordship does not *relativize* Israel; rather it *creates* Israel as his beloved possession, and that in such a way as to draw all creation into the role of fearful or joyful witnesses to his action.

> When Israel came out of Egypt,
> > Jacob from a people of outlandish speech,
> Judah became his sanctuary,
> > Israel his dominion.
> The sea looked and ran away;
> > Jordan turned back.
> The mountains skipped like rams,
> > The hills like young sheep.
> What was it, sea? Why did you run?
> > Jordan, why did you turn back?

> Why, mountains, did you skip like rams,
>   And you, hills, like young sheep?
> Dance, O earth, at the presence of the LORD,
>   At the presence of the God of Jacob,
> Who turned the rock into a pool of water,
>   The granite cliff into a fountain. (Ps. 114.)

It is an inescapable feature of Israel's faith in God the Creator that the Hebrew verb *barah*, to create, has always and only one subject in Israel's testimony: God (*Th. W. z. N.T.*, ad loc.). This should be a further warning to us that Israel's trust in God the Creator is of a different logical order from any view of "how things are" that might be developed on the basis of natural science. Natural science, as an attempt to understand the workings of things by the method of observation and the development of theories tested by further observation, would be impossible were God taken into it as one of its hypotheses, for it would thereby surrender the possibility of controlled experimentation. For the sake of good science, God must play no part in its hypotheses, and for the sake of good religion, neither Israel nor the church should attempt to bolster faith by an appeal to this or that scientific finding or hypothesis.

Since Israel's affirmation of God as Creator and the world as God's creation is, logically, a metaphysical one, it cannot be either in agreement or in disagreement with the natural sciences, for science, when it is true to itself, is not a metaphysical enterprise. Israel's affirmation, however, can and will be in conflict with other metaphysical assertions, for it is about reality, not merely about how it seems to Israel. Its subject is not Israel's faith but the object of that faith. It is about God as the loving Lord of all-there-is-other-than-God. It affirms that because God is real and good, so also is his creation. Such is Israel's conviction on the basis of the revelation of Sinai concerning the Exodus from Egypt, and such is the conviction of those Gentiles who, by the power of the One who raised Jesus from the dead, have been enabled to share Israel's trust in God the Creator.

The relationship between the Creator and his creation which Israel discovered in the Exodus by way of Sinai, the church of

Jesus Christ has discovered in a different way, namely in Easter
by way of the Spirit. It has been made known to Gentile believers by their having been awakened from the nothingness of
pagan darkness into life and light in Christ. The church knows
that the God who has done this is its Creator and, as the God
of Israel, the Creator of the world. The church, in short, has
learned this by having been inducted, in this different way,
into Israel's faith. The consequence is that it can only express
its faith in the Creator God of Easter by taking up Israel's testimony to the Creator God of the Exodus. A tell-tale witness to
this total dependence of Easter-faith on Israel's Exodus-faith in
God the Creator is the great Easter hymn of St. John of Damas-
cus (trans. J. M. Neale, *Hymnal of the Protestant Episcopal Church*,
1940, No. 94):

> Come ye faithful, raise the strain of triumphant gladness;
> God hath brought his Israel into joy from sadness;
> Loosed from Pharaoh's bitter yoke Jacob's sons and daughters;
> Led them with unmoistened foot through the Red Sea waters.
>
> 'Tis the spring of souls today; Christ hath burst his prison,
> And from three days' sleep in death as a sun hath risen;
> All the winter of our sins, long and dark, is flying
> From his light, to whom we give laud and praise undying.
>
> Now the queen of seasons, bright with the day of splendor,
> With the royal feast of feasts, comes its joy to render;
> Comes to glad Jerusalem, who with true affection
> Welcomes in unwearied strains Jesus' resurrection.

The opening words of Easter-faith (in the first stanza) are none
other than those of Exodus-faith. Easter-faith then struggles to
find its own independent voice by turning to the seasons of nature
(the second and the first two lines of the third stanza), only to
fall back again on the scriptural theme of Jerusalem, never fully
able to speak except with the tongue of Israel. Easter-faith, as
this hymn shows, has no independent voice, for Easter is the

church's way into the Exodus-faith of Israel in God the Maker of heaven and earth.

iii. Creation as Torah

Genesis 1:1, being the opening words of the Torah of Moses, is itself Torah, God's gracious gift of instruction to his people Israel — and then, through its dependence on Israel, to his Gentile church — concerning his relationship with them. It therefore seemed right to the Rabbis to teach that Creation was for the sake of Torah and thus also for the sake of Israel (M&L, 38). This will be easier to understand when we realize that Israel's Creation story is neither Genesis 1, nor Genesis 2, nor the two together, but all of the first eleven chapters of Genesis, constituting a prologue to the real beginning of Israel's story with the call of Abram (Gen. 12). Further, since the story of Creation follows upon the opening words of Torah, the Rabbis concluded that Torah preceded Creation, and that God looked into his Torah to see how he should make the world (*Gen. R.* Ber. I, 1). Since the story of Creation is itself Torah, Israel testifies that all creation shares in the covenant of which the Torah is the centerpiece. The whole creation is therefore seen to take part in Israel's praise of God, as we have seen, with the heavens joining Israel in declaring God's glory (Ps. 19).

It was a pathetic misreading of Israel's testimony when a later generation of Christians, unmindful of the fact that as Gentiles they had been invited to speak of the Creator only in dependence on Israel, pretended that Psalm 19 gave them the right to speak of a "natural" revelation of God in creation quite apart from Torah. Seen through the prism of Torah, however, the world was and is viewed by Israel as the place and context for faithfulness, more precisely, for life in the covenant between God and Israel. In this light, a saying of the Rabbis (*Ber.* 33b; M&L, 285), that all is in the hands of heaven except the fear of heaven, can open us to a testimony of Israel which the church needs to hear: precisely in that fear of heaven — that is, in Israel's loving obedience to God in the covenant — it becomes possible to see everything else as being in the loving hands of its Creator. That is why God alone is to be loved and feared. Then all else can be appreciated, but nothing else need be feared. As the context of Psalm 19 is Torah, so Israel testifies that all creation gives its echo to the praise of Torah's God.

The Jewish witness is therefore not at all against general revelation in principle. Seeing the world from the perspective of the covenant, Israel seems rather to take for granted that God's creation declares the glory of God. The church would do well to ponder the particularity of revelation which makes this universal claim seem plausible, on the one hand, and on the other, the fact the Jews immediately draw the halakhic conclusion that God's claim, and the obligation to obey such commandments as God has prescribed for them, lies upon all human beings.

Israel's basis for trust in God as Creator, and for knowing the world as God's creation, is the covenant. Israel has had no other special experiences or insights about the world which might not have been had by others. Called by Israel's God in Jesus Christ to share in this trust and knowledge, the Gentile church is privileged and pleased to add its witness to that of Israel on the same basis. Jews and Christians can therefore be as right or as wrong as anyone else about various hypotheses concerning the formation of the earth or the origin and development of homo sapiens. About Creation as Torah, however, about Creation as God's gift and act of love for the sake of Israel and the covenant, Israel can only make — and the church can only add — its confession in thankfulness and live its life in faithfulness.

iv. Creation as gospel

Genesis 1:1 is good news in which Israel rejoices and on the basis of which it calls all creation to join it in rejoicing before its Maker for the gift of *becoming*, which is more than just *being*. Israel does not rejoice simply in existence, and it does not see Creation as an act conferring only existence, for Israel (and therefore creation) does not just exist. Israel and the world exist in the hands of the loving God who made them, watches over them, and calls them to corporate with him in the completion which he intends for them. The Creator is the Redeemer, and the creation of *this* Creator has not been made to be alone. It has been created to be with its Creator and so to be redeemed from all its suffering.

As Genesis 1 through 11 is the introduction pointing ahead to Genesis 12, the call of Abram, so Genesis 1:1 points to and reaches its climax in Genesis 2:2–3, the seventh day of Creation. The whole world was made for and moves toward *Shabbat*, wh'ch is God's *shalom*. In Israel's story, the Sabbath is the real crown of creation, and not, as is so often said, human beings (made on the same day as the other animals!). And the goal of Creation is likewise the Sabbath: not simply human life, but human life in God's service. The Seventh Day, therefore, is not just one among the seven, but their queen. Israel calls it the Bride, the sign of the everlasting covenant, even God's crown (as it says in the Jewish service for Welcoming *Shabbat*). Given this vision of the goal, then, we may read Genesis 1:1 with Israel as the beginning of the story of all God's works, the heart of which is the eternal covenant between God and Israel, up to their completion in God's future. In the beginning, we are to hear, God began to move out of himself and toward an other. That movement toward an other defines God's lordship of love over that other. God is not the sort of lord who wills his own glory for himself. On the contrary, he is the LORD who wills that all that he has made be for his glory by sharing with him in his glory (Isa. 43:7). That is Israel's gospel for creation.

2. GOD'S BECOMING CREATOR

i. *God the Creator*

To know and confess God as Creator is to know and confess One "who calls into being what does not exist" (Rom. 4:17; cf. Hebr. 11:3). This knowledge and confession arise from hearing the relationship between the LORD and Abraham, with his body as good as dead, and Sarah, with her dead womb, who nevertheless receive a son. They arise also from hearing of the same relationship between the LORD and his people, called forth out of the death of slavery in Egypt into life in the covenant. They arise once again from hearing of the relationship between the LORD and the crucified Jesus, awakened to life on Easter morning in order to awaken dead Gentiles through his Spirit to a life hidden with him in God (Rom. 6:4; 8:11; Eph. 2:1, 4-6; Col. 2:12-13). To know and confess God as Creator is therefore to know and confess the sheer miracle of election, the miracle of our own calling, as Israel or as church, and to know and confess the LORD not only as our Creator, but also as Creator of our faith in him. He causes the blind to see, the deaf to hear, and dead bones to rise up and stand in his service (Isa. 35:5; Ezek. 37). That is the heart of faith in God as Creator, Israel's faith first of all, and then also the same faith into which the church has been drawn by God the Creator Spirit.

Israel comes to this knowledge and makes this confession on the basis of the gift of Torah. It makes this confession on this side of the Exodus. It knows, therefore, that although it has been called into a responsible life with God, in a covenant that demands Israel's active participation, it has arrived at this new situation on the basis of grace alone. Its testimony is clear on this point. All it could contribute to its rescue from the death of slavery was the pitiful cry of the dying. It could offer no more to its rescue than a later crucified Jew could offer to the event of Easter morning. Its God is the Creator, he who calls into being what does not exist.

The church comes to this knowledge and makes this confession on the basis of the gift of the Spirit. It makes this confession on this side of Pentecost. It knows, therefore, that although it has been called to follow its risen Lord and through him to serve Israel's God and his Father, and therefore to stand in dependent solidarity with God's Israel to which it has now been affiliated, it has arrived at this new situation on the basis of grace alone. Its testimony on this is also clear. All it could contribute to its rescue from the death of paganism was its blind groping for it knew not what. It could offer no more to its rescue than its crucified Master could offer to the event of Easter morning.

Its God is the Creator, he who calls into being what does not exist. The church's doctrine of Creation, therefore, can only confirm Israel's confession, echoing the great Yes of the Creator with the feeble Yes of its response: In the beginning God created the heavens and the earth. That is the God of whom Israel, and therefore also the church, speak.

ii. God "in himself"

If we have presented Israel's testimony to Creation correctly, it is easy to see why this confession is never argued or explained in the Scriptures: it is the absolute foundation and presupposition of everything else that Israel has to say. Having this as its starting point, Israel could only argue from it, never to it. In Israel's later history, however, as in the history of the church, pagan conceptions of the world and the gods seemed to have presented a sufficient challenge to have led at least some Jews and Christians to try to reason out the implications of their common confession of God the Creator.

The question can arise, for example, whether God created the world out of something already there, or out of nothing. The text of Genesis 1:1 does not address this question; indeed, it does not seem even to be aware of it. That will only surprise us if we forget that Genesis 1:1 is the opening verse of the Torah of Moses. When we recall the context, however, and also listen to other parts of Israel's confession (to which the testimony of the Apostolic Writings may be added), we are forced to answer that God created the world out of nothing, *ex nihilo*, for Genesis 1:1 and all of Israel's testimony speaks only of the God who calls into being what does not exist.

The doctrine of *creatio ex nihilo* is not threatened by the astronomical hypothesis of "the Big Bang" out of which all detectable galaxies may have come. If the hypothesis is sound, there must have been something there which went "bang," but this hypothesis, if it is scientific, is not and cannot be about Creation. It is, rather, an attempt to account for all the evidence which science can assemble, and God is no part of that evidence. The doctrine of Creation, on the other hand, begins with God and formulates Israel's confession that, however the process may have developed, conceivably including a "Big Bang," all that is, from the smallest detail of this earth to the outer reaches of the de-tectible universe, is God's gift of the context for our existence in lov-ing response to his love. Creation is for the sake of Torah-shaped life, for the sake of Israel in the covenant, brought into being out of the nothingness of slavery.

Christian reflection on the concept of *creatio ex nihilo* should be aware of a Jewish warning: the concept cannot mean that the world is such that only God can accomplish that which takes place in it. On the basis of the revelation from Sinai, Israel insists that God's creative love con-fers freedom, and that he has called his world and his creatures into *being*, into responsible history.

The question may also arise whether Creation is more prop-erly to be thought of as an event or a process. If again we forget the context of Genesis 1:1, we may be tempted by the processive character of organic and inorganic creaturely existence to think of Creation itself as a process. Israel's conception of Creation, however, arising as it does out of the event of the Exodus and the gift of Torah, is also that of an event. An event that sets a story in motion, however, will not be of the same kind as events within the story. The event of Creation initiates Israel's narrative. If narrative be conceived as a process, then the opening of the story is to that extent processive, but the "process" in question is essentially personal. It is God's doing, not an impersonal hap-pening. In order to do justice to this crucial aspect of Israel's testimony to Creation, it seems more precise to call it an event.

It has also been asked whether God created the heavens and the earth out of some necessity or—the only alternative—by divine caprice. Once more, we need to set the question in the terms of Israel's testimony. When we do so, we are asking in personal terms whether Creation is the necessary consequence of God's love, or is it purely the result of God's sovereign freedom? But Israel's testimony knows of no conflict between God's love and his freedom. On the contrary, as God created Israel, so he created the world by an act of his free love. Israel's doctrine of Creation tells us that God freely willed to have an other to share in his love.

Franz Rosenzweig's discussion of the supposed dilemma in *Der Stern der Erlösung* is worth listening to here. If Creation is by necessity, because God's love *had* to be expressed, then "God is robbed of his inner freedom and the world forfeits its internal cohesiveness, its ability to stand on its own" (127; cf. E.T. 115). If it is by caprice, however, "the creative emergence of God out of himself is turned into a mere factuality, inessential for him, and God's being is removed to a height that is foreign to the world and suspended over it," a purely pagan idea (126f; cf. E.T. 114). Rosenzweig's solution was to locate caprice "not in the Creator's act of creation, but prior to it in the self-configuration of God which precedes his act of Creation" (127; cf. E.T. 115). "Therefore those who ascribe inner, essential necessity to the divine creative act are right against those who assert its capriciousness. This inner necessity, however, was grounded in the transformation from hiddenness to the revealed, so as against those who exaggerated it into a passionate need, reinterpreting power as love, the ones who asserted divine caprice were on the right track by pointing to the inner core of boundless freedom in God. But of course this core, in bursting forth, forfeits its inner boundlessness and reveals itself as serene, necessarily creative, omniscient omnipotence" (128f; cf. E.T. 116).

If we translate this from Rosenzweig's architectonic scheme of thought, we may say that God's love was exercised in Creation on the basis of his soverign freedom to become the Creator. Creation is the exercise of his freedom to love and of love freely offered. In no case ought we to think of God's love as necessitating him to be other than he has freely chosen to be, or of his freedom as any other than that of love.

Other Jewish voices, those of some halakhically oriented Israelis, however, would call Rosenzweig's thought mere abstraction, the result of his assimilation into the world of Germanic Christianity. From this other perspective, the issue is far more whether God created a world free to be — and then commanded to be — responsible to him. My own judgment concerning these different Jewish notes is that they are more harmonious than discordant. What other world would a God who loved freely have created, than one in which the creature was free to love and so to obey God in response?

The doctrine of Creation, on the basis of which Israel can answer such questions as these, is grounded for Israel in the events of the Exodus and Sinai. For the church, the grounds are the resurrection of Jesus and the outpouring of the Spirit, by which the church has been introduced into Israel's faith. Israel bears this testimony, and the church gladly confirms it, as an act of trust in God's revelation, that God is truly and in all ways the LORD as he has shown himself to be in his relationship to Israel and to the church as their Creator and therefore also as Creator of the heavens and the earth. Insofar as Israel and the church speak of "God in himself," their meaning is that God is truly himself as he has shown himself to be in his relationship to Israel and the church.

iii. God Becoming

"In the beginning God created the heavens and the earth." That implies something of a beginning in God, as well as an absolute beginning for the world, either as a "coming out of himself," to use Rosenzweig's terms, or at least as an undertaking. "In the beginning," in relation to which it would be nonsense to speak of "before," God began to be the God whom Israel knows by way of Torah and the church by way of Jesus Christ. God became, we can say, what he surely had it in him to become.

Eberhard Jüngel's excellent study of a fundamental aspect of Karl Barth's doctrine of the Trinity, *Gottes Sein ist im Werden* (1965, E.T. *The Doctrine of the Trinity*, 1976; a more faithful translation of the title would have been, "God's Being Consists in Becoming"), should be read in this connection.

God's becoming Creator is God's revelation concerning himself that his very being is becoming: he is God on the move in the beginning, and as he became the Creator, so he is becoming the Redeemer, moving to redeem Israel, to gather his church, and to rescue both together with the whole of his creation. In this sense, we can say that the act of Creation is revelation. More precisely, Creation becomes revelation to an Israel created in the Exodus and at Sinai and to a church created on Easter and at Pentecost. It does not follow from this that anyone can simply look at a sunset, a mountain, or any other fruit of Creation and see God in it. Revelation is not something lying around for any person to see or not see. Revelation, according to Israel's testimony, is God's specific word to specific individuals, and God is as hidden in revelation as he is behind his creation. Indeed, not every person, not even every Jew reading Torah, will automatically hear there the word of God. Yet God does speak in and through his Torah, and for those who have heard his voice there, who know Sinai's God as their own Creator LORD, have also been able to say that the heavens declare the glory of God. The heavens and all creation do indeed declare God's glory to those whose ears and eyes have been opened by Sinai or Easter. Genesis 1:1, we recall, is the opening of the Torah of Moses, Israel's confession of Exodus trust. On the basis of this contextual understanding of Creation, Israel knows, and the church knows from and with Israel, that God's creative being is a creative becoming. It knows that God is, has always been, and will be until the End, the coming God.

3. GOD'S INVOLVEMENT

i. *God's Self-Determination*

The act of Creation constitutes a divine self-determination. A self-determining act is a step freely chosen which commits the agent of that step to the consequent course. Thereafter, things will never be the same for that agent. In the unique case of Creation, where the agent is God, we must presume that God took this step in full freedom and with full awareness of what he was doing. This act, however, involved a decision as well about himself as about Creation. Having made this decision and taken this step, there are some things which God cannot be and some choices that are no longer open to him: God can never again be anything other than the Creator of the heavens and the earth. From then on, he had creation on his hands, so to speak. From that point forward, God and creation are together, which is to say that God has time and history on his hands. God can no more be timeless and apart from history than he can cease to be what he has freely decided to be: Creator of the heavens and the earth.

It should be said that this conclusion is not reached by free speculation, nor is it the logical conclusion of an analysis of the concept of Creation. It is known by Israel from the event of the Exodus as revealed from Sinai. The church knows this in no other way than by the testimony of Israel, mediated to it by the resurrection of Jesus Christ and the outpouring of the Spirit. The basis for this conclusion, then, is the fact that the LORD's way of being God is by being in time and history the God of his people Israel and of his church.

The staggering awareness that God has determined himself by his free act of love in creating a world, as a place for the free display of and free response to his love, has been nowhere so dramatically, if untypically, expressed as in the work of the great sixteenth-century Kabbalist Isaac Luria. Luria, at least according to the interpretation of Gershon Scholem (*Major Trends in Jewish Mysticism*, 1961, 260ff; cf. *On the Kabbalah and its Symbolism*, 1969, 110f), took the event of Creation with a seriousness appropriate to the majesty of him who was the Creator. Since God was everything there was before he made the heavens and the earth, it was necessary, as Scholem read Luria (and he has been read differently, e.g., by Prof. Isaiah Tishby), that, in an act of sheer grace, God must have contracted himself, so to speak, in order to make room for his creation to exist at all. Creation, in short, must have involved an agonizing transformation of the divine.

Luria's concept of the *tsimtsum* (the divine contraction) may appear to be purely speculative, but Scholem argues that it was part of his response to the inordinate suffering of the Jewish people that followed upon their mass expulsion from Spain in 1492. In the light of that suffering, Luria could only conceive of the whole of creation as having come about through the cosmic pain of divine contraction. Although speculative, therefore, *tsimtsum* expresses the hidden involvement of God in his creation: suffering in this world is accompanied by the hidden suffering of God from the beginning. The church too has a conception of divine suffering, derived from reflection on the crucifixion of Christ. This could also be read back at least into the time of Creation, as is evidenced by the old translation of Revelation 13:8, which spoke of "the Lamb slain from the foundations of the world" (Authorized Version, Luther's translation, and of course the Vulgate; all modern translations reject this reading, agreeing that "from the foundations of the world" modifies the Book of Life, which belongs to the Lamb that has been slain, and does not refer to an eternal slaying). Luria's mystical speculation, however, informed by Jewish suffering, according to Scholem's interpretation, found divine suffering already in the act of Creation and therefore in the being of the Creator himself. This expresses more radically God's self-determination in the act of Creation.

Creation, according to the testimony of Israel, is an act of sheer giving at inestimable cost. It is grace through and through. Israel's response to Creation, therefore, has not had suffering at its center, but rather joy and thanksgiving. That joy comes from the wonder and delight of knowing oneself to be alive in a world that is the gift of the LORD who renews day by day the work of the first days. The Creator, according to Israel, is the Redeemer, for, being determined by his initial act, God will not abandon creation to the powers of destruction. Though it walk through the valley of the shadow of death, its Creator will be with it (Ps. 23:4). Israel can be sure of this because it trusts in the Creator-Redeemer of the Exodus and Sinai.

ii. *The determination of creation*

By becoming the Creator, God determined himself, but because creation is his handiwork, it too is determined by this act, first of all as something real. Creation is real as God is real. It is not a figment of God's or of human imagination. Neither God nor human beings can blink and then find that there is nothing at all. We need not worry about pagan philosophical fears that the external world may be only a product of our dreams. If creation is in danger—and it is—the threat is not epistomological. Israel's witness to the God of the Exodus and Sinai tells us that God's addressee—the newly created free people—is a genuine entity, a real hearer of God's address. Its hearing is as real as God's speaking. Its creaturely existence is as real as God's creative existence.

Creation is real, however, as God's possession. This is the other side of its determination. It is God's because God made it for his own good purpose. On this, G. F. Moore is worth hearing: "God has the power to do in this world whatever he wills, and he has the right of the creator to deal as he wills with his creatures. But nothing is more established in the Jewish thought of God than that he does not use this power willfully like some almighty tyrant, but with wisdom and justice and for a supremely good end" (*Judaism*, I, 379). Israel's witness to Creation is that the heavens and the earth belong to God, not to humanity. The idea that the earth is ours to do with as we will is an invention of the modern age. Israel's witness is otherwise. The verse from Psalm 115, "The heavens are the LORD's heavens, but the earth he has given to the sons of men" (v. 16), when read in context, is no license for human beings to exercise an unlimited mastery over the earth. On the contrary, the earth remains fully God's possession and its use is a gift of grace to human beings.

Although ancient Israel's witness to Creation did not contemplate the danger presently threatening creation, namely, that human beings may so corrupt the earth as to make it literally unfit for human or any other form of life, it did include a clear understanding of the moral relationship between the people and the land which God gave it. As we shall see at a later point, Israel knew that it could corrupt that land by its own corrupt life, and that if this were to happen, then the land would vomit this people out (Lev. 18:28). "The land shall not be sold in perpetuity, for the land is mine," says Israel's Creator (Lev. 25:23). The danger to creation lies in the realm of the moral and the political.

Arthur Waskow's *Godwrestling* (1978) is a bit of evidence that Israel's witness on this matter is alive and well. See particularly Chapter 9.

Israel's witness to Creation is more oriented to the future than to the past. Jewish thinking about the world has been and is more concerned with where the world is going than with how it began. Again we may be guided by G. F. Moore:

> God is not only the sole creator of the world, he alone upholds it and maintains in existence by his immediate will and power everything that is. The universal teaching of the Bible is equally the doctrine of Judaism: "God created and he provides; he made and he sustains." The maintainance of the world is a kind of continuous creation: God in his goodness makes anew every day continually the work of creation. The history of the world is his great plan, in which everything moves to the fulfillment of his purpose, the end that he has in mind (*Judaism*, I, 384).

That end is the completion of creation, Israel's great hope.

The connection between Israel's hope and its witness to creation lies behind the saying of the rabbis, "Creation is for the sake of Torah" (*Gen.R.*, Ber., XII, 2). Presupposed by this saying is the conviction that Creation has a purpose. God's purpose, however, is expressed in his Torah. Creation, that is to say, is for the sake of the covenant of Sinai, which is in turn for the sake of the redemption of the whole Creation. The created world is therefore God's real place for his real history with his creatures. It is determined to be the location for the march of history leading to redemption. Israel's witness to Creation, in the context of its witness to Sinai, has Israel's own history — which is God's history with Israel — as the center of its story, to be sure, but it occupies that position as the revelation of God's plan for the whole of Creation. This witness is therefore an invitation to all other peoples to see their own histories in their own places in this light. If Creation is for the sake of Torah, that is because Torah has in view the whole created order. It is Israel's witness to the whole world.

iii. God's involvement: without mixture or change, separation or division

The dual determination, of God as Creator and of everything else as his creation, entails a relationship between God and Creation which we have described thus far only as personal. We should now attempt to be more specific about the character of God's involvement in creation. The first step is to recall Israel's witness that the Creator is the Redeemer, and that redemption is the completion of Creation. Both Creation and Redemption being the work of the one God, we may reasonably assume that the character of his involvement will be the same in both cases. At first glance this would seem to get us nowhere, for we appear to be equating two unknowns: Creation is prehistorical and Redemption lies in the future. They appear as unknowns, however, only when abstracted from Israel's testimony. Taken as terms within Israel's witness, both Creation and Redemption are anchored in and defined by reference to the Exodus-Sinai event. That event was neither Creation nor Redemption, but it was surely creative and redemptive, and the relationship between God and Israel therein revealed determined Israel's testimony concerning God's involvement in creation.

In the fifth century of its history, the church, attempting to reconcile conflicting opinions within it, came to a compromise formula which did not so much define as set limits for speaking of the relationship between the divine and the human, the Creator and the creature, in the person and event of Jesus Christ. It settled on two pairs of negative adverbs: the relationship was without mixture or change, but also without separation or division. We turn to these adverbs to open up Israel's witness to God's involvement in his creation, which will then at a later point (in Part III) provide a framework for interpreting these Christological terms.

In that event of anticipatory redemption in which God drew the Gentile church into his plan for Israel and thus for his whole creation, God was involved with his creation, in the person of Jesus of Nazareth, without mixture or change, said the Fathers of Chalcedon. That is to say, the Creator remained fully the Creator and the creature remained unqualifiedly a creature. In creating the world, God remains the Lord and the creation is ever and always his possession. God did not become part of it, nor did it become any part of God. It is not God's soul or body, not some emanation from him. It is his creation, with which he can do as he pleases in justice and mercy.

On the other hand, the relationship is that of an involvement so intimate that there can be no separation or division. God is with his creation even in its bleakest and most desolate moments, sustaining it and drawing it toward its completion. From Creation to final Redemption, the world will never be without or apart from God. He is with it and for it and working within it until the end:

> Where can I escape from your Spirit?
>   Or where can I flee from your presence?
> If I climb up to heaven, you are there!
>   If I make my bed in Sheol, you are there!
> If I take the wings of dawn to dwell at the outermost
>   edge of the sea,
>   Even there your hand shall lead me and your right
>   hand shall hold me.
> If I say, "The darkness will cover me,
>   And night shall close me in,"
> Even darkness is not dark to you, and the night is
>   bright as day;
>   To you both dark and light are one (Ps. 139:7–12).

Creation cannot escape its Creator, and he will not abandon it. In Israel's witness, the model for the relationship is clearly that of the covenant. The same model of intimacy, to which distance is no obstacle, will guide us when we come to interpret the witness of the church.

iv. Creation, Revelation, Redemption

Israel learned and learns about the Creator from the event in which it was created. It learns that its Creator is at the same time its Redeemer, because it was created in an event that can be called "protoredemptive." We use this term to catch the dual aspect of the Exodus event: it was an actual, if qualified, redemption, and it leads Israel to hope for a full redemption. It was indeed redemptive, but it was not totally redemptive. It is the opening, the beginning work of a redemption still awaited. From that protoredemptive event in which it was created, Israel learned of its Creator, Maker of heaven and earth.

Israel's testimony to Creation received its definitive formulation during the course of a further event which was read through Exodus-formed eyes: the return to Jerusalem from Exile in Babylon. The unknown prophet of the Exile, usually designated Deutero-Isaiah, saw in this deuteroredemptive event the inseparable connection between Creation and Redemption: God is One—one in creating and one in redeeming. The Creator is the Redeemer, and the Redeemer is no other than the Creator. So Israel returned to Jerusalem with the Torah of Moses that opens with the good news that in the beginning Israel's redeemer made the heavens and the earth.

The Gentile church learned of the Creator from the testimony of Israel, to which it was awakened by the protoredemptive event through which it was created. The event of the life, death, and resurrection of Jesus Christ, capped by the outpouring of the Holy Spirit, was redemptive, but not totally redemptive. It led the church to hope for a full redemption of which the protoredemptive event was a foretaste. Like Israel's testimony to the return from Exile, the church's testimony to Easter and Pentecost draws upon the original protoredemptive experience of Exodus-Sinai. In the light of that event, it can rehearse the opening words of the First Book of Moses to tell of the Creator who has brought life from the dead.

For Israel, and therefore also for the church, Creation, Revelation, and Redemption are and must remain inseparable terms, three aspects of the work of God which can never be thought of properly in isolation from each other. Whenever Israel's or the church's words about any one of them is in order, their words concerning the other two will be in order. This is because God has revealed that he is Creator and Redeemer together. We can clarify this by reviewing the testimony of Israel's story of Creation, the first eleven chapters of Genesis, and then the church's variation on this, as found in the Prologue to the Gospel according to John.

4. THE COVENANTAL SHAPE OF GENESIS 1 TO 11

i. *Creation and covenant*

Israel's Creation story, which is its testimony to the context of its relationship with its Creator, and therefore of how things stand between God and all creation, is unfolded in the first eleven, not just the first two, chapters of the First Book of Moses. Reality, as Israel understands it, cannot be represented by a picture of its beginning as God's good work; it must be presented in the story of how the world as we now know it came to be. It is therefore the story of an unfinished creation, a creation in need of redemption. Israel's story of Creation opens with "In the beginning" and leads up to the story of the call of Abram in Genesis 12. Those first eleven chapters taken together tell the tale of that reality which was the context of God's call of Abram to become Abraham, eventuating in his covenant with Abraham's offspring, Israel. The rabbinic sayings that Creation is for the sake of Torah and Israel, therefore, can help us to see the literary relationship between Israel's Creation story in the first eleven chapters of Genesis and the rest of Torah.

The created world is good, even very good, because it was made by God for the sake of the covenant. It is good, but it is not perfect. One could call it a spoiled world, if by "world" one meant creation as we hear of it in only the first two chapters of Genesis. As one reads further, however, to the stories of Adam and Eve and of Cain and Abel, one must conclude that Israel did not think of the world primarily as spoiled, but as unfinished and threatened. It is threatened by Adam's disobedience and Cain's thirst for revenge, by the builders of the tower of Babel and above all by human violence, reaching its peak in the generation of Noah. Between these stories, however, there are others: of the building of cities and the making of tools and musical instruments in Gen. 4:17, 20–22 and of the succession of generations leading up to the family of Abram. This created world in which Israel lives its covenant with God is a mixed affair.

We shall return in the next chapter to the subject of evil, but in this context it must be said already that evil, chaos, and darkness are also part of this created world, as Israel understands it. These too are within the power of God, to send upon those who mock him. Evil and darkness are part of what the Creator has formed in making this world (Isa. 45:5–7). The story of the flood is a reminder of how far God can let chaos loose in creation. For all that, it is clear that Israel testifies to God's control over chaos. It is held in check by the Creator, even as it is present as a threat to creation. In sum, Israel's story of Creation is not all light; it looks ahead to a light that is yet to come, a star of redemption.

Israel told and tells this story of reality on the basis of its covenant with God and therefore in hope. It placed its tale of Creation in the opening chapters of the Torah from Sinai, for it learned of Creation by the hand of Moses *after* it had learned of redemption by the hand of God. Looking back on "the beginning" from this vantage point, it told the story of Creation as the setting for the covenant of Sinai. The created world could only be there for the sake of the covenant. One of Israel's stricter Pharisees, in speaking of suffering and evil in creation, said that God had subjected the world to this threatened condition "in hope" (Rom. 8:20). The expression catches exactly the realism of Israel's story of reality and also the angle of vision from which it is seen and presented. Because the Creator is the Redeemer, because Israel was created out of the darkness of slavery, Israel knows of the dark side of creation. But Israel knows more surely that there are grounds for hope, not in creation itself, but in him who subjected creation to the consequences of sin and evil "in hope" — that is, with an eye to the future good which he has planned for it.

ii. Creation as covenant

Israel's story of Creation is told from the perspective of Sinai. So it was in the Torah of Moses that Ezra brought to Jerusalem after the Return from the Exile and read to all the people. So it has been in the tradition of rabbinic interpretation for the continuing life of the Jewish people. The whole Creation story, from the first through the eleventh chapter of Genesis, is shaped by Israel's primal and originating experience. Creation is therefore seen as being itself covenantal. The world, as Israel knows it, is not just there; it is there for God's purpose. It is commanded.

In Karl Barth's doctrine of Creation, a detailed exegesis of Genesis 1 and 2 forms the bulk of Vol. III/1 of his *Church Dogmatics*. Genesis 1 presents Creation as the ground of the covenant, and Genesis 2 presents the covenant as the goal of Creation. While concurring with this reading of those two chapters, we are allowing a wider focus, since Israel's story of Creation is unfolded in the first eleven chapters and not merely in the first two, as Barth thought, following the Augustinian tradition of western Christianity.

The commandments of the covenant of Creation are simple, but they are none the less commandments: the fish are ordered to multiply and fill the waters and the birds to multiply on the earth (Gen. 1:20); human beings are to multiply and fill the earth and have dominion over every living thing (1:28); Adam is to take care of the garden God has planted for him (2:15), to eat certain of its produce and to abstain from others (2:16f). The covenant of Creation becomes yet more explicit in repetition when God makes it with Noah and his sons: preceded by God's commitment to preserve the seasonal order (8:22), the commandment is given to Noah and his sons to multiply and fill the earth (9:1). Again and again in more detail, God commands that some things may be eaten and others not (9:3f), and the rainbow is set in the sky of God "as a sign of the covenant between me and the earth" (9:13). The renewal of creation after the flood makes more explicit the covenantal character of the original Creation.

The covenant of Creation, like the covenant of Sinai, is presented in Israel's testimony as being less than successful. No sooner was the Sinai covenant made than the incident of the Golden Calf occurred. No sooner was the covenant of Creation established than Adam and Eve ate what was forbidden, Cain murdered his brother, and violence filled the earth in the time of Noah. No sooner was the covenant of Creation renewed after the flood than we are told of Noah's drunkenness and shame, and then the disobedience of the men of Babel.

The nature of the disobedience of the builders of the tower of Babel is not clear in the story. What was their sin? Was it that they wished to "make a name" for themselves? But what commandment would that violate? The one commandment clearly violated was to fill the earth (Gen. 1:28; 9:1), for in the story, the city with its tower was started by the men of Babel "lest we be scattered abroad upon the face of the whole earth" (11:4. So Sarna, 72.) Whatever their sin was, one rabbinic Midrash argues that it could not have been as serious as that of the men of Sodom, since the punishment of the people of Babel was only to be scattered, whereas that for the inhabitants of the latter city was total destruction. The lesser punishment, it was suggested, implies that the men of Babel must at least have loved one another (*Ab. R. N.*, vers. 1, XII, 26b. M&L, 468).

The story of Creation is nevertheless characterized by continuities. The geneological tables (the "begats") perform the theological as well as literary role of tying the story together from the beginning up to Abraham. The result is one continuous story of the working out of the relationship between God and his creation, told so as to point ahead to its covenantal realization. When we come to the story of Abraham, therefore, where we are confronted with a new step told in a new way, that *novum* has been well prepared for. And we may say further that what God did at Sinai was not foreign to his ways with his creation, for as Israel tells its story, God's mind was set on this covenant from the beginning. Already in God's determination of himself and his creation, a covenant was implicit "in the beginning." To covenant-shaped eyes, creation itself appears as a covenant.

iii. The priority of Torah to Creation

As we heard from the Rabbis, the world was made according to the pattern of Torah. This judgment contains an important exegetical insight: the first eleven chapters of Genesis, and therefore also the first two, breathe the atmosphere of the coming covenant of Sinai. They are in form and content the introduction to Torah.

Robert Alter (*The Art of Biblical Narrative*, 1981) finds this theme of the priority of Torah to Creation in the work of the writer who combined the two Creation narratives of Genesis 1 and Genesis 2. In the account of 1:1 to 2:4a (usually designated *P*, for a Priestly tradition dating from the sixth to the fifth century *B.C.E.*), "coherence is the keynote of creation" (143). Indeed, "Law is the underlying characteristic of the world as God makes it" (144). In the second chapter, drawn from the earlier *J* tradition, there is "a moral tension between man and God—a notion not hinted at in *P*—and also, as God's solicitude for man's loneliness shows, there is a divine concern for man" (145). Alter gives credit to the writer who put these two accounts together for having seen the complexity of reality, a complexity not faithfully represented in either text alone. Israel's understanding of reality requires both, and both together. God's sovereign will does underlie all reality, yet the moral struggle between God and human beings takes place within that reality. Hence, we would add, the rabbinic dictum: All is in the hands of heaven (the witness of Genesis 1), except the fear of heaven (the witness of Genesis 2f).

Alter's reading of Genesis 1 and 2 is helpful, but he has left something out of account. The Law that underlies the world of Genesis 1 is not simply "Law," but Torah, the Torah of Sinai. Torah is central to the covenant, a divine ordering which invites, indeed commands, a human responsive ordering. Whether that human ordering, which is called obedience, will follow is the great open question already implied in the first chapter, even if made explicit only in the second. Alter captured this point precisely in another place: there is, he writes, "a complex moral and psychological realism in biblical narrative because God's purposes are always entrammeled in history, dependent on the acts of individual men and women for their continuing realization" (12). That is the framework of creation in which Israel learned of Torah, and in the light of that Torah it told its complex tale of the creation of the world by the Giver of that Torah.

Consequently, Israel's full Creation story of Genesis 1 through 11 is not oriented simply to the divine will, as only appears to be the case when one forgets that the first chapter is the opening of the Torah of Moses. It is oriented to the covenant. Creation, one may say, is the setting for which Torah is the diamond. It is the question for which Torah is the answer. It is the problem of which Torah is the solution.

iv. The witness of Torah-life to Creation

Israel's life is Torah-life. Faithfulness to Torah is the calling of the Jewish people, which has kept it alive before God for centuries and has distinguished Israel from all the other nations of the world: "God gave the Israelites two [Torahs], the Written and the Oral. He gave them the Written [Torah] with its 613 ordinances to fill them with commandments and cause them to be virtuous. . . . And he gave them the Oral [Torah] to make them distinguished from the other nations" (*Num. R.* Naso, xiv, 10. M&L, 159).

Living by Torah is Israel's grateful response to the covenant of grace made with Israel at Sinai by its Redeemer and Creator. The covenant is of grace because it is a gift of God's free love and is accepted by Israel as such. Living by Torah is by no means the way into this covenant; it is rather Israel's response to the gift of the covenant. It is how Israel lives because of its election, and that election is God's free gift.

On this matter the Reformed Orthodox theologians of the seventeenth century were clear and consistent with their so-called Federal theology (from *foedus*, the Latin for covenant. For a convenient summary of their teaching, with many citations, see H. Heppe, *Reformed Dogmatics*, E.T. 1950, esp. chaps. xiii and xvi). The idea of covenant, they were convinced, was the heart of the Bible, so they made it the organizing principle of their work. God's covenant was the establishing of communion between the infinite Creator and the finite creature. This was first established with Adam as a "covenant of works," in which Adam was called to respond to God's command with obedience. After the fall, this covenant was no longer possible. Therefore by his free grace God established his "covenant of grace" with the Patriarchs, at Sinai, and then openly in Jesus Christ. As one of them argued (L. Riissen), "there may be as many covenants (and not more) as there are ways and means of obtaining blessedness and communion with God, who is the proper end of the institution of a covenant. But there are only two such means, either by inherent and proper obedience or by imputed, through *either* works *or* faith. Although we admit that the covenant of Sinai differed as to mode of administration . . . , in actual substance it is the same as the covenant entered into with Abraham, . . ." which is no other than the covenant of grace through Jesus Christ (Heppe, 399). However deficient one must find much of their understanding of the Sinai covenant, and however much warped by the use of a faith/works dichotomy, the Federal theologians at least saw that Israel's witness to the covenant of Sinai was a witness to God's free grace. What their faith/works dichotomy blinded them to was Israel's witness that concrete obedience is the primary response which God's grace requires and makes possible.

Torah-faithfulness is Israel's testimony to God. It is Israel's way of bearing witness to the Creator and Redeemer even to the point of death. To die rather than abandon Torah, to perish rather than disobey a commandment, is, in Israel's tradition, "to sanctify the Name" of God. Torah-living therefore holds before the world, if the world cares to notice, the sign of the One who created and will redeem Israel and also the whole world. Against all paganisms, ancient and modern, Israel bears witness by its Torah-faithful existence to the one Creator of all there is.

Because the Creator is the Redeemer, witness to the Creator is also witness to the Redeemer. In keeping faithful to Torah, therefore, Israel not only bears witness to but also hastens the day of redemption, the completion of the whole creation. A rabbinic Midrash has it that if all Israel would fully keep two successive Sabbaths, redemption would come (*Sab.* 118b. M&L, 665). Faithfulness to Torah is therefore a reconstructive activity. It prepares the way for, as well as witnesses to, that completion of creation for which Israel longs and the whole creation groans. It is Israel's witness to the One who said, "Let there be light," as the One who also said, "Hear O Israel, . . . you shall love the LORD your God with all your heart." That witness is therefore also to the One who promised, "Out of Zion shall go forth Torah . . . Nation shall not lift up sword against nation, neither shall they learn war any more."

5. THE CREATIONAL SHAPE OF JOHN 1:1–14

i. *Jesus Christ and Creation: Gen. 1:1, Mk. 1:1, John 1:1, Eph. 1:4*

The opening words of the Torah of Moses have left their mark on the opening of the Gospel of Mark ("The beginning . . ."),

and of the Fourth Gospel ("In the beginning . . ."), and its overtones sound in the letter to the Ephesians (". . . before the foundation of the world"—1:4). This is not surprising, for the communities which produced the Apostolic Writings had their origins
in a Jewish context. God the Creator was known to the Jews
from Sinai and so through Torah. For the first "Christians," who
were all Jews, we may say that the Creator was known to them
through Torah as interpreted by—perhaps in some sense per-
sonified in?—Messiah Jesus. (For the Gentile church that was
to follow, the Creator God of Torah was known only through
the person of Jesus Christ.) It is difficult to define how it was
with the earliest post-Easter followers of Jesus, for what evidence
we have (the Apostolic Writings) comes from the time when the
church had already become a predominantly Gentile movement.
Paul, for all we know, may be the only Jewish source we have
among its authors! Nevertheless, in the time during which the
Gospels came to be written, the church still knew Israel's Scriptures as its own and preached its gospel in the terms of those
Scriptures. The God of which it spoke was the God of Israel,
Maker of heaven and earth.

According to the witness of the Apostolic Writings, the One
who called the Gentiles by his Spirit in Jesus Christ is himself
the Creator: "In the beginning was the word . . . , and the word
was God. . . . All things were made through him" (Jn. 1:1,2).
It would be a fundamental misinterpretation of the apostolic
witness to say that God called the church into being through Jesus
Christ, and then told the church that way back there in the beginning he was the Creator. With the Torah of Moses in its Scriptures, the church could never have come to such an interpretation of what God was doing in Christ, for God had not so dealt
with Israel. Israel did not first know the call of God at Sinai and
then learn that way back then God had also created the heavens
and the earth. It knew God as Creator by knowing him as
Redeemer. So it was for the young church and for the church
ever since.

The church knows God as Creator because his initial calling

of the church, and of every Gentile into it, is itself an act of creation. By this calling God brings life from the dead, calling into being things that are not (Rom. 4:17). As with Israel, so with the church: God proved himself to be Creator of heaven and earth by creating the church. That is the word that was in the beginning, that was God in his creative, life-giving or life-making generosity. And that is the word that called the church into existence in Jesus Christ.

ii. *Torah, Wisdom, Word*

> In the beginning was the Word;
> the Word was in God's presence,
> and the Word was God.
> He was present to God in the beginning.
> Through him all things came into being,
> and apart from him nothing came to be (Jn. 1:1-3, *NAB*).

In the biblical view words underlie reality. With words God called the world into being; the capacity for using language from the start set man apart from the other creatures; in words each person reveals his distinctive nature, his willingness to enter into binding compacts with men and God, his ability to control others, to deceive them, to feel for them, and to respond to them. Spoken language is the substratum of everything human and divine that happens in the Bible, and the Hebrew tendency to transpose what is preverbal or nonverbal into speech is finally a technique for getting at the essence of things (Alter, 69f.).

> By the word of the Lord were the heavens made (Ps. 33:6).
> For he spoke and it came to be;
> He commanded, and it stood forth (Ps. 33:9).

God is as good as his word, so the Word of God is as good as God. When God speaks, God himself is creatively active, in calling the world into being, in calling Israel into being, and in calling the church into being. "In many and various ways God spoke of old to our fathers by the prophets" (Hebr. 1:1), the first of whom was Moses. God spoke in the Torah of Moses, and now "in these last days he has spoken to *us* (us *Gentiles*, the church) by a Son . . . through whom he created the world" (Hebr. 1:2). What God said in the Torah of Moses concerning his word of creation "in the beginning" reached and created his people Israel as Torah; it reached and created his church as Jesus Christ. The word spoken in the person of Jesus Christ, therefore, is God's confirmation of Torah ("all the promises of God find their Yes in him" — 2 Cor. 1:20) and together they are the one creative word from the beginning. What else can the church say coherently?

Israel's witness to God's creative activity through his word or through Torah could also be expressed by the use of the concept "the wisdom of God." The author of Proverbs has Wisdom speak as follows:

> The LORD begot me, the firstborn of his ways . . .
> When he established the heavens I was there,
>   when he marked out the vault over the face of the deep;
> When he made firm the skies above,
>   when he fixed the foundations of the earth;
> When he set for the sea its limit,
>   so that the waters should not transgress his command;
> Then was I beside him as his craftsman,
>   and I was his delight by day,
> Playing before him all the while,
>   playing on the surface of his earth;
>   and I found delight in the sons of men (Prov. 8:22, 27–31).

God's Word, Torah, and Wisdom are all one, the creative, purposeful, and supremely good activity of the One God. The author of the Prologue of the Fourth Gospel could therefore say that the Word "came to his own [place]," for the world, and also Israel, belonged to him by right of Creation. But, the Prologue continues, "his own did not accept him" (Jn. 1:11). And then, following immediately, "Any who did accept him he empowered to become children of God" (1:12).

"Did not accept," and then "did accept." How are we to understand this contradiction? Clearly it reflects the conflict which the early Jesus-movement came to produce within the people Israel. Some, even "multitudes," heard him gladly, and some, at least some of the Jerusalem "establishment," rejected him, possibly for fear of how the Roman occupying forces would react to this movement. In any case and after the fact, we can certainly say of this positive and negative that God's Word came once more to his created possession, and that his created own people received him in sufficient numbers to make it possible for many others to be able to accept him too.

"Him" means, in these verses, Jesus Christ. Does that mean the Jew Jesus of Nazareth? Is it proper to say of this Jew that he was in some sense "preexistent?" Here we must do some sorting out.

The term "preexistent" occurs nowhere in either the Scriptures or the Apostolic Writings, but there is no reason why the concept, properly qualified, could not be used to refer to the opening words of the Prologue to the Fourth Gospel and the verses cited from the eighth chapter of Proverbs. The idea certainly appears in the opening of *Genesis Rabbah*, where, commenting on those verses from Proverbs, the Rabbis argued, in their own inimitable way, that Torah was with God when he began to create the world. The thrust of their claim, however, appears to be not so much temporal as evaluative: Torah has a higher value even than creation. It is as if the Rabbis could have said that creation is a product of Torah, but would never have said the opposite, that Torah is a product of creation. We could put it in our own words by saying that "Torah produced history" is a claim prior in value and in reality to "History produced Torah." The second claim is obviously but trivially true; theologically, however, it comes second. In like manner, although the Prologue of John claims that "the Word was made flesh" (v. 14), it gives priority to the claim that the Word made all flesh (v. 3). (The verb [*egeneto*] is identical in both verses, and I cannot demean the craftsmanship of the author by thinking that this is accidental.) The term "preexistent," however, leads one to think primarily and misleadingly in temporal terms. The concept of "priority" is therefore preferable because it subsumes the temporal under the metaphysical and evaluative categories that seem to us to be more faithful to the Scriptural, Rabbinic, and Apostolic texts.

This Jewish notion of the priority in value and in reality of God's Word (or Torah, or Wisdom) to all else, appears in other apostolic texts as well, referring to "our Lord Jesus Christ," or simply "Christ" (Eph. 1:3f), or "Christ Jesus" (Phil. 2:5f), or "a Son" who is clearly Jesus (Hebr. 1:2). Especially interesting is the Adam-Christ argument of Romans 5, in which Christ is assigned a clear priority over Adam, and yet there is no clear indication that this priority was intended in a temporal sense. We may conclude that for the earliest church, Jesus was accorded the priority in reality that the Rabbis assigned to Torah.

If one were to make the claim of priority in a temporal sense, one would be claiming that Jesus of Nazareth, born of Mary, had existed with God before the creation of the world. That claim would be worse than unintelligible; it would destroy all coherence in the essential Christian claim that Jesus was truly a human being, that the word *became* flesh. The humanity could hardly be eternal in that sense and still be "like us in all things, excepting sin" (Council of Chalcedon; cf. Hebr. 2:17). Jesus of Nazareth began his life, began to exist, at a definite time in history: the Word became *flesh*.

The *Word* that began to be flesh at a definite time, however, the Word that is God's own, the divine purpose and intention that is God's very own, this Word is eternal as God is eternal. This Word is God's own eternal activity. The issue is the personal identity of personal agency. This Word was God in the beginning and with God in the beginning, according to the Prologue. This is the Word that has now moved onto the stage of history.

The Word *became*, or *was made*, or *happened as* flesh, just as the world and all that is became, was made, happened as creation. As in Creation, and as at Sinai, so in the life of this Jew, the creative Word spoke, and as a result, behold: creation, Israel, Jesus of Nazareth!

Tillich's uncertain grasp of biblical, sacramental thinking ("symbol" was the best he could do) is nowhere more evident than in his inability to see the verb *egeneto* as crucial to the meaning of John 1:14 (*Syst. Theol.* II, 149).

The subject of the Prologue to the Gospel of John is the miracle of God's involvement with his Creation in order to bring it nearer to its completion. What is preexistent, utterly one with God before the Creation of the world, is the divine resolve not simply to begin Creation but to bring it to its completion in a fully personal way. (A fully personal way, it should be noted, as distinct from either a mechanical or a logical way, will make room for a fully personal cooperation of God's creatures.) This eternal personal resolve of God's, which is with God and is God the Creator, is that which was enacted in the personal existence of the man Jesus of Nazareth.

iii. The Creator and his creation: intimacy and hiddenness

Where is the Creator to be seen? We may ask this of the event of Jesus of Nazareth as well as of the event of Exodus-Sinai. Formally speaking, the answer will be the same in both cases: the Creator is to be seen only by looking to the creature. The Word speaks or happens, and what is heard or seen is simply flesh, the Jew Jesus. This is implied in the Prologue and made explicit, later in the Gospel, when the disciple Philip asks Jesus to "show us the Father" (14:8). Jesus' answer is, "Have I been with you so long, and yet you do not know me, Philip? He who has seen me has seen the Father" (14:9). Only the creature is to be seen here, and seen precisely as a creature: we are told we must gnaw on (munch, eat noisily) this flesh (6:54), "this Jesus, the son of Joseph, whose father and mother" are known (6:42). Nothing more is to be seen. We must conclude that the Creator is never more hidden than when he draws nearest to his creation. So it was at Sinai; so it was with the Jew from Nazareth.

It was clearly the intent of the author of the Prologue, however, to establish that something definite had been seen. As with the case of Sinai, he who has eyes to see the creature as a new creation will see the glory of God's involvement in his creation, which is the glory of God himself. He who has eyes to see the Hebrew rabble of escaping slaves as the beloved Israel of God, has seen the glory of God; and he who has eyes to see the Jew from Nazareth as the living Word of his Father, has seen the glory of the Father. To see Jews as God's beloved Israel, or the ordinances of Moses as the Torah of God, or the Jew Jesus as God's eternal Word, means to see that they exist in that first way only because they exist primarily in this second way. To see them in this second way, then, is to grant the priority of this second reality of their existence, which is the priority of God's presence and action, the hidden Creator so intimately at work in and for his creation.

For his Jewish disciples, therefore, Jesus of Nazareth was the visible, intimate presence of God the Creator completing the work of Creation. For his Gentile disciples, he was the man in whom they came to know for the first time the Creator God of Israel, because as new creatures, they knew him as their own Creator. Therefore, looking directly at this Jew, they could say, "My Lord and my God" (Jn. 20:28). They said this of and to Jesus as he was, not to Jesus on his own, for he was not on his own. They said it to him as God's gift to them and so as God-in-him, utterly hidden, but utterly present. Nothing could be further from the intent of this confession than the thought of the deification of this Jew.

iv. The Witness of the Church to Creation

Walking in the Way as disciples of Jesus is the path provided for those Gentiles who have been drawn into Israel's story so as to share in Israel's trust in God the Creator. Created anew as sharers in Christ's risen life (Col. 3:1), a new creature (2 Cor. 5:17), reborn (Jn. 3:5), raised from the dead to walk in a new way (Rom. 6:4), made alive (Eph. 2:1), the church bears witness to the Creator by its very existence as the church. To follow Christ, therefore, is to bear witness to and serve the Creator alongside Israel. This is the church's witness, concordant with and confirming that of Israel, to God the life-giver, the Creator. In the famous opening words of the Heidelberg Catechism, in response to the question, What is the Christian's sole consolation in life and in death? the answer is: "That I, with body and soul, both living and dying, am not my own but the possession of my faithful savior Jesus Christ. . . . Therefore he also assures me eternal *life* through his holy Spirit, and has *made* me henceforth sincerely willing and ready to *live* unto him." (Emphasis added.) As continually being made alive for him as his possession, the church serves Jesus Christ as Israel's corroborative witness to God the Creator of heaven and earth.

CHAPTER THREE

The Reality and Risk of Creation

According to Israel's testimony, creation from "the beginning" is "very good" but unfinished. As part of this unfinished creation, women and men are called to responsible life in the service of creation's completion. They are therefore part both of creation's problem and of its possible solution. This testimony of Israel's is a reminder to the church of the particularity of its own witness and hope.

1. GENESIS 1 TO 11 AS THE BEGINNING

i. The goodness of creation

Under the heading of "The Reality and Risk of Creation," we come to a part of Israel's witness that is particularly difficult and urgent for the church to hear, especially the western church, and more especially the churches of the Reformation of the sixteenth century. The subject is the goodness of creation and the reality of human sin and evil. The difficulty arises from the fact that the (western) church's understanding of these matters has been shaped by a particular interpretation of them, stemming primarily from Augustine, which departs in important respects from Israel's understanding of its own witness. Listening afresh to that witness, therefore, without assuming that they have already heard and understood it, requires of Christians a willingness to reconsider their traditional understanding of the reality and risk of creation.

The task is made yet more difficult by the fact that the church's

(Augustinian) understanding of creation and its problem has shaped its conversation concerning Torah and the significance of Jesus Christ. The openness that is required at this point therefore exposes for reexamination the whole of the church's witness. The task is nevertheless urgent because the consequences of the church's traditional witness have been disastrous for the relationship between the church and the Jewish people. The church's witness must be its own, of course, but if this contradicts rather than confirms Israel's, something must have gone wrong: as God is one, so the witness to him, in all its diversity, must be held together. The church has certainly something more and other to say than Israel, but this addition concerns God's act in Jesus Christ: in him, according to the apostle to the Gentiles, however, "all the promises of God (to his people Israel) find their Yes" (2 Cor. 1:20). A correction of the church's witness so that it will echo this confirmation is the task of a Christian theology of Israel.

That apostle has often been accused of (or credited with!) initiating a departure from Israel's teaching which shaped the witness of the church. When read through Augustine's eyes, he merits the charge (or applause!), but just this reading of Paul is the issue. It was one thing for that strict Pharisee (Gal. 1:14, Phil. 3:5,6) to have made *himself* a Gentile (Gal. 4:12, 1 Cor. 9:20b, *not* 21!) under particular circumstances and with full understanding, we may presume, of Jewish teaching; it is quite another thing for Gentile readers, from Augustine to Käsemann, to turn him into a Gentile ignorant of the teachings of his people. Paul's understanding of Adam's sin and its consequences, as expressed most fully in Romans 5:12–21, when read through Augustine's eyes, appears to have been "that the first sin affected all mankind, and that Adam bequeathed to his descendants, by his trespass, a body infected by lust and desire, and consequently they were predestined to sin." The quotation is from E. E. Urbach, *The Sages* (E.T., Jerusalem, 1975, p. 423), but may not this eminent Jewish scholar be excused for reading Paul as the overwhelming majority of Christian exegetes have read and continue to read him? That was certainly Augustine's teaching. With the help of better-informed exegetes,

I shall argue in due course (and in the third Part of this theology of the Jewish-Christian reality) that it was not Paul's. It was in any case not the teaching of Israel.

A Christian theology of the people Israel has no choice but to wrestle with the genuine differences between the two traditions. The Jewish people have learned from experience of the dargers of apocalypticism and the stress on hope and the future redemption which play so large a role in Christian faith. Instead, they center their attention on practice in the here and now. The attempt to incorporate this witness into Christian theology will therefore sound too Christian for Jews and too Jewish for Christians.

Israel's witness concerning creation is that, as a whole and in all its parts, it is good, very good, *all* of it and as it *is*. And yet it contains darkness. "When God began to create the heavens and the earth, . . . *darkness* was upon the face of the deep" (Gen. 1:1,2), and "the earth was *tohu* and *bohu*."

Whether these Hebrew words are best translated "without form" and "void" (*RSV*), the Rabbis certainly took them negatively. According to one Midrash, the history of the Temple was foretold in the first three verses of Genesis: "God created" — that is the building of the Temple; "*tohu* and *bohu*" — that is the destruction of the (second) Temple; "Let there be light" — that is the rebuilding of the Temple in the Days of Messiah. (*Gen. R.*, Ber. II, 5).

Israel's story of Creation, from its opening verses through to the end of Genesis 11, portrays a tension between creation's goodness and the threat of chaos. The tension is revealed whenever a commandment is addressed to some part of creation or to certain creatures, especially when addressed to human beings. Creation is good in that it is addressed and is therefore addressable. It is made for responding and is thereby made responsible. Just this fact of its goodness, however, opens the terrible possibility of irresponsibility, of failure to be what creation was made to be: God's faithful and responsible creature.

Creation's very goodness involves this risk. Israel's story of Creation includes the sin of Adam and Eve with its grim consequences (Gen. 3), Cain's murder of his brother Abel (Gen. 4), the almost universal wickedness of humanity in the days of Noah (Gen. 6), the destruction of the flood (Gen. 7), the drunkenness of Noah (Gen. 9), and the building of the tower of Babel (Gen. 11). Creation, according to Israel's witness, is hardly idyllic. Yet Israel insists that all this, creation as it is, is good.

Why is it good? Why this application of "the most general adjective of commendation" (*O.E.D.*)? Creation is worthy of this commendation because it is God's. It is all his work and all his possession, every bit of it, including the darkness and all that it may represent. "I form light and create darkness, I make weal and I create woe; I, the LORD, do all these things" (Isa. 45:7)! Creation is good, however, not just because of its origin in and possession by God. It is also good because it was created for and therefore would lead to Israel praising God in his holy Temple. As the Sabbath crowned the work of Creation, so it also pointed ahead to creation's goal: "The LORD is in his holy Temple; let all the earth keep silence before him" (Hab. 2:20)! The prophet was calling all the earth to share in the worship of God that is its originating and ultimate purpose. (Cf. the passages cited and referred to at the end of the first subsection of chapter 2.) How could it then be other than good? Its meanest aspects have this as their context; therefore they are good, very good.

ii. Creation's incompleteness

Israel's witness to the directedness of creation toward the covenant and the gift of Torah celebrated in the Temple, however, reveals an awareness of creation's incompleteness. Israel never doubted that all was God's alone and that God alone had created, owned, and directed it. No second power, however feeble, was involved. Creation is God's, so it is good, but it is incomplete. It is a good beginning. So the Rabbis, in their typical style of farfetched punning, said of the "very good," that "very" (*me-od*) means "death" (*mavet*) (*Gen. Rabbah* XI, 5): the pronouncement of the exceeding goodness of creation acknowledges the fact of death.

The incompleteness of creation is nowhere so radically underscored as in its climax — *not* the creation of human beings, which is only a part of the work of the sixth day, but the Sabbath. God's rest sanctified the seventh day as a time of rest for *all* creation. This is spelled out in the commandment that not only Israel but also its beasts shall rest on that day (Ex. 20:10), and in the further commandment that the land itself shall be given rest every seven years (Lev. 25:2ff). The Sabbath therefore points ahead (as the author of the so-called Epistle to the Hebrews saw, in his own way) to the goal of all creation. Creation has a goal, Israel said and says, at which it has not yet arrived. Creation is incomplete and longs for its completion (cf. Rom. 8:19–23). The theme of redemption is therefore audible to Christian ears in the very beginning of Israel's story of Creation. The "good" (Gen. 1:12, 18, 21, 25, following the creation of earth, sea, and plants, of sun, moon, and stars, of fish and birds, of cattle, bugs, and beasts, but *not* of light, the firmament or heaven, and human beings! Interesting!) does not signal perfection, not even a "very good" which covers everything. Nothing could be further from Israel's witness than the idea of a golden age in the past, a perfect primordial paradise from which the world has fallen. Rather, the perfect is yet to come. From its beginning, creation looks ahead to what is to come. How else should we expect Israel to have told its story of Creation, seeing that this people knew itself to have been created toward freedom in the land of promise? The recurring memory of that experience of redemption — slaves on the way to freedom, but also tested forty years in the wilderness (cf. Amos 2:10; Deut. 8:2,4; Neh. 9:20ff) — shaped Israel's view of reality and so its telling of the story of Creation.

Israel's story of an incomplete creation will inevitably be heard by the church as pointing toward God's future. Without denying this, Judaism puts the stress rather on the present responsibility to which God calls. Israel's witness, as we shall see, therefore reminds the church that creation's Redeemer is creation's

Lord, and that trust in him as Redeemer can only be expressed by serving him now.

iii. *The reality of creation*

The world is real, with its goodness and its incompleteness. So said and says Israel. What happens in it matters and has consequences. In other words, creation is purposeful. Israel knows this, because the covenant by which it lives confronts Israel with a real choice. Since the choice is real, so is its context. The reality of creation, therefore, appears as the context of Israel's decision: "I call heaven and earth to witness against you this day, that I have set before you life and death, blessing and curse; therefore choose life, that you and your descendants may live, loving the LORD your God, obeying his voice, and cleaving to him; for that means life to you and length of days, that you may dwell in the land which the LORD swore to your fathers, to Abraham, to Isaac, and to Jacob, to give them" (Deut. 30:19f; cf. vs. 15–18). The choice is genuine and concrete. A real life of actually walking in God's way depends neither on esoteric or abstract teaching, nor on impossible ideals:

> For this commandment which I command you this day is not too hard for you, neither is it far off. It is not in heaven, that you should say, "Who will go up for us to heaven and bring it to us, that we may hear it and do it?" Neither is it beyond the sea, that you should say "Who will go over the sea for us and bring it to us, that we may hear it and do it?" But the word is very near you; it is in your mouth and in your heart, so that you can do it (Deut. 30: 11–14).

Israel lives from a real decision and therefore in a real world.

Israel's witness, it is frequently said, is essentially ethical rather than religious. This distinction is utterly foreign to Israel. What Israel is called to *do*, by its own testimony, is to love God, obey his voice, and cleave to him. That activity is in no way enlightened by the distinction between the ethical and the religious. In the terms of the history of religions, the "religion" of Israel is classified as "ethical monotheism." "Ethical" is the adjective; the noun is "monotheism." The grammar is in order. Israel's "ethics," its life and activity, is derived alone from the one God. More precisely, it is derived from its covenant with the one God. In one of his more daring but dangerous aphorisms, Augustine caught the sense of Israel's witness when he said, "Love God and do as you please." Augustine's hidden premise was that, if you loved God, what would please you is that which already pleases God. It might be wiser to make the premise explicit. More importantly, it might be well to acknowledge that God has already made known what pleases him. This Israel has done and, we think, has said it better: love God and do all these commandments. The Rabbis, following the lead of Torah, produced a more realistic and practical love-ethic than Augustine. This realism pervades Israel's understanding of creation.

iv. Faith in God the Creator

The key to Israel's understanding of Creation and creatureliness is its trust in God the Creator. This trust, however, is expressed centrally in the words of Israel's "confession of faith," the *Shema*: "Hear, O Israel, the LORD our God, the LORD is one" (Deut. 6:4). One, alone, unique: the LORD all by himself, and so in a unique way, is God. Thus Israel testifies to the lordship, the sovereignty of the one God. But his sovereignty is not empty. It is sovereignty over the world. The world is his as his possession.

Israel's trust in the present sovereignty of God has correlaries in both directions, past and future. He is the Creator of the world, and he will be its Redeemer. As the world is his possession by right of Creation, so its future is also his. His above all is the present. Israel's trust in the world's Creator, therefore, is at the same time trust in the world's Redeemer and Lord, for God is one. Who else could redeem it and bring it to its completion but the One who created it "in the beginning?" Israel gives this witness on the basis of having learned of the one God at Sinai, in the context of having been created a people and sent to obey God's commandments in the land of promise.

Because God is one, Israel trusts in a redemption of God's

one creation. Israel does not hope for another world than this one. It hopes in God's future for *this* world, the one God created. There is no other world, because there is no other God. It is the world in which God is to be served.

Israel hopes not only for the coming of the Messianic age for this world, it hopes also for the *olam haba*, the age to come. (From rabbinic times, these have usually been spoken of as two distinct and successive ages, the latter being final.) *Olam haba* could be translated "the world to come," but that is misleading, unless we make it clear that we mean "the world as it will come to be." "The age to come," or "the coming age (or era)" is a better translation; the expression can therefore be replaced, simply, with "the Future." (On this see Moore, *Judaism*, II, 378.) A new order, which is a new ordering of this world, not some other world, is Israel's hope. In effect, Jewish hope directs one more to present responsibility than to longing for the future.

Israel stands by this: the recitation of the *Shema* is every faithful Jew's first word in the morning of each day but also the last word Israel can and does say when pushed to the limit. With these words Rabbi Akiva sanctified God's name in the hour of death, and so have all of Israel's martyrs. This witness to the unique God is the root of Israel's understanding that everything other than God is his and his alone. "For thus says the LORD, who created the heavens (he is God!), who formed the earth and made it (he established it; he did not make it a chaos, he formed it to be inhabited!): I am the LORD and there is no other!" (Isa. 45:18)

2. MALE AND FEMALE: THE IMAGE OF GOD

i. Human beings and creation

We come now to the subject of ourselves, or rather, since this is Israel's testimony, here Israel testifies concerning itself. This is Israel's story about how it and all other human beings fit into God's creation. Given that this story is told as revealed from Sinai, so that creation is understood to be for the sake of the covenant, Israel is unavoidably central. Israel is not mentioned by name, of course. That name will appear only after Abram is renamed Abraham. Here we are told of *adam*, the first inclusive person from whom Israel and all humanity descends. *Adam* as the created person stands for humanity because the story from Abraham to Israel is for the sake of all of humanity. In that sense, *adam* is Israel.

The artist who wove together the two stories of Genesis 1 and Genesis 2, and Israel who preserved the result, did not see fit to glorify *adam*. *Adam* is not alloted a separate day but is created along with "cattle and creeping things and beasts of the earth," in the first story, or is made out of dust from the ground in the second, *adam* made from *adamah*. This creature will be central to the story that is beginning, but as a creature.

What God created, according to Israel, is not "a man," not a male human being. God said, "Let us make *adam* in our own image, after our likeness, and let *them* have dominion" over everything living. "So God created *adam* in his own image, in the image of God he created him; *male and female* he created *them*." *Adam* turns out to be "them," male and female, a couple. So also in the second story, God said, "It is not good that the *adam* should be alone; I will make him a helper fit for him." Clearly, "adam" alone is incomplete. What God created, according to Israel, is the couple, commanded to be fruitful and multiply. He created the human family.

According to the first chapter of Genesis, the human family is to have "dominion" over every living thing. This is a limited dominion, however, for it hardly includes the right to kill. Likewise in the second chapter a vegetarian diet is again specified. For food, plants and the fruit of trees have been provided. Indeed, the same is to be food for everything that breathes. The vegetarianism is relaxed at a later point in the story, but the idea is retained that even eating is within the framework of the covenant of Creation. Human dominion is therefore understood within the covenantal relationship between God and all that he has made. *Adam* is placed by God in his garden in order to take care of it for its owner.

ii. Humanity as male and female

Having itself been created as a people through the Exodus-Sinai event, Israel's anthropology, its understanding of the human being, is corporate: the individual is fully God's creature only in community, the root form of which is the family. To this day, Jews tend to number the Jewish community in any place by families. "It is not good for *adam* to be alone." Of course it is not good, for human beings are creatures and creation was for the sake of the covenant. Human beings, in Israel's understanding, were made for covenantal existence.

Covenantal existence, however, involves relationships between human beings as well as between human beings and God. Each is made his brother's keeper, and the commandment concerning love for the neighbor is "like" the commandment to love God. Made for the covenant, human beings are made for each other.

Although Israel's testimony and practice concerning the status of women are relatively good in comparison to those of other peoples and cultures, they unquestionably reflect Israel's patriarchal structure and have certainly been understood until recent times in what we are now slowly learning to call a "sexist" manner. The problem, as G. F. Moore put it succinctly two generations ago, is that, "for emancipated women there was in the ancient world only one calling" (*Judaism*, II, 127)! We have underscored the themes in Israel's creation story which can be of help in our quest for new understandings of the relationship between men and women, but we will not pretend that the Jewish people, any more than the church, has done more than begin to think through and act out a theology of the female-male relationship as that of co-partners in the covenant.

iii. The image of God: responsibility and responding

"In the image of God created he them." Wherein lies this likeness of human beings to God? The serpent, in the third chapter of Genesis, suggests that it consists of knowing good and evil, an expression that means knowing what is good and bad for human beings, and so the sum of all knowledge. This Faustian suggestion, however, is that of the serpent and is to be rejected. As the story unfolds, the author has the LORD God say, "Behold, *adam* (evidently collective for the man and the woman) has become like one of us, knowing good and evil" (3:22), but in the light of the divine displeasure at what has happened, the remark should be taken sarcastically. It is not by an act of disobedience that human beings become like God, for "in the image of God created he them."

When we set the story of Creation in its proper context, that of the covenant, it becomes clear that the image of God in human beings is their having been made with the ability to respond to God. Human beings were made for the covenant and so are capable of that for which they were made. They can respond and so be responsible. In their faithful response to God, they are the visible witnesses of the hiding God. Israel is itself the image of the God of Exodus-Sinai; no wonder, then, that it was commanded to make no other images!

This image and likeness is not something that could be or was "lost" in "the Fall." If and when Israel is spoken to by God, Israel can respond. If it does not, it can blame nobody but itself. Judaism has consistently maintained that what is real is possible. The covenant is real and therefore it is possible, Israel knows, because it lives in that covenant which God has made with it. Whatever change may have been introduced into creation by the disobedience of the first couple, Exodus and Sinai have come since. Israel itself is therefore the living witness that something can still happen between God and human beings. We are still as we were made, being able to hear God's command and promise, and capable of loving, obeying, and trusting him. That is the likeness of humanity to God. We can define it in a word: personhood, provided that we learn from Israel what it means to be a person before God.

The person that God created is a unified mind-bodied human

being in a mind-bodied relationship with other human beings and God. That is why my person can be attacked by blows as well as words. In order to respond to another person, be it another creature or the Creator, I must have ears that hear and eyes that see, hands that touch and skin that may be touched. Because of this holistic conception of personhood created in the image of God, Israel could not speak of the loss of it in the disobedience of *adam*. The one way in which it can be lost is by death. Judaism did develop the idea that death came into the world with that primal act of disobedience. Death is the end of the person and so of the mind-bodied relationships with other persons, including God:

> Dost thou work wonders for the dead?
>   Do the shades rise up to praise thee? (Ps. 88:10.)

> The dead do not praise the LORD,
>   Nor do any that go down into silence. (Ps. 115:17.)

This holistic conception of the person was maintained by and expressed in the Pharisaic elaboration of Israel's teaching, that there is a hope beyond death: the resurrection. If there is to be a future for any person, it would have to be a mind-bodied future. An immortal soul apart from its body would be no help, for we are not souls temporarily clothed in a body. So one Pharisee could say that his hope was for better or further clothing from God, not to be found naked (2 Cor. 5:2–5)! The concept of the resurrection of the whole mind-bodied person is something that the church has learned from Israel. What it has not learned so well is the holistic mind-bodied conception of the image of God which makes the concept necessary as well as possible.

iv. The reality of human history

Not only was the first couple made in the image and likeness of God, according to Israel's story of reality, but their children too were born in the image and likeness of their parents (Gen. 5:2). The story that begins between the Creator and his creatures is continued by means of reproduction, by generation. Therefore the recitation of the generations from *adam* to Noah (Gen. 5), the descendants of Noah's sons (Gen. 10), and then the generations from Shem to Abram (Gen. 11:10–32), are the vital links in Israel's story of reality. Generation guarantees the reality of human history.

There was a time, not two generations ago, when young Christians still learned to read the Bible in Sunday School, albeit often under the tutelege of teachers with little awareness of the historical and none of the narrative character of Israel's Scriptures. That they remained living Israel's Scriptures never seemed to have crossed anyone's mind. Consequently, the "begats" of the King James Version (not only in Genesis, but also in the Gospels according to Matthew and Luke!) were skimmed over as unimportant. It follows that if one fails to attend to the living, incarnate reality of the Israel of God's covenant, one will not see the importance of its mind-bodied generation.

The generations are an especially important part of Israel's story of reality for Gentiles to hear (the "begats," replaced with freer translations in all the newer versions), because Israel testifies that the covenant of Creation depends upon the covenant of Sinai. Gentile participation in Israel's story of either or both depends, therefore, on the continuation of Israel's covenant. But Israel's covenant cannot continue in a world "free" of Jews. There is consequently no more important commandment resting on Israel than to produce the absolute prerequisite for the continuation of the covenant: the next generation of Jews. Christians need to reconsider this matter of generation, of Jews making more Jews, for it concerns the reality of their own standing before the Creator and Redeemer of Israel.

History is real for Israel because that is where the covenant takes place, and there is nothing more real than the covenant. The covenant, however, as protoredemptive, promises a final redemption. History, in Israel's view, could therefore never be cyclical. It moves toward the completion of creation. This marked

Israel's story of reality, in form as well as content. It is a narrative, and it moves toward the further story that tells of that history out of which Israel came to be. The protohistory of Creation, in the first eleven chapters of Genesis, forms the introduction to and the context for the beginning of that great dialogical history that begins with God's call to Abram and Abram's response. That history, being its own, was known by Israel to be real. It was also known to involve risks.

3. THE RISK OF CREATION

i. Creation as risk

William James was no Jew, but he was the child of a culture profoundly marked by Israel's Scriptures. In the eighth of his lectures on *Pragmatism*, "Pragmatism and Religion," he expressed well the element of risk in Israel's conception of Creation:

> Suppose that the world's author put the case to you before Creation, saying: "I am going to make a world not certain to be saved, a world the perfection of which shall be conditional merely, the condition being that each several agent does its own 'level best.' I offer you the chance of taking part in such a world. Its safety, you see, is unwarranted. It is a real adventure, with real danger, yet it may win through. It is a social scheme of cooperative work genuinely to be done. Will you join the procession? Will you trust yourself and trust the other agents enough to face the risk?"

Having been drawn into a "social scheme of cooperative work genuinely to be done," the "real adventure" of its covenant with God, Israel saw the element of risk in Creation, not only for itself but also for the Creator.

Because, as Israel sees it, Creation was for the sake of the covenant, it depends for its completion on the free response of God's dialogical partner. Israel must choose life, but it could also choose death. That means that the Creator, as Israel understands him, has no guarantee that his world will "win through." The story of the flood testifies to the risk of failure for the whole undertaking. Creation is therefore a risk first of all on God's part.

Creation is not only made for the covenant. As we have seen, it is itself filled with commandments. Indeed it comes into being through commandments. But the commandments that are given to creation do not seem to offer much choice until we come to the story of the first couple in the garden. Even the command to eat freely of all the trees except one does not seem to offer much of a choice, for violation of the single prohibition means death. What God offers is life, and what God asks is that his offer be accepted. So was Israel confronted by God at Sinai, and so it presents God in its story of Creation.

The offer of life, however, does raise the possibility of death. Just as the creation of light brings with it its contrasting darkness (which Karl Barth, less boldly than Isaiah (45:7), called "that which God did not create"), so the covenant does entail a genuine decision. If God commands obedience, then disobedience lurks in the background as an alternative. God's creation is good, but it can be otherwise. If the biblical authors, and the Rabbis after them, lacked the logical sense of the Greeks (see H. Loewe's discussion of this in M&L, 658 ff), they made up for this with their sense of the moral seriousness of the world. Because their witness is to the centrality of moral choice, they confront us with a world that may not become what God intended.

The consequence of seeing the world as incomplete, with human decisions contributing positively and negatively to its course, is the realization that history counts in the story of reality. Such is surely the basic import of the rabbinic saying that all is in the hands of heaven except the fear of heaven. It was just this that worried the Rabbis: it was little comfort that all was in the hands of heaven if heaven's hands were tied by Israel's failure to live by Torah. The events of Israel's own history, therefore, had to be told in Israel's story of the world. Some of those events were painfully black. Slavery in Egypt, corruption of its own leaders and leading classes, destruction of its cities, exile in Babylon, profanation and then destruction of the second Temple, the difficulties and sometime agonies of almost nineteen centuries of Diaspora, all these became parts of its story, and all these reveal the risk in God's enterprise. Contemporary Jewish theologians who see the Holocaust and/or the foundation of the state of Israel as marking a new stage in Israel's covenant with God (those of the Diaspora generally stressing the former, Israelis tending to focus on the latter) are clearly standing in the tradition of Israel's witness.

ii. Historical evidence and uncertainty

Given the fact that Israel was created as the people of the covenant by a historical deliverance from actual slavery in Egypt, we should expect it to be sensitive to the facts of history. Believing that what it did mattered to God, Israel took its historical experience to be evidence of how things stood between itself and God. Defeat by enemies and "natural" disasters were evidence of divine displeasure over Israel's infidelity. So the Rabbis concluded that the destruction of the second Temple and Israel's dispersion among the Gentiles was "for our sins." It is not surprising, then, that the Holocaust, along with its other traumatic effects, has led to Jewish agonizing over what if any lessons are to be learned from the disaster.

It is worth noting that there has been almost no Jewish exploration of the appropriateness to the Holocaust of the rabbinic response to the destruction of the Temple — that it happened "for *our* sins." This may arise from the fact that some of those who have been writing about the Holocaust have not been careful students of the Rabbis. For the Rabbis, it should be pointed out, there was, first of all, no question of punishment as compensation. It may be that they were in fact providing a strategy for moving ahead, rather than offering any sort of explanation. In any case, the Rabbis did not say that the destruction of the Temple was visited upon those Jews who suffered in the wars with Rome because of their own personal sins. On the contrary, they made this claim with respect to all Israel. One may grant that the victims of the Holocaust were largely the most Torah-observant Jews of eastern Europe, if not all Israel. But all Israel comprises all Jews. What about the others, including, for example, those who had so assimilated to German culture as to believe Germany incapable of producing what it did? This is hardly a subject on which a Gentile can speak, for there can be no question that the judgment of the Rabbis applies directly to us: this disaster happened to *them* because of *our* sins of centuries of Christian teaching of anti-Judaism. I would therefore not have raised this painful question had it not been brought to my attention by one of my Jewish graduate students.

The Jewish theologian Irving Greenberg has pointed out that in fact Israel has been exceedingly selective in applying the insight that history provides evidence of God's truth. The one liberating event of the Exodus taught Israel that God is Israel's redeemer, but the overwhelming bulk of Israel's experience points to just the opposite direction. To this we could add that one of Israel's sages concluded that all is vanity and that the search for wisdom was a striving after wind (Eccl. 1), and another wise Israelite observed that God causes the sun to shine and the rain to fall equally on the just and the unjust (Mt. 5:45), and that although he said that every hair of our heads was numbered (Mt. 10:30), he did not say that this would prevent them from turning gray or falling out! Perhaps we may conclude from these conflicting voices of the Jewish people that Israel realizes that reading historical evidence is an art, and that for every prophet there have been many false prophets.

From these witnesses to the uncertainty of any conclusions to be drawn from historical evidence, combined with Israel's equally strong testimony that we must make our judgments on the basis of just this evidence, we may draw one sure conclusion for theology, whether Jewish or Christian: every position taken will involve a risk and lack the assurance of certainty. Israel's witness is that Israel has often been wrong, that old insights no longer apply. Further, it tells us that God has changed his mind in the past and that he is able to do new and unheard of things. This means that Israel, and a church that listens to

Israel's witness, have to be prepared to see matters differently from how they have seen them before. That applies to our theologies and also to our reading of the Scriptures.

One can read Israel's story, from Creation through Abraham and to our day, as evidence that the creation is in such jeopardy that God has been forced, so to speak, into "acts of increasing desperation," as a fairly recently awakened Christian has put it to me. Perhaps that is right. Or perhaps it tells of a series of new actions not fully planned out in advance, at least as far as we can tell. Who could have foreseen an Easter after Good Friday or predicted the flowering of rabbinic Judaism after the destruction of the Temple? How could a people possibly endure for nineteen centuries without a land or even a central authority or administration? And who could have foreseen the present new readings of the covenant between God and Israel that some Jewish theologians are exploring, or the radically new understandings of Paul and of Judaism beginning to appear in the church? Surely the conversation between God and his people, the beginnings of which are recorded in Israel's story of Creation, is not over and not determined in advance. Since the conversation is between persons, it is perhaps just as well that Israel has no guarantee that it will end well. A real conversation must include the risk of failure, and a failure of this conversation would be a failure for both parties.

iii. The problem of sin and death

The greatest danger to creation, according to Israel, is ourselves. Human creatures can refuse to choose the Way which their Creator has chosen for them. They can chose death rather than life, disobedience rather than free cooperation. They not only can, Israel tells us; they have, and right from the beginning. Israel's name for this disastrous choice is "sin." Sin introduces an element of chaos that threatens creation right at its center.

The fact, reality, and recurrence of sin is a notable feature of Israel's story of reality. *Adam's* disobedience, Cain's murder of his brother, violence culminating in Noah's time, punctuate and shape the reality of creation. The sin of *adam* comes first, but it is only the first. The others follow and there is no suggesting that the first sin caused the later ones to happen. Sin is a recurring fact for Israel. *Adam's* sin can therefore stand as a model, but Israel never took it to be the turning point of the story of creation, as it became for the Augustinian tradition in the church.

It is no part of Israel's recognition of the fact and problem of sin to call *adam's* sin or that of those who followed him an exercise of "free will." "Free will" is a problematic concept at best. What Israel tells us are stories of wrong choices, of following another lead than that offered by the Creator. Again and again, for any number of reasons, human beings have made and go on making wrong choices. Human beings have a by-no-means irresistible, but certainly a powerful inclination to make the wrong choice, the one that God has not chosen for us, the Rabbis taught. When this evil inclination is not brought under control, disruption and antagonism is unloosed in creation.

Nahum Sarna, commenting on Genesis 3, said, "man does possess the possibility of defying the divine word, and therein lies the secret of his freedom" (27). Surely Sarna has put the matter backward. The secret of human freedom lies in choosing freely the good life that God has chosen for his creatures. Defying that choice is the opposite of exercising the freedom that God has given: it is a forfeiting of freedom.

Israel's story confronts us with the fact of death in a world marked by sin. Death came into the world as a punishment for the first sin, and *adam*, standing for all humanity, has bequeathed this fact of existence to all his descendents, the Rabbis taught. Israel's Scriptures, however, after telling this story, never once refer back to it, and the Rabbis did not make much of it either. The center of their story was Sinai and the fact that Israel said Yes, although like *adam* it might have said No. Sin is the refusal of the choice that God has chosen for his creatures. It is real and it recurs, but it is not the central theme of Israel's story. We must remember that Israel's story of reality tells of a world in which the threat of sin, from that of *adam* to that of the age of Noah, is serious, but in which that threat has been countered by God's call of Abram leading to the covenant of Sinai. It has been countered, not yet overcome. The world awaits its redemption. In the meantime death remains, the unavoidable reminder of the risk of Creation.

One of the Pharisees formulated Israel's understanding concisely: "sin came into the world through one human being, and death through sin, and so death spread to all human beings—from which it follows that all sinned" (Rom. 5:12). *Adam* was the effective representative of humanity. As the blessing of the first couple passes to all—made in the image of God—so the mortality passes to all, and Paul seemed to have seen no grounds for doubting the logical conclusion that all must therefore in fact have followed the model of the prototype by themselves sinning.

We should add the witness of another Jew whose teaching on this as on so many other points places him within the general framework of the pharisaic tradition. When asked by a fellow Jew what to do to inherit eternal life, which is to say, how to conduct oneself as an heir of the covenant of grace from Sinai, he asked in turn what Torah said. Having received a correct answer—to love God and the neighbor—he is reported to have said: "You have answered right; do this and you shall live" (Lk. 10:25–28). That God's will may not be done is the constant threat breaking in upon creation, and death is there to remind us how often this occurs and how serious a matter it is. But that God's will may and can be done even by sinners is Israel's witness to the world. It is a witness that the church, especially the Augustinian western, above all the Protestant, church needs to hear.

Let us be clear about this. Neither Jesus, nor Paul, nor any other Pharisee of whom we know, neither Israel nor Judaism as a whole, thought any human being was able on his or her own to establish a relationship to God or earn God's love. How could Israel even entertain such a preposterous idea, when it knew that God's love for his creatures was the foundation of every relationship between him and them? Judaism knows only of a God whose offer of the covenant is itself a gift of grace. It knows this because it is convinced that sinful Israel is still God's Israel, and that Israel as a whole and every single Jew can turn back to God, can repent, in the sure conviction that God forgives. This relationship, established by God's free grace at Sinai, is the presupposition of Israel's seriousness about Torah-faithfulness.

Whoever those Jew-mimicking Gentiles were with whom Paul had to contend, they clearly had distorted the witness of Judaism, that the merciful God would accept the righteous among the Gentiles, if they thought that anyone could *establish* a right relationship with God on the basis of "works" of any sort. A Gentile church that has not heard Israel's witness and has constructed a faith-works dichotomy out of the writings of Paul needs to read him anew as what he claimed to be: the God of Israel's apostle to the Gentiles, a Jew standing firmly on the witness of Israel to the God of justice before whom none can stand unashamed, and to the same God of mercy whose forgiveness none can do without.

iv. The problem of evil

The threat to creation can also be given the more general title: Evil. Evil is the opposite of good. Whatever destroys, hurts, or harms is evil. The word generally refers to a result or effect, rather than to intention. I can indeed intend evil where good results, but it is no grammatical mistake to speak of an act as evil which was done with the best of intentions. Harm can and does happen to creation and to individual creatures. According to Israel's witness, God himself can bring evil upon human beings, and they can bring it on themselves, each other, and the earth. Evil is whatever destroys, hurts, or harms anything in God's creation. God's creation is good, yet it contains much evil. Evil is therefore a problem in Israel's view of creation. It is a sign of creation's unredeemed or unfinished character.

There are "natural" evils not caused by human beings. Death by disease, the failure of crops, droughts, and famines are all evil, according to Israel's view of reality. In biblical and rabbinic times, and up to the modern era, Israel tended to regard such evils as sent by God. Usually they were understood to be divine punishment for human sins. Today there is more uncertainty about this. Israel like the church has become more secularized and more inclined to view such evils as "natural," yet there remains a strong feeling that evil should not be, whatever its cause. It remains a threat to creation and a hindrance to its completion.

Israel has on the whole been more concerned about humanly caused evil and about evil human beings. The evils of grinding poverty and the systemic injustice that produces it are of human cause. War and political oppression are humanly caused. Hatred, persecution, and murder, as Israel has suffered these at the hands of Christians and pagans, are evils Israel knows well, and it regards them as evil when they happen to others as well. All these are brought about by human beings, whatever their intentions. The perpetrators may have sinned; the victims know the effects as evil.

The greatest evil that Israel has known since the destruction of the Temple and Jerusalem is the Holocaust. It must rank as the greatest evil not simply because of the numbers who died nor even because of the brutality visited upon them. It stands alone because it was directed at the heart of the covenant on which the completion of creation depends, for to eradicate Israel would annul the covenant. One-third of Israel was in fact murdered. Had Hitler succeeded in his dream of making a world "free" of Jews, it is not clear what would have happened to the God of Israel or to his creation!

Human beings, because they are created in the image of God and therefore capable of responding, are God's hope for completing his creation with its cooperation. They also pose the greatest threat to God's purposes. That God should make a world so under the influence of men and women defines the risk involved in that undertaking which God began "in the beginning."

4. CREATION AND HOPE

i. Genesis 1 to 11, and Genesis 12

The first eleven chapters of Genesis form an introduction to the story that begins in Genesis 12. They set the stage of reality; the action begins with God's call of Abram and Abram's response. Creation is not simply there; it is going somewhere, because now something decisive has happened to it. History, the history of God's creation as he leads it by the hand of his elect, has begun.

It should be noted that history takes place within creation, and creation is the setting for history. It is questionable, therefore, to call Israel a people of time rather than a people of space, or to speak of the God of Israel as a God of time, in contrast to the gods of space, as Tillich (and Abraham J. Heschel!) was inclined to do (see especially his Berlin lectures of 1953, *Die Judenfrage: Ein Deutsches und ein Christliches Problem*, G. W. III, 128–70). Of course Israel has always taken time and history seriously, but for Jewish thought, the Exodus was a rescue out of Egypt, Sinai was a particular mountain, the wilderness experience left a lasting mark, the conquest was of an actual territory, and a specific piece of Mideast geography has been central for Jewish hope for millennia. Israel's Redeemer is also the Creator of hills and valleys, streams and seas, woods and fields. There is no need to go to the other extreme; we need only point out that in Israel's witness, history takes place in a *here* as well as in a *now*.

Israel's story of Creation in the first eleven chapters of Genesis is a fully adequate introduction to what follows, because in it creation is presented as made for dialogue, for the serious mutual engagement of God and human beings in the conversation and life on which the future of creation depends. The story of Abram, on his way to becoming Abraham, is that for which the world was made, according to Israel's understanding. It epitomizes Israel's whole history: as we heard, "Creation was for the sake of Torah," and also "for the sake of Israel." Because of this conversation that began between God and Abram, there is hope for the unfinished, threatened creation. Chapter 12 of Genesis, coming as the great beginning to which the earlier chapters lead, is the grounds for the conviction of a later Jew that creation, although it had been "subjected to disolution," was not beyond hope (Rom. 8:20). Something has happened in and to it that tastes of redemption. For rabbinic Judaism, however, redemption and hope remained secondary to the issue of halakhic ex istence. Halakhic Judaism is a warning to the church not to let hope for redemption too easily take the sting out of the real risk under which creation stands.

ii. Creation and Easter

The Gentile church comes to the knowledge of and participation in Israel's hope for creation on this side of Easter and consequently gives that hope more emphasis. It knows a hope for creation because it was itself created in hope—in hope, not yet in possession of that for which it hopes. The church should therefore be able to see that Israel speaks of Creation and its hope for the future of creation from this side of the Exodus and Sinai, where it had earlier learned what it is to be created in hope. As the confirmation of Israel's grounds for hope, Easter provides the church with a sign pointing to the goal of creation. That sign points to creation's completion, rescued from all that threatens it. It points to creation's coming into its own.

Coming into its own, not as having arrived. "We know," wrote Paul, a full generation after Easter, "that the whole creation groans and suffers pangs together until now. Not only that, but also we ourselves, who have the first-fruits of the Spirit, also we ourselves groan among ourselves, waiting . . ." (Rom. 8:22–23). Waiting: for the redemption of our bodies, for the redemption of the whole creation, for the redemption of Israel. Waiting. Easter, like the Exodus, like the call of Abram, gives us grounds for hope; but for Redemption, the redemption of God's beloved creation, the church is still waiting. Until then, the threat of futility, nothingness or decay remains. Mortality remains. The dead sleep. Redemption is still outstanding. We and creation are still waiting.

We may wait with patience, however, because there are grounds for hope. Now and again, here and there, signs have been given. Abram's call was the first, then the Exodus, and then the appearing of the crucified one. They are all signs of the same hope, for with the last of these there is a reminder of the first: by this last sign, God has been able to raise up dead Gentile stones as children of Abraham (cf. Lk. 3:8).

The church has therefore been introduced into Israel's hope. Israel's hope was there already before the church was created. When the church rehearses its "sure and certain" hope of the resurrection, it rehearses what it began to learn from Israel's teachers, originating with the Pharisees. When the church expresses its hope, however, it moves beyond the witness of the Jewish people throughout their long history. As it makes this move, it would do well to ponder the implicit question of the Rabbis — and Judaism — whether it remembers this world in all its risk, and therefore whether it is attending seriously to the matter of walking as it waits. If the church has in fact entered into *Israel's* hope, then it faces the challenge of halakhic responsibility.

It was from one of Israel's sons that the church learned to pray, not only, "Thy kingdom come!" but also, "Thy will be done on earth!" A church that makes these petitions commits itself not just to wait with patience, but to serve with impatience, and to do so here and now, "on earth!" As is the case with Israel, the church's hope is not for itself, much less just for its individual members. Its hope is for God's whole creation, in which of course the church and each of its individual members are included. Its hope therefore drives it into the service of God's world.

Easter is the sign which God has given to his creation, and which the church has acknowledged, that God has not left his threatened creation to itself. God is with it and will stand by it to the end. Israel, however, is the sign which God has given to his creation, the church included, that God requires of his creatures their cooperation in overcoming the threat to creation.

iii. The particularity of the church's witness

Israel's testimony to creation and the place of human beings within it stands as a living reminder to the church that the Christian witness to God is not his only witness. Indeed it makes clear that the witness of the church is a quite particular one in several respects. It is particular, in the first place, in being assigned the role of echoing the witness and hope of Israel, which were already on the scene of history before the church came to be. When the church speaks of the Creator, it tells Israel's story of Creation. It has no independent story to tell on its own, other than that marvelous chapter, which it adds, of how it was awakened to an appreciation of this story by God's creative act in Jesus Christ. Its witness is therefore to the God of Israel, the Creator who is the Redeemer.

The church's witness to the Creator is particular, second, in being a *Gentile* confirmation of that of Israel. By the very fact that Gentiles take up this witness to the God of Israel, they confirm Israel's testimony that this God is Lord of every people. The Jewish Prayer Book speaks again and again of "our God" as "King of the Universe." The church, drawn from every nation and people around the globe, confirms this testimony simply by praying to and adoring the One God of Israel. The church's particular witness to the Creator of all is to add its voices in every tongue to the Hebrew prayers of the Jews. In this way, it bears witness to the God of Israel as Creator and King of the Universe.

The church's witness is therefore particular in the sense of being only one and not *the* only one. At the very least, it comes after and then alongside that of Israel. If the church has to reckon with the existence of Israel's witness, of which its own is a confirmation, then it has at least to be open to the possibility of yet other witnesses. It cannot pretend that its voice is the only one that speaks of the Creator, or that its life is the only sign of him. From Israel the church may learn to hear the heavens tell of God's glory and to see the mountains skip like rams. And if with Israel it must be open to all of creation praising the Creator, how much more should it be open to the possibility that other Gentiles, other non-Jews, may be singing the Creator's praise. The church was created in the context of Israel and learned a Jewish vocabulary with which to speak of God. It will ever be dependent on Israel's witness in making its own. It will therefore have to test what it hears from other Gentiles, not to speak of the stars and mountains, against the testimony of Israel, in order to be sure that it is indeed hearing of the Creator who is the Redeemer. But if it continues to confirm Israel's witness, the church can listen attentively and hopefully to other voices, for every voice is that of one of God's creatures and may in fact be speaking of the Creator.

The church's witness is particular, finally, in being, like Israel's, always strictly related to Creation. That is to say, it is always a witness to the One who brings into being things that are not. This is so because the witnessing church itself, again like Israel, speaks and lives out of its own creation by this God. It knows of no Redeemer other than the Creator, nor does it know of any God other than this one. A proof, if there were one, that "there is a God" could therefore not be part of its witness. The so-called "proofs" of a first cause, prime mover, or whatever, imply a relationship between that supposed cause or mover and the church that is quite other than that between the One who brings into being what does not exist, including specifically a church created out of Gentile darkness. In this the church is not only like Israel; its witness remains to this day dependent on Israel, the Jewish people. From them the church has learned the words with which to speak of God and of its own beginning, for its Bible begins in every age with Israel's, its opening words being those of the Torah of Moses: "In the beginning. . . ."

iv. Hope for creation

"All creatures groan (or the whole creation groans) and suffer(s) pangs until now," wrote the apostle nineteen centuries ago (Rom. 8:22). It is still going on. Whether matters have become worse is hard to say, but this present time is surely one of great suffering and anxiety. We have seen in this century mass slaughter of incredible proportions, culminating in the most systematic, cold-blooded attempt to rid creation of the people Israel that history records. The possibility of ending all life on earth, even of making this planet uninhabitable, is now within the hands of the descendants of *adam* and Cain. That is not encouraging. We do not have to follow the example of our ancestors, according to Jewish teaching, but there is a high probability that we shall.

There are in every human being two contrary tendencies at work, according to the teaching of Israel's Rabbis, one pulling us to the service of God, and another in the opposite direction. An inclination to the good is recognized, but so is an evil inclination, the *yetzer ha-ra*. With this doctrine of the *yetzer ha-ra*, Israel acknowledges the problematic character of the human component of creation.

Israel has not made the evil inclination in every human being as major a theme as has the church its doctrine of "original sin," and the church should listen with care to the reason for this difference. In the first place, Israel's teachers have spoken specifically to their fellow Jews. In other words, they were responsible theologians of the Jewish people, directing them in their understanding of God's purposes for them and their proper response to God. They therefore addressed an audience for whom they were convinced God had graciously provided a powerful and effective weapon against the *yetzer ha-ra*: the gift of Torah. Study Torah, meditate on God's revealed instruction, and the evil inclination can be overcome (see Urbach, *The Sages*, 472ff).

The Christian church, especially its western, Augustinian branch, duly impressed with its having been called into life from the death of pagan darkness, has been acutely aware of the fact of human sin. Had its theologians reflected on their proper role, had they taken the lead provided by Israel's teachers and remembered that they were talking to the living, then they might not have emphasized to such an extent the death from which the church had been called, or they might have spoken of it primarily by way of contrast, as grounds for rejoicing over God's gift of life, and as a spur to walking in the way of life now made available even to Gentiles. On the other hand, an attempt to speak to the world about human sin could, on the church's own terms, have made no sense at all, for how can the dead hear the dreary "news" that they are indeed dead? The word of human sin can only be heard by the living, by those, that is, who have been set on a path no longer under the domination of the evil inclination. Attentiveness to Israel's teaching on this matter could not but help the church to understand its own good news.

As for the world—and Israel and the church share the world's future—there is enough anxiety abroad already, without hearing further words of sin and doom. This world needs hope, for without hope, it is hard to do anything. Israel's witness is, in the last analysis, a word of hope, and this the church can confirm. The grounds for hope do not lie in creation itself. They do not lie, that is, in a world on its own, for Israel's testimony is that the world is not on its own. The world is God's creation, God's own possession. Its hope, therefore, lies in its having a Creator: "Our help is in the name of the LORD who has made heaven and earth" (Ps. 124:8).

The phrase "the name of the LORD" which occurs so frequently in Israel's Scriptures, expresses the involvement of God in his creation: he has caused his name to dwell in Israel. "The name of God" is a short way of referring to God's covenantal relationship to Israel. It therefore focuses on God's intimate concern for and involvement in his creation. It says that creation is not alone or left to itself. It is indeed creation, the possession of its Creator. The world may hang onto Israel, for the name of the LORD is there. Israel is therefore the sign of hope for a threatened creation, for Israel has no stronger conviction than that it and the world's Creator is and will be the world's Redeemer.

Israel's hope for this world is through and through a creaturely hope, and therefore so is that of the church. The church hopes, together with Israel, as a creature, and for itself as part of the whole creation. It trusts as a child trusts that its mother cares. If this seems incredible to the modern spirit, then Israel speaks with a spirit older and more experienced in suffering and hardship to tell the world that we may trust in God's maternal care for his creation. Into just this trust the church has been awakened from sleep by the God of Israel who raised up Jesus Christ from the sleep of death. That is the church's sign of hope, not as concrete as the sign of the Exodus, but precious to Gentiles as the sign that they too can serve the Creator as a responding part of his creation at the side of his people Israel.

In the course of incorporating into the church's theology the witness of Israel to the reality and risk of creation, I have heard it implying a goal — redemption — more strongly than have some Jews. A Christian theology of Israel's witness is not, as we said, a Jewish theology. However, I believe I have made it clear that for Judaism, hope is not the highest virtue. That is also true for the church. Israel's apostle to the Gentiles was speaking out of sound pharisaic tradition when he said that love was more important than faith or hope. The reason for this is that hope looks to the future, whereas love confronts the present. Love sets us face to face with the neighbor, and that is where the covenant is to be lived. Because Creation was for the sake of the covenant, so Judaism knows that deeds of loving kindness are the highest witness to Creation that is humanly possible. Love in action — and what is love that is not active? — is Israel's contribution to the completion of creation. Paul realized that the church has no higher vocation than to join Israel in this work.

CHAPTER FOUR

Israel's Election—and the Nations

Israel's election is manifested in its interpretation of its history as being bound to God for the sake of the completion of creation. As the covenant of Noah points to the final possibility, so the covenant with Abraham initiates the actual path to this goal and invites the Gentile church to find itself along that road in cooperation with Israel, learning from Israel how to see its own history and that of the world.

1. ISRAEL'S ELECTION AND PARTICULARITY

i. Election and covenant

God's election of Israel is the foundation for everything that Israel has to say and for its continuing existence as his witness. Everything else in Israel's life and testimony follows from this; nothing precedes or leads up to it. Israel is the people *of God* or it is nothing.

In his essay of 1914, "*Atheistische Theologie*" (*K.S.*, 278–290), Franz Rosenzweig made clear the difficulties in attempts by liberal Jewish thinkers to lay a different foundation. He began with an illustrative example: the collapse of the liberal Protestant Life-of-Jesus theology. Rosenzweig saw the roots of this theology in the eighteenth-century attempt to circumvent classical Christology by defining Jesus as the great teacher, with Christianity as the teaching of this master. One had then no longer to believe in the incarnate one; it was sufficient to be instructed by this teacher. Romanticism shifted the emphasis with its discovery of the individual; the great teacher was replaced by the great religious personality. But the more this personality was examined, the more he gravitated back to his time and place, impossibly remote from nineteenth-century Germany. The only recourse was to abandon the inadequate historical quest and turn to philosophical theology: the *idea* of the Christ ("Jesus *as* the Christ"?) replaced the historical Jesus. The idea, however, was proving a soggy ground on which to rest the whole edifice of Christian life and thought (as a young pastor of Safenwil, just Rosenzweig's age, was also discovering at the time).

Jewish thought, which had given so much to Christian theology in the Scholastic period, was on the receiving end in the nineteenth century, Rosenzweig continued. Personality could not be a central theme of Jewish theology, but as Christian theology turned from the incarnate one to the ideal man, so Jewish thinkers converted the divine election of the chosen people into the idea of an ideal humanity. In both cases the myth, be it of the incarnation or of the election, was displaced by the humanly understandable human bearers of the myth. Revelation was defined as mythology, and this was "the supreme triumph of a theology inimical to revelation," making possible for Judaism as well as Christiantity an atheistic theology. Unwilling to entertain "the offensive thought of revelation," atheistic theology displaced the incarnation (*Menschwerdung*) with the humanness (*Menschsein*) of God, his descent to the mountain from which he gave the Law, with the autonomy of moral law. As the universal (that which was more than Jewish) triumphed over the particular (the Jewish) in the Christian image of Jesus, so on the Jewish side, the tension between the election of the chosen people and the people itself dissolved into a single concentration on the latter.

Rosenzweig's conclusion was that, although every interpretation of Judaism had to acknowledge the inseparability of God and human beings, there was a world of difference between the human beings in whom God was dissolved by rationalist or mystic, and human beings as the recipients of revelation. For the former, God is finally dispensable. The latter, unable to evade the thought of revelation, will find they must think also of God in order to make the Jewish people central for faith. Thus, several years before Karl Barth, Rosenzweig had rediscovered the centrality of election for biblical faith.

Election, as Israel presents it, means recruitment. Election comes as command. The opening word of Israel's own story is the story of its election. It begins in Genesis 12 as the story of God's purpose for his unfinished creation, and its first word is the command, "Go!" God's eye lights upon one man, Abram, and sets him in motion, "to the land that I will show you." Election is recruitment for a task. It breathes purpose. One creature is singled out, together with his family, in order that something be done about the unfinished creation of which we hear in Genesis 1 to 11. Being himself a part of that creation, however, the elect one receives his own particular blessing, ahead of the rest of creation. Elected to be a harbinger of redemption, Abram, renamed Abraham, will know the taste of, as well as acquire a taste for, redemption. God's elect shall live in their election. That means they shall live with God. The terms of that living are given in the covenant. The covenant, consequently, spells out the meaning of election, what it means for and about God, as well as its meaning for and about the Jewish people.

The Fellows of the Hartman Institute, and particularly Noam Zohar, have pointed out that I am favoring Israel's biblical witness over that of the Rabbis, by filling the gap, so to speak, between Genesis 11 and 12 with God's free election. The Rabbis filled that same gap by speaking of Abraham's choice of God! With their pervasive concern for right human action, for moving the people to faithful living, the Rabbis presented Abram as a model for the human decision to serve God. As they saw both sides of the covenant, so election for them was a mutual act: God chose the Abram who chose him. The concern of the Rabbis is important and needs to be heard by the church, but as the church as well as Israel need also to hear the biblical witness, especially at this time, I venture to side with the witness to God's free choice. But the last three sentences in the preceding paragraph show that I do not want to deny the importance of human responsibility that such a choice creates.

ii. *The electing God: election and revelation*

The witness of the Jewish people, throughout its long history, is to a God who has made up his mind to become and remain involved with his creation, from the beginning. By the witness of their continuity, the Jews stand as testimony to that enduring involvement. Israel understands this involvement to be quite particular and personal. On this basis, it must assume a general, universal relationship of God to his creation, but if there is truth in a general claim of the fatherhood of God and the brotherhood of man, Israel can contribute only its own election as evidence in its support. The Jewish Prayerbook regularly addresses the God of Israel as also King of the Universe, assuming apparently that God must have some sort of sovereign relationship to the whole of his creation, but it has little to say about this. Israel speaks primarily of what it knows, the quite particular, personal involvement of God in choosing the Jews to be his people. It knows this because of the particular, specific, and personal covenant which God has made with this people. God chose Israel for this covenant, and Israel accepted it: "All that the LORD has spoken we will do" (Exod. 24:7). Indeed, one of the Rabbis (Jose ben Simon) taught that before Israel accepted the Torah it was just another nation, called simply "Israel," "but after you accepted the Torah at Sinai, you were called 'My people,' as it says, 'Harken, O my people, and I will speak' (Ps. 50:7)." (*Tanh. B.*, Wa'era, 9a; M&L, 81). Israel knows God as the electing One on the basis of the reciprocal covenant of particularity.

So basic and common is the affirmation of God as Israel's elector that it is found not only in Torah, but also in the books of the early prophets Amos and Hosea, the later prophets Isaiah, Jeremiah, and Deutero-Isaiah, as well in the post-Exilic Writings. It is of course a common teaching of the Rabbis, medieval Jewish philosophers, poets, and biblical commentators, and indeed all of Israel's teachers down to the present. The popular ditty, "How odd of God to choose the Jews" gets to the heart of it: the God of Israel is indeed odd, working through particulars, to accomplish his purpose for his universe. Israel, and therefore the church, the witness of which on this as on so many fundamental points is absolutely dependent on that of the Jewish people, know of no other God than this odd one, quite particularly and personally the electing God.

This God, we must conclude, has chosen to deal with the vast reaches of his creation by involving himself with a particular part of it. The biblical expression which Jesus is said to have used, "the finger of God," says it all: God does not work by a broad sweep of the arms; God puts a finger, one finger, on one people, just so, just here. And the church, chosen to confirm Israel's witness, must say "Amen." Does the church know of any God other than the One whose finger was placed precisely on the Jewess Miriam (Mary)? In the light of this understanding of the particularity of God's finger, we shall have to ask whether we can say that the Muslims, for all of their universalizing tendency, do not bear witness to that same one finger laid on the lips of the Prophet. Even the Eastern traditions of China and India, with their hesitancy in speaking of God at all, nevertheless look to the teachings of quite particular individuals, a Gautama, a Lao-tzu.

Be that as it may (and on God's workings in Islam, much less in the traditions of India and China, Israel has had little to say), Israel knows God primarily and essentially as the God of Israel, the electing God. This teaching is no secondary addition to a primary "ethical monotheism;" it is the foundation of Israel's faith. Only a generalizing presupposition in an early stage of the development of the history of religions could have lost sight of the highly personal character of Israel's teaching and misunderstood it as "a monotheistic faith of the Mosaic persuasion." Israel, on the contrary, knows nothing prior of God than his election of Israel, his decision to bind himself to them in a covenant. God is and will be Israel's God in everything else that he does.

Israel's witness to the electing God clarifies an aspect to its testimony to God the Creator: since God made men and women in his own image and likeness, they correspond to God by being able to respond to God. But if human beings are in this way like God, God is also in this way like them: God can and will also respond to Israel. Israel knows only of a bilateral covenant, in which God as well as Israel can respond to a partner. The covenantal God has involved himself in the history of his people and will therefore move with that history. Israel affirms that the covenant will stand, but not necessarily that it will stand still. Indeed, it entertains the possibility that the covenant can change.

Since the terms of the covenant are matters between God and Israel, it is not for the church to take sides in this matter, but there is at this time important discussion among Jewish theologians about the developing or changing character of Israel's covenant with God. As it is being expressed by Rabbi Irving Greenberg, for example, Israel is entering into a third stage of its covenant with God, and God is entering into a third stage of his relationship with Israel (see the publications of the National Jewish Resource Center in New York City, especially "The Third Great Cycle of Jewish History," and "On the Third Era in Jewish History," both by Irving Greenberg). On this interpretation of Jewish history, the first era of the covenant, testified to by the Scriptures, began with Abraham and lasted until the destruction of the Second Temple. God was unambiguously the senior partner and prime mover in the relationship. In the second era, which was brought to a close by the Holocaust, the partnership was far more equal, Israel through its Rabbis having to make many of the decisions about how the history of this relationship was to proceed. In the third era, so recently inaugurated by the birth of the state of Israel, the Jewish people are called upon to take the lead in the covenant, with God remaining a largely silent partner. At this point no further comment on this understanding of the changing covenant will be made, other than to call attention to the similarity of this view to Bonhoeffer's idea of God's changing relationship to a world "come of age," with the resulting call for Christians to live before God as if they had to handle life entirely on their own, "without God."

With no less an appreciation of the new situation in which Jews find themselves today, David Hartman sees the Zionist state differently. It does not mark a new era, nor does it signal a change in the covenant. Rather, it presents a new and exciting opportunity to live the covenant more fully and responsibly. Hartman's different reading of the new situation rests in part on drawing a distinction between a Maimonidean understanding of Judaism, which takes its model of history from Sinai and Israel's halakhic responsibility in the covenant, and a Nachmanidean model of God's mighty acts, modeled on the Exodus. Although Hartman sees both models at work in the tradition, he leans toward the former as a better guide for the Jewish people today, especially for those of them who have shouldered the responsibility for shaping a Jewish state. See Hartman's *Joy and Responsibility: Israel, Modernity and the Renewal of Judaism*, Jerusalem, 1978.

However the terms of the covenant be understood, Israel's witness to the electing God has always taken the form primarily of living by its election. Israel lives by Torah, as it understands and interprets Torah, and it passes down this living to each new generation: each newborn Jewish boy is circumcised like Abraham, the covenant between this people and God being thereby cut in Israel's flesh once again.

Circumcision being required only of males (except among the Falashas, the black Jews of Ethiopia), this traditional practice raises the problem of the equality of the sexes for many Jews today. How the Jewish people will work out this equality is one of the more interesting problems confronting Israel's life in the "Third Era" of its ancient covenant. The church is not in a position to offer much of a lead in this matter.

Israel understands its history to be bound to God, a history lived together with God. This understanding and its resulting practice is the Jewish witness to the electing God, who wills creation's completion to be carried out not by himself alone, but with human co-workers as his partners. Israel tells of God by telling its own history as a history with God. In order to hear Israel's witness to God, therefore, one must listen sensitively to Israel's story of Israel.

iii. The elect people

Jews are special, Jews might say, or they are different, as Gentiles might put it. Both are correct, and both remarks should be heard: the peculiarity of Israel is that of a people as a whole. The Jews are the chosen people, and chosen as a people; they are not a people consisting of individually chosen persons. Their original ancestor, Abram, himself not a Jew, was chosen alone, but he was chosen in order to become a great nation (Gen 12:2). And God made his covenant not just with the renamed Abraham, but "with you and your descendants after you" (Gen. 17:7). The descendants of Abraham, according to Israel's story, through Isaac and Jacob, renamed Israel, the Jewish people to this day are in this history together, bound to God. That is how they have understood themselves and their history.

Bound to God for ever: "for better for worse, for richer for poorer, in sickness and in health" (from the marriage service, the Episcopal *Book of Common Prayer*), the Jewish people understand themselves tied to God and so are witnesses to the eternal covenant between themselves and God. Every Sabbath observed, every kosher meal eaten, every *mitzvah* performed, every son circumcised, every act of solidarity with the people is another expression of that witness. Faithful and unfaithful, willing and unwilling, this people is defined by God's election. This and this alone marks them off and makes them different from every other people. They are not distinguishable ultimately by the purity of their conception of God; by what supposed "standard" could that be judged? Nor do their ethical values, "Jewish values," make them unique. Nor is it their civilization that marks them as different; their civilization has had and has its strengths and weaknesses like all others. One or another of these alternatives have been proposed by liberal German Jews of the nineteenth century, or by liberal American Jews of the twentieth century, but Rosenzweig's analysis of the hollowness of "atheistic theology" covers them all. God's election, not Jewish genius, is what makes the Jewish people different. That is Israel's own testimony.

"For you are a people holy to the LORD your God; the LORD your God has chosen you to be a people for his own possession, out of all the peoples that are on the face of the earth" (Deut. 7:6). That is why "You shall not walk in the customs of the nation which I am casting out before you" (Lev. 20:23), and that is also why Israel is not and cannot be a nation "like all the nations," even when it longs for this (1 Sam. 8:5). If at certain times in its history this people or a larger or smaller part of it has denied or abandoned its election, if they have "forsaken me the fountain of living waters and hewed out cisterns for themselves" — such Jewish-hewn cisterns as "Jewish values," "Jewish civilization," or the Jewish people themselves — these substitutes turn out to be "broken cisterns that cannot hold water" (Jer. 2:13).

Such is Israel's own testimony. Theological liberalism holds as little water for Jews as for Christians. If Jews are different, it is because they are God's chosen people, his elect nation. And since they are God's elect nation, then no matter how they may try, they can never—as Jews—become "like all the other nations." The contemporary consequence of this, as we shall see later, is that the state of Israel, precisely because it is the *Jewish* state, can never succeed in becoming a state like all other states.

iv. Israel and the nations

Israel is a people, a nation (in Hebrew, *goy*). Taken simply as a nation, it is not distinctive, not unique, except in the way that each nation has its own particular history and character. Every nation has its customs and practices. Many have their own religious heritages. Considered without respect to its divine election, Israel is just one nation among all the others, with all the possibilities and limitations that go with being a nation. Israel itself knows this: "It was not because you were more in number than any other people that the LORD set his love upon you and chose you, for you were the fewest of all peoples; but it is because the LORD loves you" (Deut. 7:7f). Neither size nor, we may assume, any other feature accounts for or contributes to Israel's election.

God loves and chose Israel, but what of the other nations? What about us Gentiles? Are we not peoples and nations as Israel is? Are not the other nations also God's creatures? Indeed they are, as Israel understands them, and they are objects of God's care and concern: " 'Are you not like the Ethiopians to me, O people of Israel?' says the LORD. 'Did I not bring up Israel from the land of Egypt, and the Philistines from Caphtor and the Syrians from Kir?' " (Amos 9:7). That may be an unusual verse from the Scripture, but God's concern for the other nations is even more powerfully stressed in some rabbinic sayings. One reason given for the absence of any mention of rejoicing in connection with Passover is the fact that the Egyptians died; Proverbs 24:17 is quoted: "When your enemy falls, do not rejoice"

(*Pes.K.* 189a; M&L, 465). A similar saying is attributed to Rabbi Johanan: "The ministering angels wanted to sing a hymn at the destruction of the Egyptians, but God said: 'My children lie drowned in the sea, and you would sing?' " (*Meg.* 10b; M&L, 52).

The relationship between God's special concern for Israel and his care for all of creation is nicely brought out by a saying of Rabbi Judah the Prince, commenting on Deuteronomy 11:12 ("A land which the LORD cares for"): "But does [God] care only for Palestine? Does he not care for all lands? It is as if he cared only for Palestine, but as the reward of his caring for it, he cares with it for all other lands. 'The Guardian of Israel.' But is he the Guardian of Israel only? Does he not guard all? (Job 12:10). It is, as it were, like this. He guards Israel only, but as the reward of guarding them, he guards all with them" (*Sifre Deut.*, 'Ekeb, #40, f.78b; M&L, 557). God exercises his universal care for his creation by caring paradigmatically for Israel. He shows his effective love for all nations by loving Israel. Indeed, the very love he shows to Israel brings his love to the rest of the world.

Israel's priestly roll, which it has by its election, is for the sake of the other nations: "Rabbi Joshua ben Levi said: If the nations had known how valuable the Temple was for them, they would have surrounded it with forts in order to protect it. It was even more valuable to them than to the Israelites, for Solomon in his prayer of dedication said, 'And concerning the foreigner . . . do according to all that the foreigner calls to thee to do' (1 Kings 8:41–3), but when he touches on the Israelites, he says, 'Render unto everyone according to his ways,' that is, give to him what he asks if it is fitting for him, and if it is not fitting, give it him not. And indeed one could go further and say, 'If it were not for Israel, no rain would fall, and the sun would not shine, for it is through Israel that God gives assuagement to his world, and in time to come, i.e. in the Messianic age, the nations will see how God dealt with Israel, and they will come to join themselves unto them,' as it is said, 'In those days it shall come to pass that ten men out of all the tongues of the nations shall take hold of the skirt of him that is a Jew, saying, "We will go with you, for we have heard that God is with you," ' (Zech. 8:23)" (*Num.R.*, Bemidbar, 1,3; M&L, 115).

There is of course much that the Rabbis had to say against the Gentiles. Israel's historical experience with other nations has hardly provided grounds for a positive assessment of them. The passages we have cited are therefore all the more remarkable. Two more shall be given, crucial for understanding Paul, Israel's apostle to the Gentiles, and providing a theological account of the difference between Israel and the other nations, which the Rabbis usually numbered as seventy:

"The nations of the world were asked to receive the Law, in order not to give them an excuse for saying, 'Had we been asked, we might have accepted it.' They were asked, but they did not accept it, as it is said, 'The LORD came from Sinai and rose up from Seir unto them' (Deut. 33:2)." There follow accounts of the offer to the children of Esau, of Ammon and of Moab, and of Ishmael: each found one of the Ten Commandments to prohibit some action characteristic of that nation and therefore rejected Torah. Finally, it is offered to Israel, who responded, " 'All that the LORD has said, we will do, and we will be obedient' (Exod. 24:7)" (*Mek.2*, *Bahodesh*, Yitro, #5, pp. 221f; M&L, 78).

Similarly, " 'The LORD came from Sinai' (Deut. 33:2). Hence we learn that God went about from nation to nation to see whether they would receive the Law, and they would not receive it; as it says, 'All the kings praise thee, O LORD, for they have *heard* the words of thy mouth' (Ps. 138:4). One might think that, since they heard, therefore they were *also* willing to *receive* the Law. But Micah came and explained, saying, 'I execute vengeance in anger upon the nations which have not hearkened' (5:15). Hence we learn that they *did* hear, but would not receive the Law. David came and gave thanks, as it is said, 'Thou art the God that doest wonders, in that thou hast shown thy might among the peoples' (Ps. 77:14). . . . By the word 'might' is meant the Law, as it is said, 'The LORD gives might to his people' (Ps. 29:11)" (*Pes.K.* 199b *fin.*-200a; M&L, 79).

God's Torah, and so his redeeming intention, is for all the nations. No wonder the Pharisee Paul was so concerned about the "Law" as it affects Gentiles. They know it, because it was revealed to them, according to Jewish tradition, and so they are "without excuse" (Rom. 1:20). They are therefore "under the Law," a term no Jew could use of Israel's relationship to Torah, under the "curse of the Law" for having rejected it. No hope was open to them by way of the Law that they had rejected, Paul knew, which was why God had provided for them another way into his mercy. Paul appears to have been trained in the same tradition as the Rabbis, the teaching of the Sages that Israel's election was the world's hope.

Jews have mostly known Gentiles (the nations) as enemies of Israel and so as enemies of God. It is therefore remarkable that in medieval Europe they came to regard Christians as better than idolators, and even decided that it was all right to teach them Hebrew and even Jewish exegesis of the Hebrew Scriptures. These positive notes, however, must be heard in the midst of a heavier chord of hostile polemic, for Israel's overwhelming experience of the Gentiles was negative. The result has been that Israel has had little opportunity and less encouragement to develop the positive notes which we have just heard. Jewish teaching has consistently allowed a place "in the coming world" for the righteous among the Gentiles, but this does not tell us much about the nations. Further, what it has said about the Noachide covenant between God and all creation, as we shall see later, provides no adequate theological grounds for a Jewish understanding of the Christian church, not to speak of other traditions. Perhaps a development of a positive Jewish teaching concerning God's relationship to the nations may require the prior development of the more favorable relationship with at least some Gentiles which has begun to take shape in this early stage of Israel's "Third Era."

v. God of Israel, King of the universe

Both Israel and Israel's God are particular and universal. How has it come about, then, that the element of the particular has come through to the outside world so much more strongly? The element of the universal is there in Torah, the prophets, in such rabbinic sayings as we have reported, in major figures of medieval philosophy and commentary, and on through Israel's history. Whenever Israel tried to let its "light for the nations" shine, however, it has been met with hostility, and not least from the church. It is only the most recent setback to God's plan for the witness of his people Israel that the magnificent work of Israeli doctors, nurses, agricultural experts, and all sorts of technological and development programs in Africa and other developing lands was almost brought to a halt by a propaganda attack on Israel which closed so many ears and eyes to the witness of the young state of the Jewish people. Once more the nations have conspired to extinguish Israel's light for them. Yet Israel's witness has been offered, in our day as in the past, the universal witness of this particular people to the universality of their particular God.

An outstanding expression of this witness was given in this century by the remarkable testimony of Rav (Rabbi Abraham Isaac Ha-Kohen) Kook, Chief Rabbi of Jerusalem and all Palestine from 1919 until his death in 1935. Talmudic scholar, mystic, and Zionist in one, he achieved in his own life and in his writings a unification of Jewish Orthodoxy, Zionism, and the liberal spirit fostered by the Enlightenment, thus spanning the whole range of Jewish commitments of the day. As he himself was able to affirm a positive element even in atheism (in that it challenges the fixity of religious orthodoxy), so he could affirm other religions and all cultural movements that sought in their own way to move humanity forward. His passionate commitment to his people was an expression of his even deeper commitment to God and his redemptive purpose for the totality of existence.

Rav Kook's thought is available in English in the Paulist Press series of "Classics of Western Spirituality," *Abraham Isaac Kook* (New York, 1978), from which the following are cited, first an affirmation of Israel's particularity, and then of its universal goal.

"It is a fundamental error for us to retreat from our distinctive excellence, to cease recognizing ourselves as chosen for a divine vocation. We are not only different from other nations, differentiated and set apart by a distinctive historic existence that is unlike that of all the nations, but we indeed surpass the other nations. If we shall know our greatness then we shall know ourselves, but if we forget it then we shall forget our own identity; and a people that forgets its own identity is indeed small and lowly.

"The road our nation has traveled in its general interrelationship with humanity is very long. We are a great people and we have also blundered greatly, and, therefore, have we suffered great tribulations; but great also is our consolation.

"The people of Israel yearns to exert an influence with its psyche, to bring near the great day when the influence of the spiritual in its existential aspects will find ready and prepared ground to make possible the fulfillment of the prophecy (Zech. 8:22–23): 'And many peoples and mighty nations shall come to seek the Lord of hosts in Jerusalem . . . and they shall take hold of the corner of the garment of a Jew, saying, Let us go with you, for we have heard that God is with you.' " (p. 289f).

"When the light of Israel will emerge and make its appearance in the world, after purging itself with firmness and courage of the darkness and murkiness that attached themselves to it because of its lack of self-understanding, there will at once become manifest the precious vision of unity, which integrates all forces into one complete, comprehensive phenomenon, at the same time leaving intact the particular essence of each. The spiritual world in all its dimensions is patterned into one entity, so that even this area of religion that abounds in quarrels becomes filled with peace and light. There will remain a definite distinction in the levels of the different religions, in the values of one as against another, but through their general orchestration there will be made manifest automatically the central goal at the heart of the religions, which will then radiate light and the splendor of holiness upon the constituent individuals in the organic whole, each unit recognizing its value and its place" (p. 312).

Not all Jews have had Rav Kook's deep trust in God and so have not been so free to express the universal thrust of Israel's witness. Nevertheless, that witness at its truest is that the God of Israel is the King of the Universe. At the same time, it is a witness that the King of the Universe is the God of Israel, so that the vision of universal redemption which Rav Kook presented included the particularity of each part of God's creation.

2. THE COVENANT OF NOAH: PROBLEMS AND POSSIBILITIES

i. *The Jewish tradition of the Noachide covenant*

According to the written Torah (Gen. 9: 8ff), God made a

covenant with Noah, his sons, all the creatures that were in the ark, "and for all future generations" (9:12). According to the oral Torah (Moore, I, 274), all the nations are obligated to keep the seven commandments of this covenant. These are usually given as prohibitions against idolatry, blasphemy, murder, incest and adultery, theft, and eating flesh taken from a live animal, and a positive command to establish courts of justice. All of these commandments, the Rabbis taught, had originally also been given to *adam* as part of the covenant of Creation, with the exception of the last prohibition (since permission to eat meat first came after the flood). Because all the seventy nations of the world are the descendants of Noah, they are all included in this covenant with God.

This covenant, however, has not been observed. The nations have not obeyed its commandments. Israel has regarded Islam as an exception; in view of their strict monotheism, Muslims were considered Noachides from the first, and a grudging exception was also made since the Middle Ages for Christians. Generally, however, Gentiles and idolators have been synonomous terms in Israel's tradition. Worshiping the one God, Israel has for most of its life been surrounded by nations serving other gods. The Gentile, the non-Jew, was therefore assumed to be a worshiper of idols, and because the God of Israel was a jealous God, who does not want the covenant partner to be seduced by idols, close contact with Gentiles was to be avoided. The fundamental role of the Noachide covenant in Jewish tradition, therefore, has not been to affirm any personal relationship between God and the nations, but rather to serve as God's guarantee of the continuity of creation, thus making possible the one covenant that really matters, the one with Israel.

Thus the Noachide covenant, which at first sight appears to offer the basis for serious Jewish reflections on the relationship between the God of Israel and the nations of the world, has not in fact done so. It has, rather, reflected Israel's primary witness to its own covenant. When the Jew thinks seriously about the relationship between God and creation, the covenant of Sinai will inevitably stand in the center. Because the word "covenant" occurred in the Noah story, it was logical for the Rabbis to search out a list of commandments for that covenant, for how could there be a covenant without commandments? But since they believed the tradition of the seventy nations having been offered and having rejected the Torah, they had no reason to explore the possibility of God's relationship, personal as God is personal, with the nations surrounding them. The nations were alien and usually threatening to the Jewish people; they were therefore presumed to be the enemies of God.

Jews have always known of exceptions, and the Rabbis had nothing but the highest praise for the righteous among the Gentiles, insisting that they had a place of honor in the coming world. Further, they were also sure that God's desire for human repentance applied to the Gentiles as well as to Israel. This was, after all, the theme of the book of Jonah. Nevertheless, as Moore summed up their teaching (I, 529), they believed that "for the Gentile to participate in this promise [of forgiveness], as in all others, the indispensable condition is the repentance, or conversion, in which he abandons his false religion for the true, the heathen freedom of his way of life for obedience to the revealed will of God in his Law; in a word, become a proselyte to Judaism, a Jew by naturalization. This is the logical attitude [so Moore concluded] of a revealed religion, and has always been maintained by the Christian church: repentance avails nothing — or, more exactly, repentance in the proper sense is impossible — outside the church. . . . Moslem doctrine is the same."

ii. The inadequacy of the Noachide covenant tradition

The covenant with Noah and his descendants, as the Rabbis conceived of it, when contrasted with the covenant of Sinai, is a minimal covenant at best. Only the minimal requirements of constructive living are stipulated, and God is only committed to preserving the minimal conditions for that living. What is missing is the interior of a covenant, so to speak. This covenant has no heart. No personal relationship between the covenant "partners" (should we not say "parties?") is in question. It is not even necessary for the nations to know God at all; they are only prohibited from serving false gods. It is therefore quite unacceptable for the church, which can never see itself in its relationship to the God of Israel in the terms provided by the Noachide covenant. That covenant simply does not fit the reality of the church's experience of its relationship to God. Could Israel ever come to accept that?

As we have just noted, Moore concluded that it was logical for Judaism to have a negative view of other traditions. The logic to which he appealed was that of a revealed religion. Today we must add that it is the logic of a religion of a *fixed* revelation. But if new interpretations of past revelation are possible, then this logic fails. Whether this be called a new revelation or a new understanding of a received revelation is immaterial. The issue is whether Judaism, whose written as well as oral Torah is the product of repeated reinterpretations, could come to a new view of the relationship between the God of Israel and the nations of the world, beginning with those Gentiles with whose history so much of their own has been enmeshed, the church.

As a matter of fact, fresh thinking about this matter on the part of Jews is taking place. In an essay in *Issues in the Jewish-Christian Dialogue* (New York, 1979), Manfred Vogel raised the question "Why, on principle, should the Gentile be required to give up his own ethnic identity in order to have access to Israel's covenantal relation? Why should the Gentile not be enabled to share and participate in the context of his own ethnic identity? Judaism, in our judgment, does not provide a satisfactory answer to this problem and we have to admit that on this point Christianity can provide better for the Gentile world. In fact, there is no reason why Judaism should not accept and welcome Christianity and its new covenant, provided that its role is clearly confined to this function" (79).

Vogel's essay reveals something of the spirit which we saw in Rav Kook: the Jewish view of the other appears to open up when

Jews are not on the defensive. His last clause, however, reflects Jewish awareness of the risk in letting down their defenses in the face of the church. The church is certainly in no position to criticize Judaism for inattentiveness to the relationship between God and the nations, for the church has been for many centuries the principal threat to Israel's existence.

When the Jewish people finds itself face to face with another church, one not determined to rid the world of Jews by trying to turn them into Christians, when it hears from Christians who stand in supportive solidarity with Israel, the response is immediate. Two review-essays on *Discerning the Way*, by David Novak in *Judaism* (1982, 112–120) and Shamai Kanter in *Conservative Judaism* (1982, 83–90), confirm this judgment. (When a response of a similar tone appears in *Tradition*, the evidence will be complete!) The evidence is of the possibilities of a development beyond Israel's tradition of the Noachide covenant. What that might be will concern us in the remainder of this section.

iii. The covenant of Noah and creation ·

We take as our point of departure the witness of both the written and the oral Torah to the intimate connection between the covenant of Noah and that of Creation. In both, chaos gives way to order and God commits himself to the result. In both, all creatures are commanded to do their part by being fruitful and multiplying. In both covenants, therefore, both God and the whole of creation are committed to each other.

In this connection we recall our reflections on Israel's testimony to Creation as a covenant: Creation entails God's self-determination as well as the determination of all that is made. He will be its Creator, and all else shall be his creatures. Creation, then, is made for covenant, and covenant is just that for which this creation was designed. The story of the covenant with Noah (here the word "covenant" makes its first appearance) recapitulates much in the story of Creation and makes explicit its covenantal character. Creation is renewed and ever to be made new in the cycle of seasons and *also* in creaturely procreation.

The renewed creation is, however, still incomplete, still imperfect. The flood has not really solved anything. Yet the Creator is still with his creatures; he still wills to be bound to them and them to him. It is as if it took this long, the ten generations from *adam* to Noah, for God to realize, so to speak, that he had determined himself by becoming Creator, that he could never again, at least as long as the earth remains, be just the *En Sof* of divine totality that he may be supposed to have been before Creation. Something like this is hinted at in Israel's mystical tradition and even in such an antimystical heir of that tradition as Franz Rosenzweig. The Noah story itself does not say this; it only leaves itself open to such an interpretation. If we reflect on this possibility, then we might say that the prehistory of Genesis 1 to 8 was as much the prehistory of God as of creation, and that could lead to the suggestion that there has never been and will never be a history that is not also God's history with his creation. In which case, the distinctive histories of all the "seventy" nations take on a new significance.

The rabbinic tradition of the oral Torah did not explore such a possibility, but does it exclude it? The rabbinic focus, of course, was halakhic, a concern for how to walk day by day in the covenant. But the covenant of Noah has its halakhic side: there are explicit commandments (Gen. 9:1 [and 7], 4, and 5–6). Manfred Vogel (in the aforementioned essay) is not quite accurate in calling the covenant of Noah a covenant of promise. It too contains commandments, which the Rabbis imaginatively expanded into seven. In thus elaborating the halakhic aspect of the covenant of Noah, they were emphasizing its mutuality. Creation, even as renewed after the flood, is unfinished and needs redemption, but it will not be finished until there is human cooperation. Noah and the seventy nations descended from him are thereby brought into the work of redeeming creation. Again we find grounds for taking seriously the history of the other nations.

From both the written and the oral tradition of Israel's witness, therefore, it is possible to develop the tradition of the covenant of Noah in such a way as to point toward the goal of creation and so the goal also of God's covenant with Israel. In which case there opens up a fresh way to understand the relationship between Israel and the other nations, and that between each and all of those nations and the God of Creation, the God of Israel.

iv. *The Noah covenant as promise and invitation*

The Noah covenant, as we have seen, has played a minor role in Israel's witness. We have, so to speak, extrapolated from that witness in an attempt to explore an underdeveloped aspect of Israel's witness, namely, to the relationship between God and the nations of the world. Because we did so at a relatively secondary point in Israel's story, we should not expect to do more at this point than indicate a direction for further reflection. Israel's witness to the relationship between God and the Gentiles must draw its substance from the center of Israel's story.

Nevertheless, we can make a beginning with Israel's story of Noah. The authors of this story evidently accepted a widespread Mesopotamian tradition of a universal flood (see Sarna for a full discussion, 38–59). What they made of it, however, was unique, something only comprehensible within the context of Israel's whole witness: the promise of the Creator that he would carry through what he had begun "in the beginning." There is a rabbinic tradition of God having experimented with Creation, trying out several versions and rejecting and destroying them in turn, until the existing creation was arrived at (*Gen.R.*, Ber. III,7). However that may be, the story of the covenant with Noah affirms that with this creation, the one that is real, God will not give up. Having involved himself with it by creating it, and then by renewing it, he will not let it go its own way by itself. God will be with it to support it. The creation renewed points ahead to its completion. Israel's whole story of creation, from Genesis 1 through Genesis 11, says that "so far, so good" is not good enough for its Creator. Creation will be redeemed.

The covenant with creation made through Noah contains God's promise to the world of a future. It may also be seen to contain an invitation: all of Noah's descendants, every nation or people is invited to see itself in the light of the special story of the one people that begins with the call of Abram. That special story lies beyond Israel's story of Creation. Only its essential foundations have been laid: a real world with real people, promised a future by the Creator. Their history with him will be possible because he has promised them his history with them. That this is the underlying intent of the covenant of Noah will become clear as Israel's story of Creation concludes, with a span of ten more generations, and gives way to a new "beginning," the beginning of history.

3. THE COVENANT WITH ABRAHAM

i. *The Way in history: the father of Israel*

We have been groping, with the help of Israel's witness, in the shadows of prehistory. We have dared to trust Israel's lead in doing so, because God has proved his personal and temporal involvement in his prehistorical, temporal creation by entering personally into the concreteness of world history. He did so in calling and committing himself to the single human being, Abram.

Whether Abram was a discrete individual in our modern historical sense, I am not competent to decide. Scholarly skepticism seems to have given way during this century to cautious acceptance of a historical root to the story of Abram. What matters for us, however, is the clarity of Israel's conviction, evidenced in the preservation of the story, that real history, the history that matters, of men and women in datable and locatable interaction with each other and with God, and so Israel's own history of wrestling with God and man, began then and there with God's call of the pagan Abram, who until that time had "served other gods" (Josh. 24:2).

However dimly, with Abram we begin to connect with history as it is generally understood today (see Sarna, 85ff). The connection with history, however, is brought to our attention in

Israel's Torah, in the First Book of Moses. The story of Creation in Genesis 1 to 11, which we have called prehistory, tells of Creation and the unfinished, threatened condition of the world. Now we come to a particular individual, the first whom God addressed by name (Gen. 15:1) and to whom he gave a new name, Abraham (17:2). We are thus introduced to Israel's understanding of history. It is the realm in which the Creator and his creatures address each other, where their plans and purposes interact, conflicting or sometimes cooperating. This realm is in time and space. In this realm the human beings involved have their feet on the ground, live in particular places for definite lengths of time. Here from time to time God speaks to one or another of them and some of them, from time to time, speak to God. It is, according to Israel's witness, the place where we all live. It is history.

The history that Israel tells is essentially its own, a history that began with Abram, who was renamed Abraham, continued with that of his son Isaac, and continued with that of his grandson Jacob, who also received a new name: Israel. Since each of these figures had more than one child, Israel presents a history of choice upon choice in each succeeding generation. Otherwise expressed, history, according to Israel's witness, becomes ever more definite. Whatever may be God's broader purpose for the whole of his creation, it is going to be unfolded in a quite particular history, and this history of the people Israel will be presented as that to which the history of all creation is related. History, the world's as well as Israel's, therefore, begins with election, and as the chosen people, Abraham's descendants will be a people of history, bearing a name and a memory, a people living in a definite place. That is what happens when God elects: election propels into history.

Into history, not simply into time. Tillich expressed a typically Augustinian misreading of Israel's story when he insisted that Israel was essentially a people of time rather than space. Space is of course not a category of history. History concerns places, not space, but we shall see that Israel's election is to life in a place, not just to life in time. God's first electing word to Abram was to go "to the land that I will show you," a definite place. The chosen people are elected into history.

In propelling Abram and his seed into history, however, God committed himself to this history. God's election of Israel tells us something about God as well as about Israel. He will from now on be the God of Abraham, and then the God of Abraham, Isaac, and Jacob. Israel knows to this day of no other God than this One who tied himself to these particular people and their history.

Tillich's misunderstanding of Israel as the people of time was matched by a corresponding misunderstanding of Israel's witness to God. He is not, as Tillich thought, the God of time, in contrast to the gods of space. He is rather the God of history, who will cause his Name to "dwell in this place."

History is consequently the ground of Israel's life and witness. Israel will remember history, tell history, and hope for a future that is historical. History will therefore also be the ground for a church whose witness confirms that of Israel, for with Israel the church has been set upon an actual path along which God has revealed the goal of his creation. Indeed, this path is one leading to that goal, the completion of God's creation.

ii. *The father of Ishmael, and of many nations*

Israel remembers Abraham as the father of Isaac and the grandfather of Jacob who was renamed Israel. It remembers him, that is, as the father and beginning of the line of God's choice. Israel also remembers, however, that Abraham had other children, and that God promised that he would be the father of many nations. The finger of election will fall upon Isaac (indeed will single him out before his birth) and not upon Abraham's firstborn son, Ishmael, just as in the third generation, the younger of Isaac's twin sons, Jacob, not Esau, will carry the burden of God's choice. But what of Ishmael? He stands in blood kinship to the line of election. Is he simply ignored? Has Ishmael no part in Abraham's election?

First, it must be said that the Torah of Israel is clear: God's election depends on God alone, no matter how strange his choice may seem to us. As Israel tells the story of this election, it runs through not just Abraham, but also through Sarah. Sarah too is blessed and will be the mother of many nations (Gen. 17:16). Therefore, although Abraham pleads for Ishmael's place as the heir of God's promise (17:18), God's choice is with Sarah's future son and for his descendants (17:19). Ishmael receives a great blessing, but the eternal covenant will be with Sarah's son (17:19–21).

Two remarks are in order. First, it could be argued that it is more the result of later interpretation than of Torah itself that Israel's God has come to be known as the God of the patriarchs, rather than of the matriarchs. Abraham is clearly important in the story of election, but when first we hear of an "everlasting covenant" (Gen. 17:7,13,19), Sarah is the one who counts! Abraham had other children; the covenant will be with Sarah's child and his descendants. Thus has Israel preserved and told the story of God's election.

Second, the emphasis of Torah on election as solely God's decision was picked up and confirmed by the apostle to the Gentiles in the ninth chapter of Romans. In emphasizing that election was entirely of God's free disposing, Paul, in good rabbinic form, paraphrased, totally out of context, the words of Malachi: "Jacob I loved, but Esau I hated" (Rom. 9:13; Mal. 1:2–3). It is important to note Paul's concern only to show that election tells us much about God but nothing about human beings. Further, it should be noted that Malachi was not even talking about Jacob and Esau; he was contrasting God's love for Israel with the desolation visited upon its traditional enemy Edom. In the passage cited by Paul, Edom was given the "code name" of its patriarch, Esau (cf. Gen. 36:8). Esau served as a code name for others of Israel's enemies at different times. For the Rabbis, Esau was the usual designation for Rome (M&L, 432f).

Given that Israel saw the line of election passing Ishmael by, it is remarkable what the tradition of election has to say concerning that person. The same Torah that tells of Israel's election tells us that Ishmael's name means that God has heard (Gen. 16:11). Ishmael is blessed and promised that he will be the father of princes and become a great nation (17:20). Even more remarkably, Israel preserved the story of God's choice of Sarah's son over Hagar's, interposed, it would seem, into the story of circumcision as the sign of God's eternal covenant. The covenant of circumcision is announced and defined (17:9–14), God insists that his covenant will be with Sarah's son (17:15–21), and then Abraham carries out the covenant of circumcision (17:22–27), circumcising Ishmael first of all (17:23), the story emphasizing the point by saying that Abraham and Ishmael were circumcised on the same day (17:26). Thus with Ishmael, explicitly, is enacted "how you shall keep my covenant between myself and you and your descendants" (17:10). Ishmael is therefore marked with "the sign of the covenant between me [God] and you [Abraham — and Israel!]" (17:11). Thus the "rejected" Ishmael is explicitly included in God's covenant with Abraham and Sarah's descendants! And this is *Israel's* witness, the story of God's election as Israel has preserved and passed it on for all future generations.

I call that Israel's witness, since we have it from no one else, yet it is not clear whether the Rabbis made anything of it, judging from their cryptic midrash on Gen. 17:20. The biblical text reads as follows: "As for Ishmael, I [God] have heard you [Abraham]: behold, I will bless him and make him fruitful and multiply him exceedingly; he shall be the father of twelve princes, and I will make him a great nation." The Rabbis disagreed among themselves as to the antecedent of the repeated "him" in the blessing, some incredibly maintaining that it referred to Isaac. But the reason given for this unlikely reading is yet more remarkable: those who maintained that this blessing of Ishmael really was for Isaac explained that this was so in order that "the son of the bondmaid might learn [that he had been blessed — so the Soncino translators interpolated] from the son of the mistress." Those who maintained that the blessing really was meant for Ishmael, as the text plainly requires, explained that this was so in order that "the son of the mistress might learn from the son of the bondmaid" (*Gen.R.* 47, 5, *Midrash Rabbah, I, 401f*).

A minimalist reading of this difference would be that some maintained that Isaac was blessed, not Ishmael, and therefore Ishmael had to learn (everything?) from him, whereas others let the text stand, but only to argue that if Ishmael was blessed at all, it was only to heighten the worth of the blessing given to Isaac. If, however, we adopt a maximalist reading, as the interpolation of the translators suggests, it is hard to say which position is the more remarkable. On the one side, Isaac is blessed in order to be able to tell Ishmael that he, Ishmael, is blessed, and on the other, Ishmael is blessed in order to tell Isaac that he, Isaac, is blessed. On either hand, *being* blessed is for the sake of telling others that *they* are blessed! If we follow a maximalist reading, we will have to say that even in their disagreement, the Rabbis would seem to have borne a common witness to Israel's mission to the world. Which way to take the midrash, however, is, as in so many rabbinic passages, left to the reader.

Surely the conclusion to be reached from this strange text, although a conclusion for which rabbinic support is ambiguous, is that election is for the sake of God's purpose for all those who are not the elect. Ishmael in particular, standing perhaps for all the nations of the world, although not to be the bearer of the covenant, is intimately and concretely touched by it. Its mark is left also on him. So Israel's witness to its election by God may be interpreted in a Christian theology of the people Israel.

iii. The Blessing

We are now in a position to understand the force of the blessing of Abram (Gen. 12:3): "All the families on earth will pray to be blessed as you are blessed" (*NEB*), "shall find blessing in you" (*NAB*); "By you all the families of the earth will bless themselves" (*RSV*); "Abraham's name would . . . be invoked in blessings" (Sarna, 117). However we translate the blessing, the sense is clear: when it comes to the matter of blessing, all humanity may and ought to think of Abraham. The rabbis went a step further. Punning on the word *berakah*, 'blessing,' they said, "this means a pool (*berekah*): just as a pool purifies the unclean, so do thou bring near [to Me] those that are afar" (*Gen.R.* 39:12; *Midrash Rabbah* I, 322). Blessing has entered the world and will draw all nations into its orbit, because in their midst walks the one who has been blessed by the Creator of all.

The possibility of blessing for the world has come about because God has chosen a particular people, the descendants of Abraham and Sarah, to walk in God's Way in history, on a path which leads to the redemption of his whole creation. God has chosen his own way of reaching this goal by choosing a particular people to cooperate with him in this work. Together with him, they will walk the path in history that God has chosen. The blessing of creation will come by way of God's election of Abraham and his and Sarah's descendants.

Therefore the existence of Abraham, the presence of Israel in the history of the world, the existence of the Jewish people today, are God's evidence and testimony to the world that he stands by his blessing and that the whole of creation will share in it. Because Israel is his, so the nations of the world may know and trust that they too are his. Israel's witness is confirmed by that of the church: the nations are to know that *their* "salvation is of the Jews" (Jn. 4:22). That is Israel's testimony concerning its own election.

4. COVENANT AND HISTORY: THE RIGHTEOUSNESS OF GOD

i. *Abraham and Isaac: the* akedah

The Temple was of greater benefit to the nations than it was to Israel, and Abraham was blessed in order to bring near to God those who were far off, the rabbis told us. Thus has Israel interpreted its own story. It could be, then, that the God of Israel is as close to and involved with the other nations as he is with Israel. If that is so, it has not been shown to Israel, any more than it has been shown to the church. If it is true, it has to be discovered, perhaps in our own time or in the future. The key to any such understanding, however, has certainly been given in Israel's story of God's covenantal relationship with Abraham, Isaac, and Jacob. The story of their way through history, however, is first of all that of the God who chose them, as is clear from the fact that he gave them their names. Of the three, only Isaac was not given a new name by God, but this was only because his name was divinely given before his birth. Those whose history is in God's hands must give up their own claim to it, or claim it only in the name which God alone bestows.

The feature of "giving up" comes to a climax in sharpest focus in the story of the *akedah*, the binding, of Isaac (Gen. 22:1–20).

For a summary of the rich Jewish tradition of commentary on this story, rabbinic, mystical, and philosophical, see the essay of Rabbi Louis Jacobs in *E. J.* II, 480–4.

The story is of Abraham's obedience on trial. He was asked to give up his only son, to sacrifice him to God. Isaac, however, was the child of promise, the one through whom God's covenant purpose was to be carried forward. Abraham was therefore asked to sacrifice not only his own future, but also God's. The covenant itself, for which the world was created, was to be sacrificed! Yet Abraham obeyed.

Abraham obeyed in silence. There had been a time for laughter and joy. This was a time for silence, perhaps the silence of incomprehension. Yet Abraham obeyed.

The story is of Abraham's obedience, not his faith, yet Israel preserved this story along with the earlier story of Abraham's trust in God's promise of this very son (Gen. 15:4–6). There it says that "Abraham put his trust in the LORD and counted it to him righteousness."

Against the whole tradition of Christian interpretation, we translate Genesis 15:6 with Lloyd Gaston, following the lead of the great thirteenth-century rabbi-philosopher Nachmanides and a minority Jewish interpretation. (See L. Gaston, "Abraham and the Righteousness of God," *Horizons in Biblical Theology*, 2 (1980), 39–68.) This reading, as Gaston points out, has the merit of following the plain meaning of the Hebrew and its use of parallelism.

God's righteousness is his faithfulness to his promise. He promised Abraham posterity, and Abraham, in trusting the Promiser, acknowledged God as one who would carry out what he had promised. God's righteousness consists in carrying out what he has promised. So when God's promise to Abraham is recalled in Isaiah 51:1-8, "in the concluding line of the poem (vs. 7,8) the blessing of Abraham now being fulfilled for Israel is called very impressively the 'righteousness of God' " (Gaston, 47. He adds, "It is significant that the middle strophe [vs. 4-6] refers to the Gentiles in this connection"). Abraham as God's elect was promised a son by Sarah and that he would be the father of many nations. God's righteousness was demonstrated in restoring Isaac to his father, in rescuing his people in the Exodus, in redeeming them from Exile. It was further demonstrated in calling to life many dead stones from the nations as further children of Abraham.

The merit of Abraham, to which the rabbinic tradition refers so often, that which is stored away for the future benefit of his children, is precisely this righteousness of God. God intends to carry through in history the covenant which he made with Abraham. That is how he means to right what is wrong with creation and to mend what is broken. Abraham put his trust in this God and so counted on this righteousness of this God.

ii. *Abraham and Jesus*

The author of the Gospel according to John was probably no Jew, but he knew Israel's witness that Abraham's children do the works of Abraham (Jn. 8:39; cf. Lk, 19:8-9 for a similar awareness). This is recorded in a highly polemical passage in which he has Jesus say that Abraham rejoiced to see his day (8:55).

In this and the following subsection, we come to matters that have not been part of Israel's witness, not because they could not have been, but because of the negative and polemical teaching of the church. We come to what might have been part of Israel's testimony to the electing God. Perhaps it will be that one day.

The covenant is lived in history. God and Israel together move through time. In a time that marks the beginning of the Common Era, there was born a son of Abraham, a Jew, one marked by that covenant of election. In him, Israel's light began to shine out upon the nations, the Gentiles, as it had never shone before. In him, therefore, once more and in a new way, the righteousness of God appeared, that which Abraham had acknowledged by trusting in God. No wonder that his followers could say that Abraham rejoiced to see his day, for in that day, the promise to Abraham that he would be the father of "a multitude of nations" (Gen. 17:5) began to happen.

This son of Abraham was also tested, but no angel came to stop the hand of the Roman executioners. But as Isaac was brought back from the point of death, this one's life and historical effect did not stop with death.

There was a widespread Jewish belief in the Middle Ages that Abraham actually sacrificed Isaac, who was then restored by resurrection. Was this a defensive response to the church? The grounds for this belief are in the text: when Abraham returns from the mountain, he and his "young men" are mentioned, but there is no word of Isaac (Gen. 22:19), nor does Isaac show up to assist at the burial of his mother, Sarah (23:2, 19). His name first recurs when Abraham makes plans to find a wife for him (24:4ff).

The righteousness of God consists in having restored Isaac, in having raised up Jesus, and in awakening Gentile stones to be children of his promise to Abraham. What God began in choosing Abraham he has continued and is yet continuing in Abraham's descendants, the Jewish people. What God began in Abraham, he is also continuing in raising up from the Gentiles a community, the church, to be an auxiliary of his original election, and only in our days finally just beginning to assume the cooperative role which it was designed to play alongside the people of his election.

iii. Abraham and Paul

The way of the electing God and his elect people, the course of the covenant, continued through history. In the second generation of the Common Era, a certain Pharisee received a prophetic calling, which he wrote of in terms of Jeremiah's call (Gal. 1:15; cf. Jer. 1:5), "appointed," like Jeremiah, "a prophet to the nations," or "as a light to the nations," like the prophet of the Exile (Is. 49:6), or, as this Pharisee was to put it, an "apostle to the Gentiles." Known as Paul, this Pharisee trusted, like his father, Abraham, in the righteousness of God, and indeed he was convinced that he was living at the moment in the history of the covenant in which that righteousness that Abraham had acknowledged was happening. Let us hear what he had to say as he summed up his news in his letter to the church in Rome.

If what follows seems unusual, I urge the skeptical reader to take off traditional Augustinian glasses, with their inevitably anti-Judaic focus, and simply consult the Greek text, with the help of a good dictionary and grammar as needed.

Paul had been appointed, he told his readers, to make known the good news of a new manifestation of the righteousness of God (Rom. 1:1, 17). Although the manifestation was new, it had been pointed to already in the Torah and by the prophets (3:21, 1:2). Now, "in the present time," that righteousness which Abraham had faithfully ascribed to God was being carried out: God was laying claim to the many nations, calling them to Abrahamic sonship "out of the faithfulness of Jesus" (3:26). The news of this happening, therefore, completely confirmed Torah (3:31), for God's righteousness had been counted to—that is, stored up in God on behalf of—Abraham while the patriarch was still a Gentile, before he received circumcision (4:9–11a), precisely so that he might become the father not only of his faithful descendants, the Jews, but also of believing Gentiles (4:11b–12). Gentile sinners in their helpless condition had been reconciled to God by the death of God's son Jesus Christ and were now caught up in the love of God (5:6–11). What Torah could not do for Gentiles—namely, lead those who had rejected God's Torah into the path of righteousness—God had now accomplished through Christ, so that that righteousness of God which Torah expressed for Israel might take place also in them (8:3–4). This was truly startling news of a new thing, news for Israel as well as for the Gentiles.

Paul was in agony over the fact that most of his fellow Jews had no ears for this news and no eyes to see this new righteousness of God (Rom. 9:1ff, 11:8–10). Sons of Abraham, living within the covenant, and therefore knowing the promise that just this would happen (9:4), they of all people should have been the ones to know that God's election, both of Israel and now of the Gentiles too, was totally a matter of God's free love (9:6–29). But in point of fact, what was happening was that Gentiles, who had not the vaguest idea of God's righteousness, were now being caught up in it (9:30), whereas Israel was so eagerly centered on the Torah of righteousness—for Torah is unquestionably God's righteousness for Israel—that they did not anticipate (although it was right there in Torah! 9:31) this new manifestation of the righteousness of God on behalf of Abraham's Gentile heirs. They never dreamed that God's righteousness, which they so eagerly followed according to Torah, could also be, for the Gentiles, accomplished through the faithfulness of Christ, rather than by their becoming proselytes (9:32). The very idea of God's righteousness being enacted apart from fidelity to Torah was just too new for them (9:33; cf. 3:21). Consequently, they could not see that Christ, as God's means of reconciling the Gentiles to himself, was for them the goal for which the Torah of the covenant existed (10:4). In short, God had made Christ to be that righteousness of God stored up for Abraham; in doing this, God had thereby opened the way for Abraham to become the father not only of Isaac, but also of many nations.

Paul's deepest hope and prayer was therefore that his fellow Jews would be saved [from their blindness — no small matter in the eyes of a Pharisee] (10:1). Their rejection of Paul's news about the righteousness of God did indeed make room for Paul's mission to the Gentiles (11:11, 15) and was therefore to the benefit of the latter (11:12a, 28a), but Paul longed for Israel's cooperation in this mission (11:12b, 31b). Paul was sure that God had not rejected his beloved people Israel (11:1, 2, 11, 28, 29: hence the bracketed reading of 10:1). How could he? They were, after all, Abraham's heirs and so heirs of the promises (11:1,28b).

So may Paul be read, if, contrary to the whole history of Christian exegesis, we take him at his word that he was a Jew, an Israelite, a Pharisee, and blameless in his keeping of Torah — at least until his calling seemed to demand an identification with his new Gentile converts. But from our earliest records, Paul was not so read by Gentiles unfamiliar with his Pharisaic background. Instead, his glorious good news addressed to Gentiles of the righteousness of the God of Abraham being now extended to them, was twisted into a venomous attack upon Paul's beloved fellow Jews and upon his and their hallowed and joyful Torah. The result was that the church set up an almost insuperable barrier to the fulfillment of Paul's deepest hopes and prayers. In the face of the church's anti-Judaism, how could Israel's witness include this new manifestation of the righteousness of the God of Abraham? Jesus Christ as the confirmation of the promises of God to Abraham has therefore not appeared within the testimony of Israel to God's particular way toward achieving the completion of his creation. Whether Paul's prayer will yet be answered and Israel's witness include also this act of God's election remains to be seen. This would clearly depend upon how the church will decide to read the words of the God of Abraham's apostle to the Gentiles.

iv. *The righteousness of God: God's historical generosity*

First and last, Israel bears witness to the righteousness of God, God's fidelity to his decision in calling Abraham, so that, through him and his descendants, God's promises would reach to his whole creation. The church of him in whom "all God's promises find their Yes" (2 Cor. 1:20) can therefore do no other than echo Israel's witness. The Creator will finish his incomplete creation; he will make right what is wrong; God will make whole what is broken. Israel was called in order to know that this would happen, that it was "counted," stored up in God, for the good of the Gentile Abraham and his Gentile descendants, as for the circumcised Abraham and his Jewish descendants. Israel was chosen to make this known by its life and its words and to take part in its accomplishment.

Israel bears witness to Abraham's election by living its covenant with God. It is therefore essential to this witness that Israel testify that God has promised he will make things right for Abraham's Jewish descendants. The birth of Isaac was the first installment on that promise. The rescue of Isaac on Mount Moriah was the second. The Exodus was the third. But the gift and acceptance of God's Torah is the enduring form of Israel's witness and the abiding memorial of these earlier installments on God's promise and of all that are to follow. As with all these installments of the past, may not every Jew give thanks for the birth of the state of Israel as the most recent installment on that promise? The God of Israel is the living God and the promise of his righteousness is alive in history. He promised that he would make it right for Abraham.

But God also promised that he would make it right *in* Abraham, and therefore not just for the child of Sarah, but also for all Abraham's descendants. This is the thrust, the goal toward which Israel's election drives. Were Israel's witness of the election of Abraham to cease, creation would have lost its foundations for hope. In Israel's story of Creation, before we hear of Abraham's election, we end up with only the heirs of Noah, saved from the flood, but in effect no better off than before. The earth will endure, we heard, but how can creation be completed? Noah and his children only provide the base on which to build. There is no word of an actual building until we come to God's choice of Abraham. In him there is hope for creation, because history begins to move. "How odd of God to chose the Jews," but that choice is the hope for every Gentile, every non-Jew. That is Israel's testimony. It is about Israel because it is fundamentally about what God has done for Israel for the sake of his creation. It is the sum of Israel's testimony about God, about the righteousness of the God of Israel, Creator of heaven and earth.

By God's utterly free generosity, Israel is enabled to give this testimony to God's utterly free generosity. God's generosity to creation is that he gives it real independent existence, and that he ever renews it toward its completion. God's generosity to Israel is that he gives it to know this divine purpose of the completion of creation and invites Israel to cooperate with him in this task. God's generosity is therefore identical with God's righteousness, whereby Israel was selected to be a co-worker with God in pursuing the goal of God's generosity toward creation.

The exemplary case of Israel's witness is of course Abraham, especially in the story of his role in God's plan to make right what was wrong in the city of Sodom (Gen. 18:16–33). The story is introduced by God's remarkable announcement that he would not hide from Abraham what he intends to do (v. 17), for this follows from his having chosen him and his descendants "to keep the Way of the Lord by doing righteousness" (v. 19). He who trusted in the righteousness of God was also to walk by that righteousness, and in that walking, Abraham would know all that he needed to know in order to be a full co-worker in God's plan to accomplish that righteousness.

Abraham, sensing that the wicked Sodom had no place in God's plan for righteousness, then begins the work of cooperation that is his by his election. Raising the question whether the righteous should be destroyed with the wicked (v. 23), and by appealing to God's own righteousness (v. 25), Abraham wins the concession from God that the city will not be destroyed if but ten righteous men can be found in the place (v. 32). So Abraham set the pattern for Israel of accepting God's invitation to join in working out the terms of and conditions for the realization of the righteousness of God. Israel testifies with this story to its election as a co-worker for the righteousness of God in history, even as it bears witness to its own calling to live a corresponding righteousness in history.

Many centuries after Abraham, by a further demonstration of his righteousness, God was to gather and invite his Gentile church into a co-responding role of cooperation with him and therefore with Israel. Elected in Abraham's son Jesus, they were to learn through him of the generosity of the God of Israel in electing Abraham. Israel's testimony, in the form of its sacred Scriptures, would therefore be sacred Scriptures also for them. From Israel, therefore, they would be able to learn of their calling to do the works of Abraham (cf. Jn. 8:39), seeing as they were being adopted into Abraham's inheritance. From Israel, finally, they would be able to learn that both the righteousness of God and the corresponding righteousness of God's elect were connected fruits of the generosity of God. History suggests that this connection has been an especially difficult one for Gentiles to understand.

The church did learn, from its first beginning, to see its history in the light of Israel's history, but here too a failure to listen led to a fatal confusion. Israel's testimony has been consistently that its own history was where God's righteousness happens. The church misread the sacred Scriptures as if Israel had said that its history was where God's righteousness happened — solely in the past. It failed to see that so long as creation remains incomplete, God's righteousness has yet to work its way out in the world, and that therefore Israel's cooperative task is not yet finished. Had the church really acted as Abraham had, it would have entered into a discussion with Israel with all the respect that Abraham showed in accepting his role as a co-worker in the cause of righteousness. As a new fellow co-worker, the church would have done well to listen more carefully to its elder brothers. Then it might better have realized that its own history in the world, and the world as the context of that history, are what God means to make right, and that he means this to happen through the cooperation of his elect.

Such a self-understanding on the part of the church would be the fruit of its recognition of the Jewish people as Abraham's descendants and its awareness of the dependence of its own witness on that of Israel's. It would rest upon seeing both as part of the history of God's generous righteousness that began with the call of Abraham. The consequence, however, would be an understanding of the world as also caught up in the drama initiated in the election of Abraham. Nothing in all of creation can fall outside the generosity of God's righteousness made known to and stored up for it on Abraham's behalf.

And yet, the Gentile church finds itself called from its beginning to just such a self-understanding, by its engagement in the prayer for the coming of the kingdom. It learned that prayer from that son of Abraham by whom it was elected into the history of the righteousness of God begun in Abraham's calling. It prays, understanding or not, for the *coming* of the kingdom, the completion of God's good creation, for its *coming*, right into the here and now, in history! And it prays that this take place "on earth," not in the clouds or in some "other" world! Could it but recall that in the generosity of God it is an heir of Abraham, not of Augustine (!), then it should realize that, in praying, it must also *work* for the coming of the realization of the righteousness of God, and that this is in no way contrary to grace, to God's generosity. This work for the righteousness of God in history is only a response to the invitation of God's generosity.

CHAPTER FIVE

The People of Israel

At Sinai, Israel accepted the inheritance of God's election, which it had received in its forebears, to be a kingdom of priests, a holy nation. Its elected reality as a peculiar people is a witness to the church of God's way of particularity for the completion of creation, and its living existence is an invitation to all peoples to recognize God's hand in their own histories and to join hands with Israel in the particularity of witness provided by their own peoplehood. As the invitation is of God's generosity, so it comes with the promise of God's support.

1. THE CENTRALITY OF SINAI

i. Sinai past and present

According to Israel's traditions, somewhere in the peninsula of Sinai, from a mountain of the same name, God gave Moses Torah—instruction—for the people Israel, and Israel accepted God's Torah. That event has been central for the Jewish people throughout its history. It has shaped Israel's memory and its continuing life. Israel's identity has continually referred to this event: Israel is that people to whom God gave his Torah from Sinai and who accepted God's Torah at Sinai.

Israel remembered Sinai as a definite place at which a definite event occurred, there and then: it was a definitive meeting of God with Israel as a people. Israel remembers Moses as the greatest of all its prophets, but Sinai was not primarily an event between God and Moses. Constituent of Israel's testimony to the event of Sinai is that all Israel was involved in the event: "Moses came and told the people all the words of the LORD and all the ordinances; and all the people answered with one voice, and said, 'All the words which the LORD has spoken we will do' " (Ex. 24:3). And again, "Then he took the book of the covenant, and read it in the hearing of the people; and they said, 'All that the LORD has spoken we will do, and we will be obedient' " (24:7). The covenant of Sinai was between the whole people and God.

Sinai was an event not only for all the people at that time: "Nor is it with you only that I make this sworn covenant, but with him who is not here with us this day" (Deut. 29:14–15a). The Rabbis took this to include all of Israel in the future: "All souls were present then, although their bodies were not yet created" (*Tanh. B.* Nizzabim, 8:25b; M&L, 108). Every Jew to this day is therefore to consider him- or herself as having stood before Sinai and as having responded, "We will do." The covenant of Sinai is an eternally present relationship between God and the whole Jewish people, past, present, and future, and the emphasis is on the present. Generation after generation, in the words of the *B'rith Milah*, the rite of circumcision, all male children are "introduced into the covenant of Abraham our father." The covenant is ever new, ever renewed, ever continued, living on in the blood of this people, in the continuing life of the Jewish people. Sinai is central to Jewish identity because Sinai is central to Jewish reality. All Israel stands always before Sinai.

ii. The covenant and the covenants

The covenant of Sinai is central for Israel, although it is but one of many appearing in the scriptural story. It is preceded by the covenants with Abraham (Gen. 12:1ff; 12:7; 13:14f; 15ff; 17:4–27), Isaac (26:2–5), and Jacob (28:13–22; 35:10–14). All of these are covenants which seal and renew the election of the patriarchs of Israel and of Israel in its patriarchs. The covenant of Sinai is, as it were, built upon the covenants with the patriarchs.

There are also those other covenants at which we have looked that were not made with Israel, that with the earth after the flood, and that with Ishmael. One could add the word of Amos (9:7), setting the Ethiopians, the Philistines, and the Syrians on a par with Israel. It is characteristic of Israel's testimony, however, that it is given on the basis of Israel's own history with God. Israel has never had much to say about how it stands between God and the rest of his creation, other than that it is all his and will all be redeemed. Israel bears witness to its own life with God, and that has been determined by the Torah-covenant of Sinai. It knows of the rest of the world, therefore, as being different from Israel, and different precisely in the fact that Israel has accepted Torah, whereas the rest of the world has not.

There are also remembrances of other later covenants coming after Sinai. First there is the covenant of Shechem, in which the whole people of "all the tribes of Israel," called together by Joshua and swore fidelity to the God of Israel (Josh. 24:1–27). Although the patriarchs, Moses and Aaron, the Exodus and the conquest of the land are recalled, not a word of Sinai and the gift of Torah occur. Then there is the covenant of David, with God's promise to protect the house of David forever (2 Sam. 23:5; Ps. 89:3–4, 19–37), which also omits any reference to the covenant of Sinai. There is never any suggestion in Israel's testimony, however, that these were other than further expressions of Israel's Sinaitic relationship to its God.

For a provocative interpretation of the Shechem covenant as a reflection of the beginnings of the confederation of the tribes of Israel, see N. Gottwald, *The Tribes of Yahweh* (1979). K. Rylaarsdam ("The Two Covenants and the Dilemma of Christology," *J.E.S*, 1972) has argued that the Shechem and Davidic covenants are two types of covenantal relationship which stand in tension in the Scriptures and also in the Apostolic Writings. In the context of Israel's Scriptures, however, and as those Scriptures were preserved by rabbinic Judaism, the extra-Sinaitic covenants form no competition to Sinai. The same may also be said of the promise of a renewal of the covenant in Jeremiah 31:31–34, for the "new" covenant is none other than God's original covenant with Israel, made effective in Torah-shaped hearts and lives ("in your mouth and in your heart, so that you can do it." Deut. 30:14). The Jewish apostle to the Gentiles was true to his tradition in speaking of "the covenants" (Rom. 9:4), while knowing full well the centrality for Israel of the Torah from Sinai.

All Israel in every generation stands before Sinai. There it receives ever anew the covenant that incarnates its election by God. That election is Israel's inheritance from Abraham and Sarah, but it is new each day in the continuing covenantal existence of the Jewish people.

iii. Sinai and the Exodus

The Gentile church has heard clearly Israel's testimony to its deliverance from Egypt. It has not heard Israel's testimony that Israel became free not at the Red Sea, but at Sinai! "When Torah came into the world, freedom came into the world" (*Gen. R.*, Wayera, 53:7 M&L, 128). Sinai was no afterthought to the Exodus. On the contrary, God redeemed Israel, according to the Rabbis, on the condition that he command and Israel obey (M&L, 118). "If it were not for my Torah which you accepted, I should not recognize you, and I should not regard you more than any of the idolatrous nations of the world" (*Exod. R.*, Ki Tissa, 47:3; M&L, 116).

Other examples can be given of this frequently sounded note. " 'Why is Israel called God's people?' 'Because of the Torah.' Rabbi Jose ben Shimon says: 'Ere you stood at Sinai and accepted my Torah, you were called "Israel," just as other nations . . . are called by simple names, without addition. But when you accepted the Torah at Sinai, you were called "My People," as it says, "Hearken, O my people, and I will speak" (Ps. 50:7)' (*Tanh. B.*, Wa'era, 9a; M&L, 81). "It says in Lev. 11:45, 'For I am the Lord your God who brought you up out of the land of Egypt to be your God: ye shall therefore be holy, for I am holy.' That means, I brought you out of Egypt on the condition that you should receive the yoke of the commandments" (*Sifra* 57b; M&L, 117).

Israel assigns priority to Sinai because it knows of no identity and no freedom but that which it has by being chosen by God to be God's people. But to be God's people means to be bound to God's Torah. Life in the Torah is the concrete form of its election. Election, for Israel, is an incarnate reality. It happens in the flesh, in Israel's flesh, and so it takes the form of walking, of *halakhah*, according to God's Torah.

It seems incredible that a church which has made so much of the obedience of Jesus to the will of God should have failed to see the importance of Israel's acceptance of God's Torah to the meaning of its election. God did not simply "choose the Jews." He chose them to be his people, to be holy as he is holy, to walk in his ways. He chose them for Torah-shaped existence. Therefore Israel cannot celebrate the deliverance from Egypt without at once giving thanks for Sinai, for the gracious gift of Torah and the relationship with God which Torah makes specific and concrete.

The logic of a Gentile theology that moves directly from the Exodus to the general statement that God is a God of the liberation of the oppressed, is too simplistic for Israel. To be freed from slavery is not in itself freedom. Freedom from slavery under Pharaoh took the form of becoming slaves of God, and this logic of Israel's theology was clearly understood by the Pharisee whom God sent to the Gentiles (Gal. 5:13–14; Rom. 6:16–23). Therefore, when Israel wishes to testify to deliverance and freedom, it points first of all to the Torah. There is delineated the shape of the freedom for which God set Israel free. Torah is the content of liberation.

A Christian theology of the people Israel, as it has been defined, is obliged to point out to the church that it has failed to listen to the witness of Israel on this matter of the substance of election. The content or substance of Israel's election is life lived according to God's Torah. That is freedom. This may not be discounted under a misconceived charge of "works-righteousness." Israel, in its written as also in its oral Torah (the Talmud and the rabbinic tradition) has been unwavering in its testimony that its liberation into the Torah is all a gift of God. In the most Augustinian or Lutheran sense, it is all of grace. But "grace," God's generosity, is not *tohu vabohu*, not waste and void. It has form and content. It is concrete. It is incarnate. In total generosity, God provides in it a way for Israel to walk, the way of Torah. Israel has been elected into God's Way.

iv. Sinai and Torah: the commandments (mitzvot)

Israel's testimony to the church and to the world is that the God who elected Israel commands obedience. It is therefore of the essence of Israel's elected reality, and therefore of its witness and of its whole life, that it *accepted* its inheritance of God's election. Israel said, "We will do!" By the grace of God's election, the covenant of Sinai was a genuine covenant: it initiated a relationship that entailed action from both sides. Christians, and especially Protestant Christians, should recognize that these terms of the covenant were initiated by God.

Sinai, according to Israel's testimony, was and remains God's revelation. Torah, by Israel's unqualified testimony, is "the Torah from heaven." Israel accepted the Torah, not as the price, but as the shape of its election. Torah is therefore to be lived by because it is from the God who loves and chooses Israel.

Although medieval Jewish philosophers, from Saadia Gaon in the tenth century on through the giants of the twelfth and following centuries, especially Maimonides, believed that there was a reason for every single commandment, including divine statutes which appeared wholly arbitrary, they did not challenge the rabbinic conviction that the precepts of the Torah were given by God and were therefore in any case to be obeyed. If these philosophers are to be classed as rationalists, they were surely religious rationalists. What God had commanded could not be contrary to reason, just as reason, when at its proper work, could never arrive at conclusions foreign to God's revelation. Nevertheless, the rationalist tendency, and especially as it appeared in nineteenth-century Reform Judaism, by maintaining that there is a reason for obeying the statutes other than the fact that they have been commanded by God, opens the possibility that reasons may be found for not obeying this or that commandment. This may account for the fact that the Rabbis, in their practical concern for the faithfulness of the life of the people, sided clearly with the thesis that the commandments are good because God commands them, rather than with the alternative position that God commands them only because they are good.

The Torah is God's revelation from Sinai. Sinai, for Judaism, means revelation. But revelation, according to Israel's witness, creates participation. God's revelation creates a community of response, a *we* that says "we will do." God's revelation from Sinai set Israel on God's way into history, forged as a responding community, a participant in God's purpose for his creation.

Sinai as revelation is therefore God's effective election. Election made effective is incarnate election, embodied in Israel's fidelity to Torah. The *mitzvot*, the commandments, define the actual shape of Israel as a people, from arising in the morning to falling asleep at night, in war and in peace, at work or at rest, in eating and drinking, in every part or aspect of its life. The *mitzvot* of the Torah shaped and shapes this people. They define what election by God's generosity looks like in this world.

By what logic does God's election take the particular shape of the Jewish people's fidelity to Torah? The only possible answer is: by the logic of God. Israel's witness to God is to the One who shapes this people to his Torah. God, Torah, and Israel, those three central themes of Israel's life and witness, are bound intimately together. Because God is holy, he has given his holy Torah to the Jewish people in order to craft them into being a holy people. The Torah is God's way of leading Israel into the "imitation of God."

2. HOLY PEOPLEHOOD

i. *Election and response*

Israel has been chosen by God to be a holy nation, a kingdom of priests (Exod. 19:6). "Ye shall be holy unto me, for I the LORD am holy. Even as I am holy, so be you holy. As I am separate, so be you separate. And I have severed you from the other peoples that you should be mine. If you sever yourselves from the other peoples, then you belong to me" (*Sifra* 93d; M&L, 105). Israel witnesses to this total claim of God upon the total life of the whole Jewish people. The whole people is claimed for holiness, that is, for the commandments of the written Torah and for those of the oral Torah, the first to fill Israel with righteousness, and the second to make Israel distinct from other peoples. This claim of course touches the life of each individual Jew. It is also God's claim upon each Jewish family. But it claims each Jew and each family as a part of the people, the people who said, "We will do."

From the beginning and throughout its history, the failure of Israel to live up to its call to holiness has been all too evident. Israel recalls the beginning of its life under this calling by telling of its worship of the golden calf at the foot of the mountain. It tells of grumbling and complaining about Moses' leadership. It preserved the bitter denunciations of its prophets. The emphasis of the Rabbis on the need for repentance and God's mercy reflects their acute awareness of Israel's failure to live in the holiness to which it is called.

In the face of Jewish lapses from the holiness of the Torah, the idea of a faithful remnant has been resorted to, but Franz Rosenzweig's comments on this should help correct a recurring Gentile misunderstanding of this concept. The remnant is not made up of those who alone carry forward the election of Israel. It is rather that *part* of Israel that keeps *Israel's* election and response, its covenant, alive. The Jewish people, Rosenzweig wrote, is unique among the nations in that it "maintains itself by subtraction, by contraction, by forming ever new remnants" (*Stern*, 450; E.T. 404).

The Rabbis, and indeed the whole Jewish tradition, resisted the temptation to give up on any of Israel who failed to meet the call to holiness. God's mercy and his offer of *teshuvah*, repentence, reversion, turning back to God. The call to the individual to come home to the way of holiness was sounded so often because the whole people, and the people as a whole, were destined for holiness. Israel is to be a holy nation.

ii. Peoplehood and Torah-life

Torah is for the sake of Israel, the Rabbis said, not the reverse. Jews are far from being of a single mind about the Torah and how it should be lived. From various strands of Orthodox Judaism, through Conservative and Reform to secular Jewry, attitudes toward Torah observance cover a wide spectrum. It may be said in general, however, that Jews take the stands they do on Torah observance for the sake of the Jewish people. Regarded as a people — and no other view of the Jews is consistent with their own self-understanding — the Jews are to the Torah, both written and "oral," as a nation is to its constitution. Whether strict-constructionist or the freest of liberal, the Jew sees the constitution as existing for the sake of the nation, not the reverse.

The relationship between Jewish peoplehood and Jewish relationships to the Torah has been made much more complex and more difficult for Gentile understanding by the developments in the nineteenth century coming out of the Emancipation of the Jews, and also by the birth of the state of Israel. The former led in many quarters toward a relaxation of Torah observance, as Jews, for the first time since the rise of Christendom, gained full status as citizens under the constitutions of the various countries in which they lived. The utterly unJewish distinction between civil and societal life on the one hand, and religion on the other, was thereby imposed on them.

The birth of the state of Israel has added to the complexity: Israel is a self-proclaimed Jewish state, but it is a matter of controversy whether its constitution is the Torah. Indeed the insistence by some Jews that Israel can have no constitution except the Torah is the reason why the state of Israel to this day does not have a written constitution. This being a matter in which Jews themselves are of sharply divided opinions, it is not one for Gentiles to attempt to decide. A Christian theology of the

Jewish people can at most ponder the dangers and the possibilities to which Jews themselves have drawn attention.

The danger for Israel today is the peculiar form which secularization can take among Jews: the danger of centering their loyalty on their peoplehood without any attachment to the Torah. In assessing this danger, there is no point from which to consider it that is neutral. One either stands upon Israel's own theological tradition and takes this people to be the people of God by God's election and Israel's acceptance of the Torah, or one does not. In doing a Christian *theology* of the people Israel, one can only understand the peoplehood of the Jews as a divine calling. God called them to be his own possession as a people. Ethnicity, assuming it could be defined as a general category, could not be decisive, and a Jewish "ethnicity," whatever that might be, would be of no more interest than any other. Presumed racial characteristics are hardly the stuff on which a theology of the God of Abraham and Sinai can build solidly. A Gentile church that is absolutely dependent, ontologically and teleologically, on the continuing existence of God's Israel, can hardly demand but must certainly trust that the Jewish people will continue to produce out of themselves that remnant by which it has maintained itself in its covenant with God.

From this theological perspective, the injunction at the opening of the *Mishnah* takes on a special meaning for the church. The command to "build a fence around the Torah," appears as a vital defense of the Jews as a people. The fence took the form of the oral Torah, the development of rabbinic *halakhah*, that careful elaboration of the details of Jewish life which insured that Israel's life would be more than faithful to the written Torah. The fence proved a remarkably successful defense to Jewish peoplehood from the first to the nineteenth century of the Common Era. In some renewed sense which only Jews will be able to determine, it may prove as trustworthy in the future.

iii. Not like the other nations

Israel has been called to be a holy people. This means above all that it shall be different, distinguishable, not like other peoples. It was called to be a kingdom without a king, other than the King of the Universe; it has become a priesthood without priests. Israel is different; Israel is holy.

We come here to a matter that highlights the ambiguity of Israel's life, an ambiguity that needs not only to be noticed but to be underscored if the Gentile church is to hear God's word to it through his chosen witnesses. Jewish tradition is markedly nonsacerdotal, precisely as it mourns the destruction of the Temple! Judaism, and no less the modern state of Israel, is pointedly democratic, even as it confesses God as King of the Universe and looks to the coming of King Messiah! Israel's memory of the institution of the monarchy underscores the ambiguity of kingship: how can Israel have a king, indeed how can God command the prophet to anoint Saul as king, when God is Israel's only King (1 Sam. 8:4–22)?

As for the priesthood, when Israel had a temple, it had priests, but when the Second Temple was destroyed, the function of the Temple and its sacrifices was replaced, so the Rabbis taught, by prayer, deeds of loving kindness and repentance.

God gave Israel his Torah, we have heard from the Rabbis, the written Torah with its 613 commandments to pack the Jewish people full of righteousness, and the innumerable ruling of the oral Torah, the halakhic tradition, to make them different. *Halakhah* makes the Jewish people different by conforming their life to the oral Torah given by God. It is, then, the covenant that makes Israel different. The Jewish people are unique because they have been uniquely chosen by and covenanted to the unique God.

The uniqueness of the Jewish people is no more easily discernible than its election or its unique God. This must be remembered above all in Gentile attempts to decipher the reality of the Jewish state today. Ancient Israel was surely an ambiguous entity for its neighbors. King David was one thing for Israel, quite another for the Jebusites. When the Jewish people in Palestine declared the birth and independence of their state in 1948 and gave it the name "Israel," they did not make the name thereby more ambiguous; they only continued the ambiguity inherent in the reality of God's election in history.

According to Israel's Scriptures (1 Sam. 8:4f, 20), the reason the people gave for demanding a king was that they wanted to be "like all the nations." Israel got its king, but it did not thereby become "like all the nations." Jews demanded a nation-state, and some of them did so because they wanted to be like all the nation-states. There are Jews who say that the state of Israel is unique only in the sense in which every state is unique (e.g., A.B. Yehoshua, *Between Right and Right*, 1981, esp. 63f), that there is nothing different about the Jewish people. From a secular perspective, that is correct, but it contradicts the massive weight of the Jewish tradition. Even the secular Zionists intended for the Jewish state to be different, at the least a secular light to the secular nations. And, still on a secular level, the peculiarity of Israel is striking, for what other state has anything resembling Israel's special relationship with the Jewish Diaspora?

What makes the Jewish people—and therefore inevitably also their state—different, however, is their election by God to be a holy people. That is a theological judgment, not an empirical one. It will have empirical ramifications, for Israel is a historical people, but the empirical evidence will always be ambiguous. It is called to be holy as God is holy. God's holiness consists in his being the Creator and therefore not like anything else. The holy God is beyond all comparison, indeed beyond all our conceptions of him. God is, as the kabbalists taught, the *En Sof*, the utterly transcendant. But God is also himself in all the ways in which he relates himself to his creatures and especially to Israel. Bound to this God by God's own choice, this people may long to be like all the nations, but that cannot be. However ambiguous the historical and political and social evidence may be, this people is set in the world with the call to holy peoplehood stamped upon it.

The Gentile church, expressing but misunderstanding its dependence on Israel, has called itself "the people of God" and has understood itself to be called to holy peoplehood. A Christian theology of the people Israel must point out that if this expression is to be used, it should be accompanied by some qualifier that acknowledges that the word "people" is being used in a quite different sense from that which applies to Israel. Israel was called as a people; the church has been called together out of many peoples. Israel is called to be a holy nation; the church has been called from out of the nations to be a community within the nations. Such titles as "The Church *of* England" or "The Church *of* Sweden" are remnants of the distortions of "Christendom," now well behind us. Properly speaking, there can only be a church *in* England, *in* Sweden, or in any other nation. There is something profoundly wrong about speaking of a "Christian state," theologically as well as empirically. There is something profoundly right, however, in speaking of a Jewish state; the expression is ambiguous empirically but not theologically. That is because its name is Israel, a name given by God.

iv. A kingdom of priests

A kingdom of priests, of which God is the king, has no need of priests to mediate between it and God. The Rabbis attacked none of the rules concerning the priests, for they were there in the written Torah, but they made it clear that priests did not stand as a necessary link between the people and their God (see M&L, 153f). Indeed, with the Temple destroyed, there was no further role for priests. Their work was now taken up by all Israel: " 'Grieve not, we have an atonement equal to the Temple, the doing of loving deed,' as it is said, 'I desire love, and not sacrifice.' " (*Ab.R.N.*, vers. 1, 4:11a; M&L, 431).

Israel itself is a priestly people because of the intimacy of its relationship to God. This has not meant that Israel has always known God's presence. There have been times in Israel's history when its most sensitive souls were convinced that God had hidden his face from his people, was deaf to their prayers and did nothing to help them in their distress. Yet even in such times, Jews have felt they had the right to take their complaints directly to God. After all, God had given them his Torah. He was their God and they were his people. They have often been sustained by the conviction, therefore, that God's presence, the *Shekhinah*, had gone with them into exile and shared their sufferings. "Beloved are Israel, for, even when they are defiled, the Shekhinah is among them, as it says, 'wherein I dwell.' Whithersoever they go into exile, the Shekhinah accompanies them" (*Sifre Num.*, Masse's, 161,f.63; M&L, 104). Yet more daringly, "Whenever Israel is enslaved, the Shekhinah is enslaved with them, as it says, 'In all their afflictions He was afflicted (Isa 63:9)' " (Ibid., 84,f.22b; M&L, 64).

So long as the Jewish people exist in this world, then, the world should know that God has not abandoned his creation. An attempt to destroy God's holy people, therefore, is an attempt to have a world without God. The evil of the Nazi "Final Solution of the Jewish Question" is thrown into sharpest focus by recalling the election of the Jewish people as a kingdom of priests. The rabbinic passage last cited is preceded by the following words: "He who hates Israel is as if he hated God. . . . And he who helps Israel is as if he helped God."

3. ISRAEL'S EXISTENCE

i. *Exile and return*

The fundamental reality which a Christian theology of the people Israel has to make clear, and of which it is required to develop the implications, is that God has chosen this people to be his light for the nations, for all the peoples of God's creation. The *people* are this light, not just their Scriptures; their life, not just some of their words. We have been drawing and shall continue to draw heavily on Israel's Scriptures in attempting to understand the witness that God has chosen Israel to be, but in doing so, we have intended to hear those Scriptures as the Torah of living Israel. Since living Israel is God's light for the nations, the church should be concerned to hear the words of the Scriptures as heard and interpreted by the Jewish people, the people who preserved, edited, canonized, and continue to live by those words. It is therefore necessary to attend to Israel's more recent voices, those of its Rabbis and others, in order to hear them as the Jewish Scriptures.

Israel's Scriptures can properly be called the Jewish Scriptures, because we owe their preservation, final redaction, and even a good deal of their composition from the time, beginning with the Babylonian Exile, when the people came to be designated "the Jews."

The term "Jew" (*Yehudi* in Hebrew, *Ioudaios* in Greek) became common among Jews living outside the land of Israel, as well as among all Gentiles. Jews living in the land of Israel continued to refer to themselves as Israel (*Yisrael*, or "Israelites"). According to Mark 15, the Jerusalem Jews called Jesus (mockingly) "King of Israel," whereas the Romans called him "King of the Jews." See ad loc., *E.J.*, X, 22.

The books that Ezra brought back to Jerusalem, or in part brought for the first time, form the backbone of Israel's Scriptures, and we owe the whole of them to the Sages and the Pharisees who made them into the holy writings and the effective Scriptures of the Jewish people. They are the ones who made it possible for there to be "the Scriptures," the Torah and the Prophets, for Jesus of Nazareth and his disciples, and therefore for the church.

If the church is more interested in ancient Israel than in the living Israel, beginning with the Israel of the Second Temple period, it is closing its eyes to the way in which God has worked with his people to produce the Scriptures which make up the bulk of the church's own canon. But for the Sages and the Pharisees who carried through the reform initiated by Ezra, Israel's memory of Abraham, of the Exodus and Sinai, of Isaiah and Jeremiah, would probably have perished. Early Judaism of the Second Temple period is therefore the gateway through which both later Judaism and the church must enter in order to hear what God has to say through his elected witness in the Torah, the Prophets, and the Writings of Israel.

The church's traditional "hourglass" picture of God's revelatory work, beginning with his mighty works in ancient Israel, narrowing down, following the Exile, to less and less, until it came to a single strand in the person of Jesus, and then widening out once more in the church, is not simply false. It totally distorts what actually happened. The post-Exilic period was rather a time of growth and deepening that proved to be a mighty springboard for the launching of two remarkable developments in the four centuries following the destruction of the Second Temple, that of rabbinic Judaism and that of patristic Christianity. Such powerful documents as the composite book of Isaiah, many of the Psalms, and the book of Ben Sirach, reflect the spiritual vitality of this period.

ii. *Existence in the Diaspora*

Am Yisrael khai! The people Israel lives! Its temple destroyed, its capital city Jerusalem laid waste, the land occupied by foreign troops, the Jewish people not only survived; it entered a period of remarkable growth, of which the publication of the *Mishnah* and then the full *Talmud* of Babylon and of Jerusalem were the products. Scattered through all the major centers of the decaying Roman Empire, rabbinic Judaism took shape and developed a form of life for Israel's covenant with God which was to keep the Jewish people alive through incredible hardships of intermittent and sometimes continuous persecution at the hands of Christian Europe, up until today.

It is crucial for the church's interpretation of its Apostolic Writings that it realize that they come from a time in which Israel was entering upon one of its most spiritually creative periods. The disastrous theology of displacement could never have arisen had the church been sensitive to the new departure in the covenantal relationship between God and Israel that began right after the destruction of the Second Temple. When the flowering of the Gentile church is seen as an accompaniment to the flowering of rabbinic Judaism, the tensions between the young church and the synagogue in the first century of the Common Era appear as a shared misunderstanding in that ever difficult task of discerning the hand of God in the ambiguous history of the covenant.

Galut, exile, being in Diaspora, has played a vital role in Israel's long history. First in Egypt, then the Babylonian exile, then the long, long Diaspora. No wonder the rabbis could say, "Poverty suits the Jew as a red bridle on a white horse" (*Lev.R.*, Shemini, 13:4; M&L, 95; cf. 446). It must be noted that Israel has never regarded exile as normal, natural, or desirable. Its periods of exile, however, have in fact been profoundly creative times, when God and this people have done remarkable things together.

The long Diaspora, the partial ending of which was marked by the founding of the state of Israel, was not entirely black. The Jewish people knew periods of peace and even prosperity. But beginning with the First Crusade, through the decisions of the Fourth Lateran Council, successive expulsions from one country after another (starting with England in 1290), persecutions following the Black Death (blamed on the Jews), and innumerable cases of blood libel, on to pogroms of smaller or larger scale, the Jewish people has known Diaspora as a time of great hardship and pain.

No wonder then that Emancipation, the removal of special restrictions and the granting of citizenship and normal civil rights, was greeted by the Jews of Europe as a relief from past distress. Emancipation, beginning gradually in the eighteenth century in England and then more rapidly with the French Revolution and the spread of egalitarianism, and finally reaching Russia after the Bolshevik Revolution, proved to be a mixed blessing. It was, after all, emancipation on the terms of the dominant culture, not on Jewish terms. It opened European life to the Jews, but it also opened Jews to European life, with an increase of assimilation as the price. Finally, it did not bring an end to anti-Judaism. Under the newly coined pseudoscientific term "antisemitism," the old anti-Judaic mind-set of Christendom was stirred to new life, finally breaking out in deadly fury in Nazi Germany.

The Holocaust, on the one hand, and the birth of the state of Israel on the other, mark a watershed in the history of the Jewish people. Those two so different events, however, stand themselves within a larger, more complex development, beginning with the Emancipation and ending — perhaps (?) — with the Six-Day War of 1967. That whole development constitutes a major transition in the long history of Israel's life and so of its covenant with God. Beginning with Emancipation, the peculiar people of God's election came, for what has seemed at times to be the better, but has been more often for the worse, into closer contact with Gentiles. The isolation of the ghetto died and does not seem likely to return. The way of Emancipation, however, proved finally to be disastrous in Europe, although it has been successful to a large extent in the English-speaking countries. Now, and especially since 1967, the Jewish state is on the map of God's creation. How the people Israel is to live its covenant in this new relationship to the rest of the world remains to be seen, but clearly we are witnesses today to the opening of a new era in the continuing life of God's people.

iii. *The witness of particularity*

To have survived so many centuries of such appalling persecution, without benefit of land, power, or even a central administrative structure, is remarkable. Is there any other people like this people? To have lived through the radical transition of the past two hundred years is no less remarkable. One would think that Jews would just give up being Jews — and indeed, many of them have. Yet the people Israel lives! Its very existence is its witness. Having been chosen by God, this people has continued to affirm that choice. It has stubbornly maintained its existence.

As the primary witness to the God of Israel, who is the Father of Jesus Christ, the Jewish people stand before the world, and not least before the Gentile church of Israel's God. The form of their witness is their life in their covenant with God. That existence needs to be deciphered by the church. It has something to say.

It says first of all that God is not yet finished with what he began in calling Abraham. What God started there continued at Sinai and has been developing ever since. The short name for it is "the covenant." The visible reality of it is the people of Israel, the Jewish people.

The continuing life of the Jewish people says, second, that God is still working at the completion of his creation in his same old way, the way of particularity. The universality of Christianity, which the church once thought to have displaced the particularity of Israel, is of course under fire for many reasons, not least the encounter of world religions. It is primarily and directly under fire, however, from the continued reality of the people Israel, which presses the church to rethink its commitment to universality. Can it continue to wish the whole world to become the church, now that it has affirmed the eternal covenant between God and the Jewish people? Can it wish in that way for a world without Jews? In the meantime, the Jews refuse to go away, either in their state or in the Diaspora.

The life of the people of Israel asks the church to consider, among other things, a radically new periodization of its history, which we may begin by looking at the one proposed by Karl Rahner. (I am indebted to David Burrell for bringing Rahner's proposal to my attention. See his essay "Jerusalem and the Future of Theological Inquiry," *Tantur Yearbook*, 1981.) Rahner proposed that the church has gone through two fundamental transitions: the first was the movement from a sect of Judaism, based in Jerusalem, to a church open to the Gentile West, a transition taking place in the first century. The second transition was from the Gentile church of the West, based in Rome, to a world church, presumably (?) without a center, presaged in the worldwide episcopal constituency of the Second Vatican Council. The fact that the first era lasted only fifteen to forty years, depending on how one fixes the point of transition (Rahner writes as if he thought it might have lasted a century), whereas the second lasted nineteen centuries, was for Rahner immaterial. The periodization is based on more fundamental changes than the number of years.

Rahner arrived at his novel periodization by using a new criterion: the *sphere* of the church: "First, the short period of Jewish Christianity. Second, the period of the church in a distinct cultural region, namely that of Hellenism and of European culture and civilization. Third, the period in which the sphere of the Church's life is in fact the entire world" (*Theological Studies* 40 [1979], 721). Yet the question can be asked whether any periodization of the church can make theological sense if it ignores the concurrent history of the people of God. I would concur in locating the major transitions at about the same time as Rahner, but I would find them by looking to the turning points of the church's relationship to the Jewish people. The sphere of the church may now indeed be the whole world, in which it is scattered as a minority. But what if it carries through with the about-face it has proclaimed concerning its understanding of God's covenant with the Jewish people? What if it were to open itself to the witness of particularity confronting it in the continuing life of this people? The church has yet to consider what its response should be to Israel's continuing witness of particularity. A Christian theology of Israel is needed at this point to help the church reflect on Israel's witness of peoplehood.

4. PEOPLEHOOD AS INVITATION AND PROMISE

i. Invitation to the church

If we take the church's response to God's chosen witness, Israel, as the criterion for defining the theologically fundamental points of transition in its life, we arrive at precisely the same periodization as Rahner. The earliest period saw the young church fully acknowledging its unity with and dependence on Israel's witness, its Lord as the affirmation of God's promises to the patriarchs, even its Gentile members as grafted into the ancient promises, and having no other Scriptures than Israel's. Then, evidently well before the end of the first century, the church began to turn its back on the Jewish people and to regard itself as the sole bearer of the continuing history of God's ancient covenant. Many other interesting and important changes took place in the nineteen centuries of the second period (as Rahner too admits), but a consistently negative attitude toward the Jews prevailed. Then in the second half of the twentieth century, an about-face began to take place and the Jewish people were recognized as the Israel of God once more.

One important result of the second transition has been the beginning of a reconsideration of the first. At the time in which it was taking place, the first transition was understood as God's transfer of his election and love from the Jewish people to the church, expressed in what has come to be called the theology of displacement. Since the second transition is still working its way out, it is too early to detect a consensus, but perhaps we can say that the first transition may now be seen as a new development in God's covenantal relationship to his creation, which is to say, a new development of the covenant.

The renewed covenant was new in two respects. As at Sinai, it created community, but it did so now in two ways. First, it opened the door to Gentile participation as Gentiles, as non-Jews. God spoke this word of covenant to the Gentiles in the Jew Jesus Christ, to whom by his Spirit he drew them and in whom he accepted them. Thus did God's righteousness begin to become effective among the Gentiles. But second, the renewed covenant with Israel was set on a far more cooperative basis than in the past. God delivered into the hands of the Jewish people the authority and the responsibility to interpret and even to define the details of the relationship. God spoke this word of Torah in the Rabbis of Israel, who became in God's name the judges, teachers, and shepherds of the Jewish people. Thus did God's righteousness continue to be effective in Israel.

It is hard to say which of these developments was the more radical. The one represented a departure from the original form of the covenant in that it reached out to the Gentiles. On the other hand, the renewed covenant, as it was worked out in the Gentile church, represented little change: the relationship with God was, in theory, fully as passive, receptive, and responsive, as it was of old. All was grace, and the church could only respond with thanksgiving. So it was in theory (i.e., in the church's theology), although in practice the church proved to be a most active enterprise.

The renewal of the covenant that was worked out in rabbinic Jewry was perhaps more radically new, for here the covenant became a cooperative relationship not only in practice but also in theory. God and the Jewish people were in this together, suffering together, rejoicing together, in Exile together. The prayers, repentance, and deeds of loving kindness of the Jews replaced the sacred rites of the holy Temple and carried God's word and witness on in history. In practice, the Jewish people never came up to the demands of their activist theory, but according to that theory, if Israel were truly to do its part, it would accomplish the completion of creation: "If the Israelites would but repent for one day, they would be redeemed, and the son of David would come straight away" (*Cant. R.* 2,2, on v. 2; 30a; M&L, 318).

The first transition, which had been seen by the church for so long as its displacement of Israel in the covenant, may now be seen as a new development in God's covenantal relationship with the world. This new view of the first transition has been made possible by the second transition, in which the church is beginning to turn toward the Jewish people in a spirit of cooperation. This new turn is widely interpreted as an act of Christian repentance, of correcting old mistakes. If we consider the present transition in the light of a revised understanding of the first one, however, we may come to see that we are living once more through another development in the covenant. Jewish wrestling with the meaning of Torah and the character of fidelity to Torah in the modern world, and above all the Jewish understanding of how the state of Israel came into being and survived against all odds, may be God's witness to the church today that God wants his covenant partners, indeed all his creatures, to assume far more responsibility than in the past for moving creation toward its completion. Such a witness invites the church to a new self-understanding and a new view of its relationship to God.

If that be the case, the invitation is not impossible to read. It says to the church that it is all right for it to be itself in all its limitation. The church may joyfully and peacefully abandon its earlier dreams of being a world-church, much less a church comprising the whole world, and accept its particularity as a minority in God's world. The invitation to the church is, since it exists for the sake of the rest of the world, to enter into a dialogical relationship with all of creation, beginning with Israel, and to cooperate with all that seems to work for the completion of creation. Creation needs completion, not conversion, and for this new era of the covenant, that calls for cooperation.

ii. Invitation to the nations

Israel has been called to be a light for the nations, not just for those among the nations gathered into the church. In the present era, one condition for the exercise of this task has surely been fulfilled: perhaps never in its whole long history has Israel been so unavoidably set before the world. This is because of the state of Israel. The Jewish people are brought to the attention of the nations of this earth almost daily in the newspapers, by radio and television, and not least in the United Nations.

Israel's witness, however, is largely blocked by such serious misunderstandings of its witness as that manifested in the resolution of the United Nations' General Assembly condemning Zionism as racism. That absurdity is the result of a failure to listen. Zionism is not racism. Zionism from its beginnings to this day has been and is the conviction that the Jewish people ought to and must reestablish themselves in the land of promise, the land of their ancestors. Zionism is the name of a movement whose goal was and is to bring the Jewish people back to its own land under its own control. Zionism, then, is a distinctively Jewish version of peoplehood-plus-place. There could only be a racist component to Zionism if Jewishness were a matter of "race," whatever that is supposed to be. But Jewishness is a matter of peoplehood, not "race." It is a matter of history and culture and language, of a shared destiny, all founded on a common calling by God. It has nothing to do with the pseudoscientific, late-nineteenth-century Germanic myth of "race." Zionism is the modern expression of Israel's age-old longing to unify its response to its calling by the unique God: to be itself in the place to which God called it to serve him. (For secular Zionists, this is translated as a response to Jewish history.)

Israel stands before the nations today, even in the foolish resolutions of the General Assembly, as a witness that God has not given up on peoplehood, even when the nations unite against him to call his chosen people a "race." Israel's witness is an invitation to each of those nations not to regard its own peoplehood as a liability, nor to degrade it by thinking of it as a race. Peoplehood means shared history, common culture, a sense of one's own significance. Be one Irish, or Armenian, Afro-American, or Argentinian, be one even an American WASP, before us stands Israel to demonstrate that God has not abandoned particularity. Its invitation to all these and other nations is that God wills to make use of particularity for the good of his creation.

Creation contains, according to the Jewish tradition, the seventy nations other then Israel, and it contains each of the seventy. Israel's existence stands as God's invitation to all seventy, and to each of the seventy, to take their own peoplehood seriously as one of the many agents in cooperation with which God wills to complete his creation. Israel, alive to this day, stands in its peoplehood as an invitation to the nation of Islam, the Hindu nation, the native American nations, and to all the rest, to see in their own peoplehood the hand of the Creator of heaven and earth, who through the cooperation of his creatures means to preserve and move toward completion his beloved creation.

iii. Israel as God's invitation to the "Third World"

The encouraging invitation of God presented in the form of

the living Jewish people appears at this time to be addressed particularly to the nations of the so-called "Third World," the developing nations of Africa, Latin America, and Asia. Again, the invitation is being ignored as a result of total ignorance or complete misunderstanding of Israel's history. Ignored or forgotten are the facts that the Jews have been the paradigmatic oppressed people of western "civilization," and that there has been a Jewish tradition and an utterly antagonistic Christian tradition, but never a "Judeo-Christian tradition." Failing to recall that the Jewish people built the foundation of their independent state more in defiance of rather than with the aid of the western colonial powers, the developing nations of the Third World have been deaf to God's invitation offered in the body of the Jewish people.

Nevertheless the invitation stands for any who have ears to hear or eyes to see. The invitation is clearly that other peoples take heart and take matters into their own hands, as the Jewish people have done. The experiment is as ambiguous as it could be, yet here is a demonstration of nation-building in God's world that warrants careful attention. In its mistakes no less than in its accomplishments, it is a lesson that any nation will ignore to its disadvantage.

Above all, the ideal of Zionism which the Jewish people have held out before themselves, may be seen as an invitation to the nations of the world to set for themselves a goal of justice. That the Zionist state has not met and is not meeting the Zionist goal of justice is nowhere more sharply expressed than in the Israeli press. The controversies in Israel over some of the policies of the Israeli government testify to the centrality in the Zionist movement of the concept of justice, and the belief that national survival depends upon the establishment of justice. The agony expressed in so many Israeli voices protesting the decisions and actions of their government should open the ears of the "seventy nations" to listen to the invitation offered them by the existence in this world of the people of Israel.

iv. The promise of God's support: God's providence

A Christian theology of Israel must draw attention to the fact that, according to Israel's witness, God's invitation to the nations is open to all, for all are his. Every individual member of every nation is made in God's image. As their creation in his own image is by God's generosity — God's grace — so also is the invitation to acknowledge God in the particularity of their own peoplehood. The Jewish people has never asked of the nations that they deny or abandon their particularity for that of Israel. It has neither expected nor worked for the conversion of the nations to Judaism, although the door has always been open to anyone who wanted to join the Jewish people. What it has expected, or at least hoped for (Ps. 22:28; 67:3-6; 72:8-11; 117:1; Mic. 4:2; Zech. 8:22), is that God would be known and praised by all the nations, for it has been convinced that God already rules over and guides the nations in justice and mercy (Ps. 66:7; 67:5; 96:10).

Israel's testimony is that God will provide what is needed from his side for the continuation of that which he has begun for the completion of his creation.

The doctrine of God's *providence* takes its name from Abraham's trust that God would *provide* the needed lamb for the burnt offering, without the sacrifice of the child of promise (Gen. 22:8). Understood in this context, the doctrine does not claim to tell us more than we can know. It says nothing about God guiding all things, but precisely that he will see to the continuation of what he had begun in Abraham. For an extended treatment of the issue, see K. Barth, *K.D.*, § 48, III/3.

Abraham trusted that God would stand by his promise, and Israel witnesses, both in its Scriptures and by its continued existence, that Abraham was right. God is faithful to his covenant with Israel: the covenant will endure and therefore the Jewish people have endured and will endure. But God has also shown his fidelity to those Gentiles who have heard and trusted God's promise to Israel, the Christian church. This is the church's grounds for trusting that God will provide what is needed to sustain the nations of the world to hear and respond to Israel's witness of peoplehood.

5. ZIONISM AND BLACK CONSCIOUSNESS: AN UNDEVELOPED EXAMPLE

i. *Anti-Judaism and racism*

There are many examples of the failure to hear God's invitation expressed in the enduring peoplehood of the Jews, but none is more painful — because more self-defeating — than that of blacks in the United States. Rare exceptions apart, blacks have come in recent years to regard the Jews as their enemies. This unfortunate development calls for reflection.

North American blacks know the bitter taste of oppression. They have this in common with the Jewish people. To ask who has suffered more or longer would seem to be a futile question. It misses the point that slavery is slavery and that victims of prejudice are victims of prejudice. To be despised and held down for no other reason than that you are what you are has been and continues to be a common experience of Jews and blacks. Both have felt oppression in their flesh and bones.

This common experience, however, has been lost sight of because the histories of these two peoples have been so different, and because each side, by and large, has looked only to its own experience of suffering. They have not listened to or learned each other's story. Each people therefore believes that it is the paradigmatic sufferer. Jews resist, for example, any form of quotas for admission to professional schools, because they remember their own experience of having been excluded by quotas in the past. Blacks, on the other hand, demand "affirmative action," knowing from their own past that "open admission" in a white society has always meant black exclusion. So blacks conclude that Jews are racists, and Jews conclude that blacks are anti-Judaic. Their common experience of suffering only serves to set them at odds.

It is difficult for a white Christian to reflect on this sad situation, because white Christians have been responsible for so much of the suffering of both blacks and Jews. The oppressor for both has been, by and large, the white Christian.

Blacks share something else with Jews. Possibly because of a common experience of oppression, yet utterly unlike the oppressed of Latin America, North American black Christians have been nourished on Israel's Scriptures to a degree unknown by white Christians anywhere. "Let my people go!" has become a part of their vocabulary, and they have identified with Israel, longing for Exodus, to an extent not found in any other part of the church. Without consciously deciding to do so, North American black Christians have therefore a tradition of understanding themselves in the light of Israel.

ii. *Jewish self-understanding and black consciousness*

The Jewish people understands itself as different, as a peculiar people. This remains true even if many Jews today have abandoned their traditional self-understanding as the people of God. A secular Jewish self-understanding, however, provides no solid base for understanding the Jewish people as unique, for that can stand only on the basis of their calling by the unique God. The Jewish people could only be thought to be destined to be a light for the nations on the assumption of this calling. It is therefore understandable that responsible Jewish teachers (i.e., its rabbis) are concerned to raise Jewish consciousness, to make Jews better Jews. That means, being Jews according to Jewish self-understanding.

Blacks too are different, and many of them have had a problem with their difference that is similar to that of many Jews: the world about them tries to define their difference. "Different" consequently comes to mean "inferior." Blacks could take courage from Jewish efforts to insist on defining themselves. Black consciousness is just that freedom of blacks in defining themselves in their own way. In this task, blacks and Jews could be mutually supportive. Each people could learn from the struggles and successes of the other the way to their respective self-understandings, and from this even white Christians would have something to learn.

The issue confronting us in this context might appear to be that of general revelation. The question concerning general revelation has traditionally been raised in the white church. The question is whether there is anything outside of the (white) church's own tradition and experience of revelation, specifically in Jesus Christ as he is attested to in the Scriptures and the Apostolic Writings of the church, to which the church should attend and from which it should expect to learn something of the will of God. The natural world has been the chief candidate as a source of general revelation, but sometimes also the course of human history. A theology of the people Israel, by arguing that the church has something to hear in and learn from the witness of the Jewish people, commits one who engages in it to be open to at least this extra-ecclesial source of revelation.

Israel's witness, however, is not general. It is specific, particular. The question which Israel poses for the church is not that of general revelation, but rather the question of a quite particular revelation, that of a witness to God, chosen by God, but outside the framework of the church. That question is as relevant to the black church as to any other part of the church.

Here, however, we have suggested the possibility that black Christians could and should learn to see their own peoplehood in the light of Jewish peoplehood. The possibility which we are exploring is of blacks learning from Israel's history how to see their own history, to learn — as Israel has — to detect there the hand of God at work for the sake of the completion of creation. If this were learned, by blacks or anyone else, it should not lead one to turn one's back on the source from which it had been learned. It should rather lead one to recognize this as an invitation to go on learning from this source. It should finally lead one to want to cooperate, to join hands with Israel, in being also a witness in the particularity of one's own peoplehood. Israel does not ask Christians to become Jews or blacks to become Jews. It asks them rather to be themselves and from their own place to give praise to the God of heaven and earth. Israel's witness to blacks is to know themselves as God's people, God's *black* people, in cooperation with God's Jewish people.

iii. Zionism and Black Power

The link which we have just forged in thought is that between Zionism and Black Power. Superficially seen as antagonistic, they are in important respects correlative. Since its beginnings over a century ago, the Zionist idea and the Zionist movement have had an extremely complex history. If an exhaustive definition of either is possible, it will not be attempted here. The central motif in the development and history of Zionism has been the concern for a Jewish state for Jews in *Eretz Yisrael*. An important result of the movement (one intended by some within it from an early stage) and its accomplishment, however, has been to strengthen the sense of Jews everywhere of their Jewishness. As a by-product of having contributed immeasurably to the creation of the state of Israel, Zionism stands for Jewish *self*-definition and *self*-determination.

In this respect, Zionism could become a model for North American black theologians in the task of raising the self-consciousness of their people and of winning self-determination under the banner of Black Power. From the perspective of blacks, Zionism could be taken as a pilot experiment in everything they desire in the way of self-affirmation and the achievement of self-determination. Sharing with the Jewish people a history of oppression and also the resources of the Scriptures, black theologians have the opportunity not only of learning useful lessons from Zionism's strengths and weaknesses, but even more of taking courage from the birth and survival of the Zionist state, as a sign that God can yet do a new thing on behalf of the oppressed among his creation. They would then be in a position to make a radical challenge to the white church and its entanglements with the forces of oppression. Such a Christian theology of liberation could form links between black Christians and Jews that would open a whole new era in the relationship between the church and the Jewish people.

CHAPTER SIX

The Land

*God elected Israel to landed life in a promised place, from Dan to Beer-
sheba. Israel has been called to live in and be responsible for this place
as a light to other nations, in their lands, of God's will for the life of
his creatures in and as a part of his creation. Israel's special landed witness
to the church is to the creatureliness of the service to which God calls.*

1. THE AMBIGUITY OF SETTLEMENT — AND OF REVELATION

i. *The reality of landed life*

Israel is a living, actual people. It is therefore a people with
its feet planted solidly on the earth. This is true for Israel not
only because it is thus with every living, actual people, but also
because it has been so determined as a people by its election.
God's covenant with Abraham and Sarah, reiterated in the
covenants with Isaac and Jacob and above all in the covenant
of Sinai, directed Israel explicitly to a definite place. Designated
at first simply as "the land" (Gen. 12:1), then more specifically
as "from Dan to Beersheba" (1 Sam. 3:20, 2 Sam. 3:10, 17:11,
and so on), the former land of Canaan became by divine election the land of Israel, *eretz Yisrael*. In this definite place Israel
was to live its life of fidelity to Torah.

Israel testifies that this land was promised to it as the place
in which to live its covenant with God, but it also remembers
that it came to this place by way of conquest and settlement.

Torah frequently refers to this territory as "the land which the LORD your God gives you/us" (Deut. 1:25, 2:29, 11:31, and so on). Nevertheless, the gift came by way of battle. Israel had to win the land which God gave it.

Whether the conquest and settlement of the land happened as it is recounted in the books of Joshua, Judges, and Samuel is another matter. Historical scholarship may lead us to question more than just a few details of the story. We are listening to Israel's testimony, however, and the Torah tells of a conquest and settlement of a land inhabited by others. Moreover, it makes provision for all the details of actual life in that specific land. In his lively study, *The Land*, Walter Brueggemann (1977) can even say, "Torah consists in guidelines for land management. . . . It is . . . interested in care for the land, so that it is never forgotten from whence came the land and to whom it is entrusted and by whom" (60). Thus Israel's memory of its conquest of the land always emphasized that God fought for Israel and the land was consequently regarded as God's gift for Israel's life. It is therefore integral to Torah that it makes provision for the precise location of each of the tribes of Israel (Josh. 15ff). Commandments about sowing and harvesting (e.g., Lev. 19:9f, Deut. 24:19f) and economic affairs (e.g., Deut. 15:1–11, 24:10f, and so on) are as much a part of Torah as the commandment to love God.

Landed life means living in history, for better and for worse. Israel knew landlessness both before and after its biblical history in the land (on this and the following, cf. Brueggemann, op. cit.). Its first historical period was its way to the land, and its second was in the land on the way to losing it. Then came the return to the land, but a land controlled by others. Thus Israel's biblical history was always shaped by its relationship to the land: the more nearly it possessed the land, the more decisively it lived in history. In the land or out of it, however, Israel's life has continued, but it was consistent with its biblical memory that God wills landedness, when Gershom Scholem called Israel's return to the land in the twentieth century the "reentry into world history of the Jewish people" (*On Jews and Judaism in Crisis*, 1976, 295).

ii. *The ambiguity of landed life*

Israel testifies not only to but also out of its landed life. Its witness to God takes place where Israel is—in history. It takes place in the life of this people, not just in their words. Israel's witness therefore is as ambiguous as landed life, and landed life is inherently ambiguous. Landed life committed Israel to military, political, and economic activity, with all the possibilities of injustice that follow from such involvements. One people's gain is another people's loss, militarily, politically, or economically, and not always justly. The inevitable ambiguity of Israel's landed life was the recurring occasion for the clash between the kings and the prophets of biblical Israel.

Israel had and has no escape from this ambiguity, however, for life in the land was and is its calling. Torah centers on how Israel is to manage the land and itself in the land, and Israel was called by God as a people to be a nation, even if always God's nation. The calling to be a holy nation involves, minimally, being a nation.

The understanding of Israel's ancient testimony is helped immeasurably by looking closely at the witness of Israel's present life in the land. Unhallowed by age and reported daily in the press and on television, rather than in a sacred text, Israel's present life in the land is open to inspection in all the ambiguity of the fully human life of God's elect. It is as if, alongside of 2 Samuel 5 and 1 Chronicles 11 on one page of our newspaper, we had on the next page the reports of the Jebusites and the Philistines of those same battles. When David took Jerusalem, only his side was reported; in 1967 we heard from both sides. Thus recent events accentuate the ambiguity already present in the biblical accounts of Israel's ancient history.

The modern story is indeed ambiguous. On the positive side, the concern to plant trees, grass, and flowers reflects Israel's love for a land long neglected and its joy in seeing it cared for. On the negative side is the failure to carry out the injunction of the Torah that there shall be one law for Israelites and for the resident aliens who live among them (Ex. 12:49; Num. 15:15f). As prophets and kings clashed over such matters before, so Israelis argue today. There is nothing pure about landed life, whether in ancient times or today. Then as now, to conquer a land means to dispossess others. Landed life brings with it moral ambiguity.

iii. The ambiguity of revelation

Israel's landed life, we should remember, was God's idea. According to the biblical testimony, God promised just this to Israel and made it the center of the covenant. To acknowledge the ambiguity of landed life, therefore, is to acknowledge the ambiguity of revelation. Islam may be a religion of a book, and Christianity may be a religion of faith. Israel, however, knows only of the LORD who gave it the land as the place in which to serve him.

God might conceivably have chosen to reveal himself in infallible propositions, or in ideas, principles, or ideals. Instead, so Israel testifies, God chose a nation, with a land in which to live and for which to care. If any would wish to hear Israel's witness, they will have to attend to Israel's life and therefore Israel's land, for the latter is integral to Israel's covenant with God. Listening to Israel, in a word, requires suppressing every tendency to Neo-Platonism.

This is a difficult requirement for a western church trained in the school of Augustine. It is also not easy for the eastern church, as was revealed by the negative response of the Middle East Council of Churches to some proposed "Guidelines" for Jewish-Christian Dialogue, drawn up in 1981 by the World Council of Churches' Consultation on the Church and the Jewish people. The Judaism which the Middle East Council could affirm was one shorn of Zionism, and the Israel which it wanted was one whose covenant with God omitted all reference to actual land. Indeed, it seemed to be unable to recognize God's Israel, seeing instead only a religion called Judaism.

The ambiguity of Israel's present life in the land raises the question whether it was ever otherwise, and therefore whether God's revelation has not always shared in this ambiguity. Jewish as well as Christian theology in the past few decades (that is, *since the founding of the state of Israel*, although usually without reference to that event on the part of Christians) has both emphasized God's "mighty acts" of biblical times (cf. Ps. 106:2, 145:4, 12; 150:2), and then come to question whether God acts in this same powerful way today. If we read Israel's ancient story in the light of its present story, however, we must question this development. Did Israel's conquest of the land and David's capture of Jerusalem look any less ambiguous to contemporaries than the Israeli capture of Judea and Samaria and of east Jerusalem appears today? Were God's "mighty acts" ever clearly his, to the eyes of any observer? Were there not always human agents involved? Was it ever clear whether it was God's mighty arm at work, or only Israel's army? When God spoke to his prophets, was there ever a time when it could not have been asked, "Or was that only the fruit of human imagination?" My questions, obviously, are rhetorical, for I think the case is not convincingly made that God's relationship to Israel is quite different from what it has been since the beginning of the covenant. The reality and therefore the ambiguity of landed life is the only context which God has chosen for his revelation to his people Israel. We are forced to conclude, therefore, that God has chosen ambiguity for all of his revelation.

Why has the God of Israel chosen to make his acts and his revelation so ambiguous? From the fact that he has done so we may hazard two possible answers. He has done so, we surmise, in order to remind us that God remains free even in his most intimate relationships with his creatures. Everything we say of him, including this, will ever be tinged with an element of uncertainty, for his thoughts and ways are not ours (Is. 55:8). Second, the uncertainty that is always part of God's revelation is a reminder to us of our own creaturely freedom and a challenge to use our freedom in deciding God's will and purpose in our specific situation. God's action and revelation call forth rather than suppress the action and response of those touched by them. Israel's witness to God includes this double witness to freedom, to God's and to that of God's people. These are the positive aspects of Israel's witness to the ambiguity of its landed life with God, the second of which especially the Gentile church needs to learn from the Jewish people.

2. LAND AND PEOPLE

i. *Land for the people*

God called Abraham and immediately commanded him to "go to the land that I will show you." The calling of Abraham, therefore, was not an inner matter between God and Abraham's soul. Rather, the call set Abraham in motion toward a definite place. *There* was where Abraham was to live his calling.

It is a matter of record, in Israel's Torah and in Jewish history, that Israel has spent more time out of than in the land. Abraham lived many years among the Chaldeans and then settled in Haran before he was called to go to the land of Canaan. Jacob, his grandson, ended his days in Egypt, settled with his whole family. The children of Israel were called into a new reality of peoplehood under Moses and reentered the land under Joshua. In the sixth century before the Common Era, the tribes of Israel having already been deported, the tribes of Judah were taken captive to Babylon. Many, but probably not the majority, returned in the next century, and their descendants were driven out in the wars with Rome in the first and second centuries, to begin the longest exile of their history. For most of its history, Israel has needed and longed for its land, not possessed it.

Israel's time out of its land has included some of its most formative periods. Abraham's call, the gift of Torah, the shaping of the canon of Torah, and the composition of the principal version of the Talmud, the oral Torah, all took place outside *eretz Yisrael*. Every one of these events, however, calls out for the land. All of these parts of Israel's testimony agree that Israel was made to be Israel in the land of Israel.

For nineteen centuries, in the long exile that has come to a partial end in this century, the Jewish people survived without a land, but they remembered it and never thought of themselves as a people who did not need that land. There was a land for this people, they knew, and that land was *eretz Yisrael*. The Zionist movement in its various forms may be a relatively recent phenomenon; its roots, however, are as old as the people Israel.

ii. A people for the land

So basic is the place of the land in Israel's witness that it seems at times to be more fundamental in God's purpose than Israel itself. This is reflected in the second chapter of Genesis, where it is told that God planted a garden and placed *adam* in it in order to take care of it. So Israel was set in a land that was God's, not Israel's: "the land is *mine*, and you are my foreign tenants" (Lev. 25:23)! Although the place is called the land of Israel, it is in fact, according to Israel, God's land. The Torah is God's instructions for caring for and living in it. The land is God's chosen place in which to serve him.

If Israel fails to serve God, it defiles not only itself, but also the land, and if Israel defiles the land, then the land will vomit Israel out, just as it vomited out those who had previously defiled it (Lev. 18:24–28). Such is the holiness of this land that it can stand with God its owner as the judge over the behavior of the people. The land is therefore not only God's gift but also God's challenge to Israel.

Because of this understanding of Israel's relationship to God's land, the Rabbis interpreted the destruction of the Temple and the beginning of the long exile as punishments for Israel's sins. As the agonies of exile grew to such staggering proportions in the nineteenth and twentieth centuries, however, the positive side of Israel's relationship to the land reasserted itself in the rise of Zionism. In this movement, both sides of this relationship came together: Israel was a people that needed its land, and the land, desolate and untended, needed its people to care for it. And that is indeed what has happened. It would be hard to imagine a land more lovingly and carefully tended by its inhabitants than *eretz Yisrael*.

iii. The Election of Israel and Exile

Although the people Israel has passed more of its history outside than in the land, and although biblical and rabbinic Judaism interpreted the condition of exile as punishment, Israel's election has never been in doubt. God may punish his elect, but they remain his elect. This rabbinic conviction was clearly anticipated by the apostle Paul (Rom. 11:1). That is because Israel has always understood its election to have been God's own free and unmerited choice. Israel in exile is therefore still the Israel of God.

During the longest exile of its history, following the destruction of the Second Temple, rabbinic leadership, the written Torah, and above all the oral Torah (the Talmud), kept the Jewish people alive. The house of study in effect replaced the Temple, and repentance and deeds of loving kindness took over the role of the Temple sacrifices (as did also the study of the rules given in the Torah for the performance of the sacrifices— *Pes.K.* 60b; *Meg.* 31b; M&L, 25f). But the rabbis never legitimized the condition of exile and dispersion. The hope for a return to the land remained alive, although pushed into the indefinite future, when Messiah would come and restore Israel. Over the centuries, there were always at least a few Jews who managed to maintain themselves in the ruined land, as well as others who managed to fulfill the common hope of finishing their days and being buried there, but for most this could only remain a dream of the messianic future.

Zionism is grounded on this long tradition of Diaspora longing for the restoration of the Jewish people in *eretz Yisrael*. There are secular as well as religious Zionists, of course. Vladimir Jabotinsky's arguments before the British Royal Commission on Palestine of 1937 (the Peel Commission), for example, are based on humanitarian not theological grounds. The Zionist idea (see Arthur Hertzberg's work so entitled, 1959, for Jabotinsky's argument and those of many others who contributed to the rise and development of Zionism) may indeed have arisen in the context of European secular nationalism, but Hertzberg's evidence supports his claim that "messianism, and not nationalism, is the primary element in Zionism" (16). Zionism was a peculiarly Jewish response to the secular nationalism of the nineteenth century and the trials of Diaspora existence, but its cornerstone is the conviction that Israel has been called by God to life in the land of Israel.

iv. The election of Israel and the return

Ha-siddur ha-shalem, the Daily Prayer Book of Judaism, now contains the following Prayer for the Welfare of the State of Israel, composed by the Chief Rabbinate of Israel (following Philip Birnbaum's translation):

> Our Father who art in heaven, Protector and Redeemer of Israel, bless thou the state of Israel which marks the dawn of our deliverance. Shield it beneath the wings of thy love; spread over it thy canopy of peace; send thy light and thy truth to its leaders, officers and counselors, and direct them with thy good counsel.
>
> O God, strengthen the defenders of our Holy Land; grant them salvation and crown them with victory. Establish peace in the land, and everlasting joy for its inhabitants.
>
> Remember our brethren, the whole house of Israel, in all the lands of their dispersion. Speedily let them walk upright to Zion thy city, to Jerusalem thy dwelling-place, as it is written in the Torah of thy servant Moses: "Even if you are dispersed in the uttermost parts of the world, from there the LORD your God will gather and fetch you. The LORD your God will bring you into the land which your fathers possessed, and you shall possess it."
>
> Unite our hearts to love and revere your name, and to observe all the precepts of thy Torah. Shine forth in thy glorious majesty over all the inhabitants of thy world. Let everything that breathes proclaim: "The LORD God of Israel is King; his majesty rules over all." Amen.

In this prayer, Israel's return to the land which has taken shape in the state of Israel is seen as a mark of "the dawn of redemption." Redemption means more than just the return and the state. Redemption means "peace in the land and everlasting joy," and it means that "everything that breathes" shall "proclaim: The LORD God of Israel is King." But the state, the fruit of the Jewish people's independence in their own land, is surely a step in the direction of the fulfillment of the promise of Israel's election.

The state of Israel was the culmination of a series of returns, beginning in 1882, on the part of some 600,000 Jews by 1948, and greatly increasing when the state was founded. The practice of the state from its beginning was formulated in the Law of Return, which allowed any Jew to become a citizen and settle without restriction. This ingathering spurred by the Zionist movement clearly marks a new era in Israel's long history. It brings to mind a passage of Jeremiah:

> Behold, the days are coming, says the LORD, when it shall no longer be said, "As the LORD lives who brought up the people of Israel out of the land of Egypt," but "As the LORD lives who brought up the people of Israel out of the north country and out of all the countries where he had driven them." For I will bring them back to their own land which I gave to their fathers. (16:14f.)

Jeremiah may have had in mind the return from Babylon. The Prayer for the State of Israel which we have cited clearly has in mind the return from the pogroms and the Holocaust of Europe and persecutions in other lands. In both cases, Israel's return to its land marks a new stage in the history of its election.

It must be observed that only about one-fifth of the Jewish people have returned to the land of promise. The vast majority has chosen to remain in the Diaspora. In some sense, then, we must say that Israel's existence transcends, at least physically, Israel's return. Diaspora Jews and Israelis may differ on the

Jewish legitimacy of a continuing Diaspora now that the Jewish state exists, but the Prayer for the State of Israel is at the same time a prayer for "the whole house of Israel." In exile and in the land, Israel's election is fundamental in its witness.

The Prayer for the State of Israel as well as the passage from Jeremiah invite us to make a choice about how to speak of succeeding events in Israel's history. In the historical sequence of *B* following *A*, the orthodox tendency, Christian no less than Jewish, has been to say that *B* is the unfolding of or a commentary on that which is already complete in *A*. But the Prayer and Jeremiah speak of *B* as a new and further step which adds to or changes that which was good-as-far-as-it-went in *A*. If we follow this lead, then we may speak of the founding of the state of Israel as a new step in God's eternal covenant with Israel, but we would do well to listen to the orthodox alternative, for it warns us to listen not just to Israel today, but also to Israel throughout its history. Only thus will we hear Israel's full witness to the God of Israel.

3. A LAMPSTAND FOR THE LAMP

i. *The meaning of place*

The Jewish witness concerning human existence is not exhausted in its testimony to the unity of the whole person, body and soul, and to the social or communal dimension of human life. It says also that human beings require a place. Place is more than physical space. Physical space is an extended and delimited area. Space points us to the boundaries. Place, for Israel, as Brueggemann put it, "is space in which important words have been spoken which have established identity, defined vocation, and envisioned destiny. Place is space in which vows have been exchanged, promises have been made, and demands have been issued" (*The Land*, 5).

Place is storied space; its precise boundaries are not so important as the narrative of what has taken place in it. Because Israel kept alive its stories of the land, the land remained the place which Israel remembered in exile and for which it longed. When the people began to return to the land over the past century, it was coming home. It was and is a home for Israel, however, because Israel remembers the story of God's gift of this land to Israel. It is Israel's home, but it belongs to God. So runs the story of this place.

Israel's witness to the land is part of its witness to creation. The creature has a place in God's creation. Every creature has a place in God's creation. Israel's sense of place is and should be heard by all creatures as its witness to God's purpose for his creatures. From the testimony of this nation, every nation may take courage to believe that it too is in the hands of the God who gives it a place — not strictly of its own — but in which important words may be spoken which "establish identity, define vocation, and envision destiny." Israel's discovery of the meaning of place is an invitation for all peoples to make a similar discovery.

ii. The Land and Torah

Because Israel as a distinctive people is different from all other peoples, so its land is different from all other lands. The difference is due to the relationship between God and Israel. That relationship is defined by the gift and obligation of Torah; the land of Israel is therefore where Torah is to be lived. Indeed, the land as well as Israel is determined by Torah. Not only Israel but also the land is to keep the Sabbath. The land too shares in the sabbath rest, and every seventh year "there shall be a sabbath of solemn rest for the land, a sabbath to the LORD" (Lev. 25:4). This land is different because it is the land of Torah.

Eretz Yisrael is the land to be managed and governed according to Torah. Its settlement, the allotment of sections to the different tribes, the agriculture, the civil law for the inhabitants, resident aliens as well as Israelites, all this is prescribed by Torah. Cultic, economic, and sexual behavior are also prescribed, with special concern that these be conducted so as not to pollute the land. Of course Israel is called and has accepted to live by Torah outside of the land as well, but one of the driving motifs of religious Zionism has been the recognition that many of the provisions of the Torah can only be carried out in *eretz Yisrael*, for the simple reason that they pertain peculiarly to the management of this place.

Secular Zionists of course do not accept this and have resisted the efforts of orthodox Israelis to make Torah the constitution of the state of Israel. Nevertheless, the orthodox understanding of Torah as the law of this land has prevented the secularists from establishing a written secular constitution for the land. If the land has a constitution, it is the Torah of God.

Eretz Yisrael is also the land from which Torah has in fact gone forth into all the world, and the place from which it is to go forth in power. "For out of Zion shall go forth the Torah and the word of the LORD from Jerusalem" (Isa. 2:3; Mic. 4:2). In one sense, this prophecy has already been fulfilled. The dispersion of Israel throughout the world, and of course the spread of the Christian church, has been the means of fulfillment. In a more important sense, however, the prophecy stands unfulfilled and remains a part of Israel's and the church's messianic hope for redemption. To the extent that Torah *has* gone forth, and in the day in which it *will* go forth in power, it issues from *eretz Yisrael*.

Finally, *eretz Yisrael* is the place to which Torah calls. The Prayer for the State of Israel, in its petition for the well-being of "the whole house of Israel, in all the lands of their dispersion," asks that they may "speedily . . . walk upright to Zion thy city." Many Israelis understand this call quite literally and cannot condone the action of their fellow Jews who do not obey the call and make *aliyah* (return to the land; literally, "going up"—to Jerusalem). Many other Jews interpret the call in a less than literal sense. For them it is not God's will that every Jew in every land move at once to *eretz Yisrael*. Indeed, many of them believe that Israel's witness in the world is best served by a continuing Diaspora as well as by a healthy state of Israel. It is clearly no duty of a Christian theologian to try to settle this matter of central dispute among the Jewish people. It is sufficient for a Christian theology of the people Israel to take note of the fact that in several different forms, Israel bears testimony to its land as that to which God's Torah calls.

This call has a special meaning for the Christian church. It means that the land has a place in Christian reflection on the ways of God also for the future and not just in the past. The call of Torah toward Zion takes, for Gentile Christians, the form of Zechariah 8:22f: "Many peoples and strong nations shall come to seek the LORD of hosts in Jerusalem, and to entreat the favor of the LORD. Thus says the LORD of hosts: In those days ten men from the Gentiles of every tongue shall take hold of the robe of a Jew, saying 'Let us go with you, for we have heard that God is with you.' " Israel's witness to the land as the land of Torah is therefore a further reminder of the church's future dependence on the people Israel.

iii. A priestly kingdom

Israel is called to be a light to lighten the nations, the Gentiles. As one rabbi put it to his fellow Jews, "You are the light of the world." But then he is reported to have added, "Nor do men light a lamp and put it under a bushel, but on a stand, and it gives light to all in the house" (Matt. 5:14, 15). Jesus was true to the tradition of his people in teaching that Israel had a mission to the world and that this meant something public. He may have realized that not every public road was open in his time — for example, that of winning Jewish independence from Rome by force of arms — but he would have been a strange Jew indeed had he not taken what public roads he could. The one he chose was a public demonstration that led to his death. Israel's calling to be a light for the world necessarily requires that Israel be out in public. A lamp has to have a lampstand, and such is the state of Israel.

Israel in its land, and with a state represented in the councils of states, is a nation called to a priestly role. It exists for the sake of all the other states as God's elect means for the completion of his creation. What God wills for Israel is surely his will for Israel, but it also involves his will for all nations. Did he not offer his Torah to all the seventy nations? He wills justice and mercy for Israel, and also for all other peoples. He wills righteousness and peace for Israel, but also for the rest of his creation. He wills that Israel care for its land, but he wills all the nations to care for their lands, for the whole earth is God's. And if Israel has been given God's presence and blessing, and with this a purpose and destiny, then all the nations may take courage from the witness of this one nation that God has all this also in store for them.

It might be objected that I am arguing that Israel has the role of a model for other nations, and that this undermines the concreteness of the specific land to which Israel is called. My answer to this objection is that the logic of witness is not the same as that of a model or pattern. Israel's role as a witness to the nations not only does not take away from the specificity of its election to landed life; on the contrary it positively requires it.

Israel's landed life is a light in a dark world. Since Israel too is a part of this world, its own darkness becomes especially evident in the light that it holds up. When Israel fails to temper justice with mercy, when it is goaded by its neighbors or more general conditions to act as other nations tend to act, then the Torah puts its failings into the sharpest relief. The Jews frequently object to Gentiles having a double standard and expecting more from Israel than from any other nation, but this could not be otherwise. Israel has already cast enough light into the world for the world to be vaguely aware that there exists a higher standard, the very one which Israel introduced into the world, and Israel can no more escape this annoyance than it can annul God's election of his lamp and his lampstand. The nations err, not in sensing the standard proper to Israel, but in their blindness to the fact that God judges them too by that higher standard.

Israel's witness, however, is that every other nation is as much God's by right of creation as is Israel. God cares for his whole creation, and therefore other nations in their lands are also God's concern. Israel lives in its land as a call to every other nation to live in its land with an equal awareness of its responsibility to the Creator and to the land which he provides.

4. THE LAND AND THE STATE

i. *Then and now*

When Israel came out of Egypt, it was led to a place in which to serve God, not foreign kings. It was given the land to possess and manage, not to inhabit as resident aliens. Landed life, as Israel testifies to it, entails having political control over that land. Land means self-rule under God. To have a land entails having what today is called a state.

For centuries the Jewish people has not had political independence. The political sovereigns under whom the Jews lived were always Gentiles, and Gentiles ruled over the land of Israel. The Jews lived in many different lands, under many different rulers, some of them Muslim, some of them Christian. Now, however, a sizable part of the Jewish people have returned to their land and have established, in the face of great difficulties, their independence: they are in the land as those who govern it. They have founded the state of Israel.

There are Christians who claim to be sympathetic to Jews and even to Judaism, but who object to the existence of the state of Israel. Such a position can only result from having an understanding of Jews and Judaism which the Jewish people have never had of themselves. Christians who hold such a view often insist that they are not anti-Jewish ("antisemitic"), only anti-Zionist. This means, however, that they have taken *galut*, exile, to be normal for the Jewish people. But Israel has never condoned landlessness and statelessness. Had such a condition ever become normative for Jews, the Zionist movement could hardly have arisen. Any Christian who would understand the Jewish people must allow the Jews to define themselves. That means listening to Israel's witness. That witness has been consistent, from biblical times, through all of Jewish history, and to the present. Israel belongs in *eretz Yisrael* free of foreign domination. The realization of this central Jewish hope, under contemporary conditions, requires the state of Israel. Anti-Zionism therefore is in fact an anti-Jewish position. To be against Zion is to be against Israel. It was so in biblical times and it is so now.

ii. Return and Diaspora

The people Israel is one, but it exists in the land and in the Diaspora. We shall have to reflect on this strange new situation in the context of Israel's mission in Chapter Ten but it should be mentioned here also in connection with Israel's relationship to its land. For Israel's understanding of this relationship, the fact is important, if disconcerting, that the one people Israel now lives in two ways: in its land and also in the Diaspora. Historically considered, this is not a new situation at all, for Israel lived in the same two ways from the time of the return from the Babylonian captivity. And throughout the long exile of the past eighteen or nineteen centuries, there have always been some Jews who lived in *eretz Yisrael*. What is new about the present situation is that, although the dramatic return during the past hundred years and the founding of the state has meant Jewish sovereignty in its land, yet this has not been a signal for a general *aliyah* of the whole house of Israel. This dual existence has consequences for the relationship between Israel as a people, the land of Israel, and the state of Israel.

The Jewish people now living in the land of Israel are known as Israelis. They are in some cases the founders, and in every case citizens and (in one way or another) defenders of the state of Israel. So much is relatively clear. However, there are Muslim and Christian Israelis too! And there are Jews in the state of Israel who to this day refuse to recognize the legitimacy of that state, although they cannot help but share in the benefits which its existence provides them. Non-Jewish Israelis and non-Israeli Jews, however, are the exception. The rule is that Jews in Israel are Israelis, citizens and defenders of the Jewish state. Some of them may be critical of the policies and practices of the government, sometimes vehemently so, but they are still Israelis. For them, people, land, and state are one.

The people Israel also exists in the Diaspora, either almost without persecution, as in the United States, Canada, Great Britain, France, and other countries, or subject to varying degrees of dislike or duress, as in the Soviet Union, Poland, and Argentina. Almost without exception, they rejoice in the existence of the state of Israel. They visit it when they are able, for shorter or longer periods of time. All of them know it is there, "just in case." But generally, they have decided not to make *aliyah*, to return to Israel to become Israelis. They have made this decision for any number of reasons, good and bad, high and low. However, they have supported and continue to support the state, financially and with goodwill and wishes, seeing it as essential to the preservation of the Jewish people.

It seems reasonably clear that Jews in Israel and Jews in the Diaspora both support and are supported by the state of Israel. All acknowledge that it is a benefit to the whole house of Israel. There is, however, a fair degree of tension between many Israelis and many Jews of the Diaspora. The relationship is one which is still being worked out. Notable among the unresolved issues are the amount and extent of Diaspora Jewish criticism of the policies of the Israeli government that should be tolerated, and whether the Diaspora can long exist, given the present high rate of intermarriage and assimilation.

iii. Like all the nations?

Given Israel's election, its centuries of continuing existence without its land, and the fact and tensions of its present dual existence, both in its land and in the Diaspora, there seems no likelihood at all that the state of Israel could become a nation "like all the nations," however much some of its secular Zionist citizens might wish it. No, the state of Israel is different, just as Zionism is unlike any of the nineteenth-century nationalisms among which it grew up. The state of Israel is a Jewish state, and as long as Jews are Jews, then this state will be different.

The Jewish state is and will be different because Jews are different. I do not refer to social, physical, racial, or historical differences. On all these matters there is considerable room for debate. A Jew cannot be adequately defined by such considerations or by criteria drawn on these lines, for all of them omit the one essential reality that distinguishes this people: God's election of Israel, and Israel's acceptance of God's Torah. The covenant is that which distinguishes Israel, for better or worse. Every Jew that is born is born into that covenant, no matter how much he or she as a secularist may later come to deny it. What makes the Jew different is that of which the biblical story tells.

Because the Jewish people are different, that is, God's elect servants and witnesses, their state is going to be different, since it is a part of the continuing history of which the Hebrew Bible tells the first part. Whatever the Jews do, for better or worse, is part of their life in the covenant, and that surely applies to this new thing which they have done in establishing the Jewish state. The state of Israel is nothing other than a vital expression of the Jewish people. It can therefore not possibly escape the destiny and calling of this people. But this people is called to be the God of Israel's light for the nations. The state of Israel is therefore caught up in Israel's election and purpose. There is no way that it could ever become just a nation "like all other nations." Well or poorly, it will share in the destiny of this people to bear witness to the One who is Creator and will be the Redeemer of the whole of creation.

iv. *Hindrances to the witness*

There are serious hindrances to Israel's landed witness, the primary one being that Israel has yet to know peace. It has had to maintain itself since birth in constant military preparedness for yet another attack by its neighbors, who from the beginning have sought the disappearance of the Jewish state. The partition of the land, for which many of the neighboring Arab states would now settle, was rejected by them when it was offered by the United Nations General Assembly (with Jewish agreement) in 1947. Instead, the Arab countries all attacked the new Jewish state, and Israel's borders ever since have been armistice lines. Israel's border with Egypt is the first to be established by a peace treaty, the stability of which, after thirty-four years of hostilities, is more a matter of hope than certainty. With the uncertain exception of Egypt, Israel's neighbors have forced Israel to be constantly prepared to fight, hardly an ideal condition for a people called to bear witness to the Creator and Redeemer of all.

Israel's witness is further clouded by the fact that the state was born in the aftermath of the horrors of the Second World War and founded largely by Jews who had fled European persecution before and during that war. The result was that the young state appeared to its neighbors to be a European intrusion into the Middle East and has been viewed by many in the Third World as an outpost of western imperialism. Ironically, as James Parkes loved to point out, the Arab countries were the principal cause of turning Israel into a genuinely Middle Eastern country: by forcing their resident Jews to flee to Israel, they are responsible for the fact that the population of Israel is now more Middle Eastern than European in background. Nevertheless, the misconception of Israel as a European rather than a Jewish state has not made Israel's task easier.

The cost of war, not least in lives lost, but also financially, has been a serious drain on Israel's resources. Efforts that might have gone into reclamation of wilderness, housing, cooperative ventures with neighboring countries, and other actions that would have been part of Israel's light for the nations have had to go into building and maintaining the Israel Defense Force and its necessary armaments. That so much has been done in those other areas is remarkable under the circumstances, but it is clear that war has been a hindrance to Israel's witness.

Perhaps the most painful cost of war has been to the soul and spirit of the country, or so many sensitive Israelis feel. Hardly an issue of the International Edition of the *Jerusalem Post* appears without some article or editorial bemoaning the spiritual price to the country of being in effect an occupying power over the Arab population in the territories gained in the Six Day War of 1967. Israel bore a remarkable witness to the nations by trading territory for peace in the Camp David accords with Egypt. What it will do about the far more complex problem of the so-called West Bank remains to be seen. Had Jordan not ignored Israel's urgent plea to stay out of the war in 1967, this painful and difficult problem would not have arisen, but the burden of occupation that has resulted is no help to Israel's witness.

5. HOW NOT TO BE "NOT OF THIS WORLD"

i. In but not of the world

Franz Rosenzweig observed that being "in the world but not of it" (cf. John 17:15, 16) was simply a fact of Jewish existence, whereas for Christians it was a calling and a task (cf. *Discerning the Way*, 26n). In a way neither anticipated nor desired by Rosenzweig, Israel is once more in its land and therefore fully in the world, yet at the same time not of it, by virtue of the fact that its being there, however much the fruit of secular Jewish sweat and blood, could hardly have come about but for Jewish trust in God's promise of this land to Israel. A Christian theology of the people Israel has therefore to ask concerning the particular witness of Israel's landed life for the Christian church. How does this renewed fact of Jewish existence speak to the calling and task of the church?

The first and obvious call to the church is to affirm God's promise of the land to Israel and therefore to stop spiritualizing this promise in a vain attempt to make it apply to the church. The church has no sacred *place* other than where God is present to it in the Spirit through Jesus Christ. Sacred *space* is a pagan concept, but for the church every *place* may be sacred if Christ is there with the church. The promise of the land, however, concerns a quite particular place, the land in which God called Israel to serve him. The church has no choice but to affirm this promise if it believes God to be faithful and if it believes that God has confirmed all his promises in Jesus Christ (Rom. 15:8; 2 Cor. 1:20).

Israel's landed witness, however, says more. It tells the church that it too has been called as a community of creatures, mortal as Israel is mortal, flesh and blood as Israel is flesh and blood, a wielder or a victim of power. The church of the God of Israel could hardly live in the clouds. It is really in the world and involved in politics and in the power struggle that is characteristic of living in a world in which God gave Israel an actual place to maintain, care for, and defend.

The world of landed life is the world of power struggles and politics. If God willed this for his people Israel, we may suspect that he wills something not totally alien to this for his church. And indeed, the church is involved in power struggles and politics, both within its own life and in the life of all the nations within which it lives. The church has tended to ignore, excuse, or cover over these struggles, as it has tended to sprititualize Israel's promise of landed life. In acknowledging the one, it may acknowledge the other, and humbly accept this creaturely condition of all that it does. Christians may differ among themselves about how power is to be used and political issues settled, as is also the case in Israel, but there is no place in the church of the God of Israel and the Father of Jesus Christ for a life divorced from the issues of power and politics.

Accepting the fact that the church has been called in the world, the church is no more than Israel *of* the world. That which makes Israel to be Israel is that which makes the church to be the church: God's election. God's election is no more visible or self-evident in the church than in Israel. It manifests itself only ambiguously in the conviction of being called to be faithful to God. The church, like Israel, is answerable to God, not to the world. To be "not of the world" is to be dependent on and answerable to God, and to be so concretely in the world. It does not mean to be "otherworldly," as if there were another world than the created one, the one for the redemption of which it prays and works. With its feet firmly planted on this earth, the church is to be not of this world. Deeply and openly engaged in the power struggles and politics of this world, the church is to be not of this world; it is called to be *incarnatedly* not of this world.

ii. The form of a servant

The church of one who was among us as one who serves (Mk. 10:45) and who became, according to Paul, a servant to the circumcised (Rom. 15:8) is called to serve. The service to which the church is called will certainly need its appropriate Christological development, which we shall address in the third Part of this *Theology of the Jewish-Christian Reality*, but in the context of a Christian theology of the people Israel, we have to ask what the church has to learn from the witness to it of the Jewish people, and more particularly here, from the landed life to which Israel has been called by God. The church has not been called to serve God in a particular land, so there can be no question of trying to imitate Israel. But the church has been called to serve the world alongside of Israel in its service to the world. It will be useful, then, to reflect on the form of Israel's service to the world.

Israel serves the world primarily by being itself, that is, by being faithful to its own particular calling to live according to God's Torah and not according to the ways of the world. It serves the world by not joining in the idolatry of the world, thus presenting the world with a sign of the reality of the one God. For Israel serves by being a witness to God. Therefore the Rabbis taught that it was far worse to steal from a Gentile than from a Jew, "because of the profanation of the Name" (*T. Bab. K.* x, 15; M&L, 398), echoing the concern of Ezekiel 36:16–25. Israel profanes God's Name when it acts shamefully, so that the nations have grounds to speak against the people of God. When in the Middle Ages, for example, Jews so conducted themselves that Christian merchants thought it preferable to borrow from them, rather than from fellow Christians, because Jews were held to be more upright (see J. Parkes, *The Jew in the Medieval Community*, 1976, p. 336), then Israel was carrying out its witness to the God of righteousness.

Israel's service to the world was characterized by one of its Rabbis in the familiar saying, "Let your light so shine before men, that they may see your good works and give glory to your Father who is in heaven" (Matt. 5:16). Israel serves by being true to its God and its covenant, by being Israel, the people of God. Its service to the world is not something additional for it to carry out. The world is best served when Israel serves God in the covenant.

There is a long-standing spiritual tradition in the church of service by way of personal identifications with those in need. A Christian serves the poor, for example, by identifying with them, by becoming one of them. Remarkable lives have resulted from this tradition. Israel's witness does not challenge this tradition, but it does warn against romanticizing those to be served. Indeed, every human being is a brother or sister, because all of us are the children of the one Father, but each human being is also him- or herself. The truth in the theme of solidarity needs to be balanced by the truth of individual particularity. Thus in fact no one can be identical with another and identification by an act of the will has creaturely limits.

Israel's service to the world is to be the Israel of God. It bears witness, then, that service is performed by being, not by doing. This witness, so far as I can see, is one that the church needs to hear and think about. If the church can hear this witness, it might better learn that its first service to the world is to be the church, to be faithful to its God and to the life to which it has been called. It needs to hear from Israel that it is to live by trust, not by busy activity.

iii. The servant and the world

> The LORD has made known his victory;
> he has revealed his vindication in the sight of the nations.
> All the ends of the earth have seen the victory of our God.

These lines (vs. 2, 3b) from Psalm 98 reflect as well as many others Israel's incredible conviction that the ups and downs in the history of this tiny nation had the whole world as their rapt audience, that all of creation held its breath, as it were, to see what would happen next to this minuscule people. Mountains, rivers, and hills, as well as nations and mighty princes shuddered or rejoiced before the events of Israel's life. Nowhere is this preposterous belief expressed more strongly than in the Servant poems of Deutero-Isaiah. The world may laugh at this absurdity; were the Christian church to do so, it would be putting to scorn its own foundations.

This conviction is the consequence and expression of Israel's trust that the whole world of humanity and nature is all God's, that it truly belongs to him, and that this one Creator God has chosen Israel as his servant in the work of redeeming creation. It follows from this that right there in God's history with Israel God was doing something that was of vital concern for the whole of creation. Israel's servant role is thus the consequence of trust that God is indeed the Creator and has indeed chosen Israel, and the Servant poems of Second Isaiah are precisely where this two-sided trust that the Creator has chosen Israel, and that the God of Israel is the Creator, is expressed again and again.

Israel's witness to the church, then, is that servanthood stands on that dual conviction. Servanthood follows inevitably from being the elect of the Creator. In a sense, one does not have to *do* anything at all to be a servant of this God. The church, with Israel, has only (!) to trust that the whole of reality belongs to God, and that this God has put his finger deliberately on Israel, and then also on the church through Jesus Christ. One may not wish to say, with Tertullian, that one believes *because* it is absurd, but for Israel — and therefore also for the church of the God of Israel and the Father of the Israelite Jesus — there is no getting around the absurdity.

What then is the church to *do*? The question was put to John the Baptist and the answer was simply: do your own work in this absurd conviction. To be a servant of God's purpose to complete his creation means to think and act on a small scale, not on a vast one. A cup of cold water to one in thirst was recommended by a reliable Jew, and perhaps turning out to vote, where one has a vote, could be added. Planting a tree where one is not growing has been recommended, and one could add: treating the physical world as befits the property of God. Being a servant is to live with the sure but incredible conviction that the Creator is the Redeemer and that he has called us to cooperate in his work. Israel's landed life combines both sides of this conviction and makes this witness to the church. It does so because the land for Israel is the place that God has chosen for Israel to be his servant in fidelity to Torah.

CHAPTER SEVEN

TORAH: Israel's Life in Generosity

Israel's living witness to God takes the form of Torah-life, a willing, creative acknowledgment of the authority of God's revelation of his involvement in his creation. Israel's fidelity to Torah as a Yes to God and as a No to the church is a supporting witness to the church of the incarnation of God's commanding word and of creaturely responsibility, both of which the church was first invited to see in the Torah-true Jew, Jesus of Nazareth.

1. TORAH: GOD'S GENEROSITY

i. Torah as grace

God, Torah, and Israel, the three central themes of Judaism, have as their center the Torah—which binds together and defines the other two. As Israel has devoted itself to Torah, so a Christian theology of Israel has to devote itself to making clear Israel's understanding of Torah as God's gracious gift to his people. Our concern at this central point is Israel's understanding of Torah, not Augustine's understanding of his *lex*, or Luther's understanding of his *Gesetz*. *Lex* and *Gesetz* are properly translated as "law," and that in the context of a world which knew the tradition of Roman Law. *Torah* is only misleadingly translated "law," for its primary meaning is God's instruction, guidance, and constitution for Israel. But since Torah's role is so central and its ramifications so extensive, it is surely best not to translate it at all. Our interest is not merely in Israel's understanding of law or laws, nor in just its ideas about instruction, or in only its constitution. Our interest is in Israel's understanding of Torah, which includes all these and much more.

The church throughout most of its history has thought that when Paul spoke of *nomos*, that too meant "law." Had Paul been read as the Jewish author and thinker that he was, the church might have realized that the *nomos* that mattered for Paul had to have been the Torah, the Torah which, with the rest of Israel, Paul knew to be holy (Rom. 7:12), spiritual (7:16) and good (7:16). It was the Torah of God (7:25), the set form of knowledge and truth (2:20). God forbid that the good news preached by the Jew Paul should have had any other effect than to uphold the Torah (3:31). What made Paul's complex statements about Torah especially liable to misunderstanding was the fact that this Jew believed himself called by God to be an apostle to the Gentiles. Consequently, Paul's special concern was Torah's consequences for the Gentiles, the seventy nations that had rejected it. One would therefore have had to know the teaching of Judaism well in order to understand the Jewish apostle to the Gentiles. Neither Augustine nor Luther understood Judaism; they thought Judaism was all about law. In fact, it was and is all about Torah.

How do you live by grace alone? How do you live as a faithful and cooperative servant of the God who gives everything, beginning with life itself, out of his pure generosity? How do you bear witness to that sort of God? Israel's answer is, you live by Torah. You study it, you meditate upon it, you practice it, you bind it on your forehead and wrists, you nail it to your doorway. You saturate yourself in Torah so that your life becomes Torah-shaped. For Torah is God's gracious gift to Israel; therefore to live by Torah is Israel's thankful and joyful response to God's generosity.

According to a rabbinic midrash, "David said: My Father, who art in heaven, be thy Name blessed for all eternity, and mayest thou find pleasure from Israel, thy servants, wheresoever they dwell! For thou didst rear us up and make us great, thou didst sanctify us and grant us praise, thou didst bind [on us] the crown of Torah, of which the words spread from end to end of the world! If I have fulfilled aught of Torah, then it is only through thee that I have fulfilled it. Any charity that I have given, from that which is thine have I given it. And in return for the little Torah which I have done, thou has granted me to possess this world, the days of the Messiah, and the world to come" (*Tan.d.b.El.* p. 89; M&L, 65). The church may think that it knows a law that is in conflict with the Gospel; for Israel, Torah *is* gospel, the best of all possible news.

ii. Oral Torah as creative participation

Written Torah, whether the Five Books of Moses or the whole of *Tanakh* (the Hebrew Bible), is the substance of the covenant between God and Israel. It is God's invitation to his creatures to enter into a cooperative relationship with him. In accepting the gift of Torah, Israel became a co-worker in God's enterprise. The cooperative feature of the written Torah was underscored by the character of the oral Torah, the so-called unwritten Torah, which in fact came to be written down in the *Mishnah* (by about the beginning of the third century of the Common Era) and the *Gemara* (by about the end of the fifth century), together making up the Talmud.

The oral Torah, according to the Rabbis, was as much God's revelation from Sinai as the written Torah, but "it was not given in writing, so that the Gentiles should not falsify it, as they have done with the written Torah, and say that they are the true Israel" (*Num.R.*, Naso, 14, 10; M&L, 159). Anti-Christian polemics aside, the Rabbis saw the oral Torah as that which truly distinguished Israel from the rest of the world, and in fact it has shaped Judaism and the Jewish people. But in spite of the conviction that the oral Torah was all given by God to Moses and passed on from generation to generation, it is clear that it represents Israel's living, growing practice of developing the application of the Torah to changing circumstances. Halakhic judgments, that is, rabbinic decisions on all manner of questions of conduct, constituted Israel's creative participation in formulating the oral Torah, and this participation has continued to the present.

A famous story illustrates this creative participation. A group of Rabbis were arguing a halakhic point, and one of them, Rabbi Eliezer, performed several remarkable miracles in order to impress the others with his interpretation. The assembled Rabbis refused to allow the evidence of miracles. "Then he asked, 'May the walls of this House of Study prove it.' Then the walls of the house bent inwards, as if they were about to fall. Rabbi Joshua rebuked the walls, and said to them, 'If the learned dispute about the Halakhah, what has that to do with you?' So, to honor Rabbi Joshua, the walls did not fall down, but to honor Rabbi Eliezer, they did not become quite straight again. Then Rabbi Eliezer said, 'If I am right, let the heavens prove it.' Then a heavenly voice said, 'What have you against Rabbi Eliezer? The Halakhah is always with him [his view is always right].' Then Rabbi Joshua got up and said, 'It is not in the heaven' (Deut. 30:12). What did he mean by this? Rabbi Jeremiah said, 'The Torah was given us from Sinai. We pay no attention to a heavenly voice. For already from Sinai the Torah said, "By a majority you are to decide" ' [Exod. 23:2 as homiletically interpreted]. Rabbi Nathan met Elijah and asked him what God did in that hour. Elijah replied, 'He laughed and said, "My children have conquered me" ' " (*Bava Metzia* 59b; cf. M&L, 340f).

Remarkable in this talmudic witness is the conviction that in giving Torah to Israel, God gave with it the full responsibility of deciding what it means and how it applies. No heavenly voice is even to be listened to; instead, a majority vote is decisive. Israel is responsible for the course of the covenant, and God laughs and says he can do nothing about it! A stronger testimony to the creative character of Jewish halakhic rulings is hardly imaginable.

Israel's creative participation in the covenant with God is made possible, according to Israel's witness, by the intimacy with God which the Torah both provides and assures. Because the Torah is so close to God's heart, when Israel embraces the Torah, it embraces, as it were, also God.

A lovely rabbinic midrash brings this out: "Can there be a sale in which the seller sells himself along with the object he sells? God says, 'I sold you my Torah, and with it I, as it were, sold myself.' The matter is like a king who had an only daughter, and another king sought her and got her in marriage. The father said, 'My daughter is an only child: I cannot be parted from her and yet to say to you, Do not take her away, is also not possible, for she is your wife. Do me, therefore, this kindness; whithersoever you go, prepare for me a chamber that I may dwell with you, for I cannot forsake my daughter.' So God says to Israel, 'I have given you my Torah; I cannot be separated from her; yet I cannot say to you, Do not take her; therefore in every place whither you go, make me a house, wherein I may dwell.' . . . When a man buys a desirable object in the market, does he usually buy also its owner? But God, when he gave the Torah to Israel, said, 'With the Torah you, as it were, take also me' " (*Exod.R.*, Terumah, 33, I, 6; M&L, 171).

iii. Revelation as commandment

Israel, the Jewish people, has lived by Torah and Torah has kept Israel together and alive. The Torah that has been so central to Jewish existence over the centuries, however, is not simply the Five Books of Moses, but the evolving, growing rabbinic interpretation of Torah, namely, the Talmud and the ongoing halakhic creativity of generation after generation of rabbis. This is what Israel means primarily by Torah.

Torah in the broad, halakhic sense, according to rabbinic understanding, is all *Torah min ha-Shamayim*, "Torah from heaven" — that is, directly from God. "When God was about to give the Torah, he recited it to Moses in due order, Scriptures, Mishnah, Aggadah, and Talmud, for God spake *all* these words (Exod. 20:1), even the answers to questions which distinguished scholars in the future are destined to ask their teachers did God reveal to Moses, for he spake *all* these things" (*Tanh.B.*, Ki Tissa, 58b; M&L, 159f). Thus the whole halakhic tradition of the application of Torah to new situations and changing conditions is regarded as itself Torah, and all of it is seen as divine revelation.

Whatever reserve the modern critical mind may have at this incorporation of what appears to have been a growing, creative enterprise into the revelation from Sinai, the point should not be overlooked that with this teaching, Israel has underscored its conviction that revelation takes the form of commandment.

We have considered Israel's witness to revelation as narrative, and the Aggadah (usually defined negatively as all those parts of rabbinic teaching which do not refer to Halakhah) reflects this, but its primarily form for Judaism is clearly halakhic. Revelation, in short, is primarily commandment.

Revelation, therefore, is not primarily God's self-revelation, although God's will, purpose, and, so to speak, character are also revealed in his commandments. Revelation is also not primary the unveiling of an I-Thou relationship, although that too is the consequence of God's commanding address to his people. Certainly revelation is not primarily propositional in form, although propositions may be deduced from it. The primary form of revelation, and also its primary content, is "Do this and live!"

To obey a commandment is to obey God. The Rabbis stressed the importance of *kavvanah*, intention, concentration, directedness. "It matters not whether you do much or little, so long as your heart is directed to heaven" (*Ber.* 17a; M&L, 272). To obey a commandment, even to want to obey a commandment, is therefore to acknowledge God's love for Israel and to answer with a responding love. To obey is therefore an act of intimacy between Israel and God.

To obey a commandment is also, in most cases, to form and solidify community. It is an act of solidarity, because so many of the commandments have to do with life in community. They touch on every aspect of the life of the family, and of course love of neighbor is second only to love for God. The commandments to love build the solidarity of Israel, and the commandments were given to Israel as a people. To obey a commandment is therefore to affirm one's being a son or daughter of Israel.

To obey a commandment is to let life take the shape that God desires, from rising in the morning to retiring at night. It is to let one's life be shaped from birth to death according to the will of the Father. To obey a commandment is therefore to accept the generosity of God who has graciously given Israel a way to walk, step by step, toward the redemption of God's Israel and, with it, the redemption of the whole creation. It is to acknowledge

Torah as good news. That is Israel's witness to revelation as commandment.

iv. *Commandment as revelation*

The conviction that revelation comes primarily as commandment, that the commandments have been revealed by God to Israel, has implications worth notice. The first is that the commandment is evidently what the creature needs to know and can know. Human beings are not inclined to be righteous. In fact, they have an evil inclination (*yetzer hara*) which they are seldom able to resist. The great blessing of the commandments of Torah is that they provide just the support that is needed to overcome the evil inclination. God has given his commandments to Israel as the cure for this condition (see M&L, 295ff for numerous rabbinic formulations of this teaching). Torah, both its study and its practice, is the best defense against the power of the evil inclination.

The gift of Torah also reveals that God is concerned for the total life of his creatures. He is as concerned about family life, agriculture and commerce, and social and political behavior, as he is about so-called religious matters. Indeed, the distinction between religious and other matters is obliterated by the commandments. Neither the written Torah of the Scriptures nor the oral Torah of rabbinic tradition provide the least grounds for distinguishing between so-called moral and so-called ceremonial commandments, not to speak of distinguishing between religious and other duties. All commandments are from God and all express his will for Israel. A Christian theology of the people Israel must draw the church's attention to this aspect of Israel's witness and ask whether the church is being faithful to the same God in making such distinctions. Israel's testimony is clearly that they have no grounding in God's revelation.

Further, the commandments reveal God's concern for community. Indeed, revelation creates and sustains community. Torah was God's gift to the people to form them into a holy nation, and Torah has shaped the common life of the Jewish people down through the ages. Of course the individual Jew is addressed by the commandments, but the rabbis speak primarily of the commandments for the whole house of Israel. The commandments address Israel as a people; they address the individual as a son or daughter of that household.

Finally, the commandments reveal that God wills the active cooperation of his creatures in his covenant. God's truth is to be *done*, to be acted upon. The covenant of grace — and there is no other — is a covenant of works, calling Israel to stand on its feet and be about its Father's business of creating a world of righteousness. That covenant, according to the Rabbis, was offered to the seventy nations of the world before it was offered to and accepted by Israel. Israel therefore stands before the other nations as a reminder of God's purpose for them too. And for the Gentile church of the God of Israel, the witness is clear: grace is for the sake of works, God's generosity is meant to lead our turning and walking in the direction God has revealed (cf. Rom. 2:4–10). Since the church has had difficulty in hearing this from Israel's apostle to the Gentiles, however, it may be expected to have equal difficulty in hearing this from the testimony of Israel's living tradition. It is, nevertheless, the witness of the Israel of God to the commandments as revelation.

2. TORAH-LIFE

i. *Study and action*

"He who does not study deserves death" — Hillel; "Make your study of the Torah a regular habit" — Shammai; "Provide yourself with a teacher" — Gamaliel. The *Pirke Aboth*, the Ethics of the Fathers (a part of the Mishnah), from the first chapter of which these sayings come, attributes to many of Israel's Rabbis the recommendation to study Torah. It also attributes to them many equally strong recommendations to obey the commandments. A life devoted to Torah is a life of study and good works.

The Rabbis spoke of "acquiring Torah" (*Pirke Aboth* 6:6) and said it required forty-eight qualities, of which study leads the list, but reverence, intellectual honesty, love of God, and love of one's fellow human beings are included. Of all these, however, study is the most important; should there ever arise a conflict between the study and the practice of Torah, the Rabbis voted for the priority of study, on the principle that "study leads to doing" (*Kidd.* 40b, Moore II, 247).

The study of Torah, oral and written, together with all the necessary aids to exegesis and interpretation, was conceived as a form of worship, so the proper intention or directedness was considered essential. Torah is to be studied for its own sake, without thought of reward, although the Rabbis were sure it would receive its reward, both in the present world and the world that was coming. It is clear, however, that study was never understood to be divorced from action. Doing Torah was rather seen as the natural and inevitable result of study. "Rabbi Meir said: 'Whoever occupies himself with the study of the Torah for its own sake merits many things; nay more, the whole world is worthwhile for his sake. He is called friend, beloved; he loves God and he loves humanity; he pleases God and he pleases humanity. The Torah invests him with humility and reverence; it enables him to become righteous, godly, upright, and faithful; it keeps him from sin, and draws him near to virtue' " (*Pirke Aboth* 6:1).

It is an important feature of the Jewish concept of the study of Torah that it not be undertaken alone. The Torah was for Israel and Israel was to share it. The Rabbis warned that to study alone is dangerous. One must seek out a teacher, study with colleagues, share one's study with students. The study of Torah was and is a corporate enterprise for Israel. That means it was and is a democratic enterprise: every Jew is encouraged to enter into this lifelong schooling in the revelation of God, and each may learn from and be corrected by the others. "Rabbi Hanina said: 'Much Torah have I learned from my teachers, more from my colleagues, but from my students most of all' " (*Ta'an.*, 7a; M&L, 186).

The rabbinic ideal of a life of study was, one may assume,

just that: an ideal that not every Jew has had the opportunity to realize. It presupposes a tranquility that has seldom been present in Israel's troubled history. Nevertheless, it is and has been the ideal, and it has surely had its influence on the Jewish people, although, in their recent history, more in the direction of secular learning than in the study of Torah, a development that the Rabbis would not have found to their liking.

ii. *The joy of Torah*

Torah-life is joyful. The element of joy in Israel's life with Torah needs particular attention from a church which has for so many centuries falsely depicted the Jewish people as sad and sorrowful. God knows the church has given the Jews more than enough to be sorrowful about, yet Israel rejoices in its one sure possession: the Torah. Indeed and on balance, in spite of all the suffering inflicted upon them, the Jews are a joyful people, able and quick to sing and dance and to make a joyful noise unto the LORD. The Sabbath is a day of joy and welcomed as a bride in the Jewish liturgy. The festivals are also joyful occasions. Only Yom Kippur has no place for rejoicing, being the major penitential feast of the year, and rejoicing is not emphasized on Pesach, in commemoration, the Rabbis said, of the Egyptians who were drowned in the sea. Otherwise, the Festivals are all joyful celebrations.

Special attention, however, should be given the recurring theme of "the joy of the commandment" (see M&L, 202f), the witness of Israel that the actual doing of the commandments is a source of joy, that Torah-living is a joyful enterprise. If the Christian church has seen Torah as a burden, that may be because Torah is not and has never been for the Gentiles what it was and is for Israel: the seal of God's love and presence. The Gentile church may see in Torah what would be a burden for itself, if that is the best it can do. It has no grounds whatsoever to see it as a burden for Israel. Rather, it needs to listen to Israel to hear its witness to the joy of the commandments. And the more commandments the better, since each is a gift of God! Their very multitude testify to the depth of God's love for Israel.

The joy of the commandments covers not only the fulfillment of the particulars of the Torah, but also its study, the careful discrimination of case from case, in short, the legal mind at work.

In this connection "Legalism," Chapter XII, in Z. V. Falk's *Law and Religion* (1981) should be read. Professor Falk shows the variety of ways in which the term "legalism" is used, and brings out the positive connotations when it refers to the legal mind. The legalism of the Jewish halakhist or lawyer includes the pleasure and satisfaction in careful reasoning, attention to common sense, and the pursuit of justice and a good life, a "balanced view of man's relations to God and to his fellowman" (156).

Halakhic study and practice were evidently a joy for the Rabbis, and they continue to be a source of joy for halakhic Jews today. Christian reeducation on this matter could well begin with a reading of David Hartman's *Joy and Responsibility* (Jerusalem, 1978), in order to learn something about halakhic joy 'in the belief that one has the power to act, to direct one's life and assume responsibility,' 'joy in the completion of an act as an end in itself,' and 'joy in going beyond oneself, in being loved and of feeling capable of love' (17f). So may halakhic life be described from the inside.

Israel also bears witness to its joy in the commandments by the element of playfulness which marks its midrachic commentary on Torah, and which forms an often lighthearted counterpoint to its halakhic concerns. Bialik has argued that these two major aspects of Torah, halakhah (regulations and rulings on the application of commandments to specific cases) and aggadah (narratives, legends, admonitions to good conduct, words of encouragement) are complementary, not contrary: "Halakhah is the concretization, the necessary end product of Aggadah; Aggadah is Halakhah become fluid again." "Aggadah gives you air to breathe; Halakhah, a place to stand on, solid bedrock. The one introduces something fluid and liquid; the other something fixed and rigid. A people that has not learned to combine Halakhah and Aggadah delivers itself to eternal confusion and runs the danger of forgetting the one direct way from the will to the deed, from the effort to the realization" ("Halakhah and Aggadah," *Contemporary Jewish Record*, VII, 6, 1944). Both are found in the oral Torah and reflect Israel's joy in the commandments.

Finally, mention should be made of the place of song and dance in Jewish tradition and life, not least, but certainly not only, in Hasidic circles. These expressions of joy root back in biblical times, but Jewish dance has evolved in time and is still changing and alive. (See the entry on *Dance* in *E. J.*) In dance and song, Israel bears witness to the joy of Torah-life.

iii. *The danger of Torah-life*

It has been a long-standing habit of the Gentile church to worry excessively about the misunderstanding and misuse of God's gift of Torah, which it has done usually under the heading of the misleading concept "Law." It has begun by forgetting that the Torah was never given to the church, but was God's gracious gift of love to his people Israel. If there is a problem, a danger in Torah-living, then one would think it should be Israel's problem and danger to think about. In order to hear the witness to the Jewish problem on this matter, the church would do well to forget about its Augustinian "introspective conscience" (Stendahl, *H. T. R.*, 56, 1963) and listen with an open mind to Israel's own witness.

Any good thing can be misused and its purpose misunderstood, as the church should know from experience. Christian faith, which is trust in God's merciful acceptance of the ungodly, has often enough been turned into a work of a misconceived piety and thought to justify the ungodly before God. Torah too can be misunderstood and misused. Strictly speaking, this is not a danger of Torah-living but of living *against* Torah. If one lives *by* Torah, then one could hardly think that obedience to its commandments could win a place in God's affection that one would otherwise not have. The Rabbis, of course, were fully aware of the *appearance* of living by Torah and the pretense to knowledge of it, as is witnessed by their strong condemnation of hypocrisy. Their strongest condemnations, however, were reserved for various forms of *not* living by Torah: for lying, cheating, being unjust, and committing slander, the last being said to be worse than idolatry, incest, and murder put together (*Jer. T., Pe'ah* 1, 1; M&L, 406)!

Reversing what the Rabbis recommend, one could imagine (and surely find examples of) a joyless, fussy, privitized attention to the commandments that was done for the sake of reward and without a thought of him who loved Israel so much that he had graciously given it his Torah. Or, in a more modern idiom, it is possible to debase Israel's humble and joyful knowledge of its election into a self-congratulatory chauvinist nationalism (and this too happens). Again, these are not dangers of living by Torah. On the contrary, they are dangers of *not* living by Torah, dangers for which Torah has been given to Israel as the best antidote.

In this context, a word of caution is in order concerning the talmudic references (or such they have been widely held to be) to seven classes of Pharisees, of whom only the last, "the Pharisee of love," is pleasing to God (cf. Moore, *Judaism*, II, 193f; M&L, 487f). If we could be sure of the meaning of these passages, we would have a nice example of the self-critical sensitivity of those who understood themselves to be the heirs of the Pharisees. Unfortunately, as Michael Cook has argued in a careful article (*J.E.S.* 15, 1978, 441–460), we are on shaky ground as to the meaning of the classes and cannot even be sure that it is the Pharisees that are being classified. Perhaps we had best confine ourselves to less uncertain sources. There is ample rabbinic denunciation of hypocrisy apart from these uncertain passages. In any case, the danger against which the Rabbis warn lies in neglecting, not in following the Torah of God, for the latter has been given precisely to produce the righteousness, love, and humility that God desires in his creatures.

iv. Torah faithfulness

"The righteous shall live by his *emunah*" (Hab. 2:4; cf. Rom. 1:17, Gal. 3:11 and Heb. 10:38). *Emunah* means trust, and it also means faithfulness. Faithfulness to God's Torah is an act of confidence in God. Israel trusts that God loves and has chosen this people, and this trust in turn takes the form of faithfulness to God. Fidelity to Torah, for Israel, is itself an act of trust in God.

One could also translate *emunah* as faith, in the sense of "faith in," not in the Lockian sense of "belief that," although the two different senses (faith or belief *in*, and faith or belief *that*) are not totally separable. If Israel did not believe that God has redeemed and chosen Israel, it would be unlikely that it could trust (believe in) God. Nevertheless, Israel lives its call to righteousness by fidelity to God and his Torah. Israel's fidelity to Torah is its living affirmation of and witness to God.

The Rabbis emphasized that Israel's redemption was for the sake of its fidelity to the commandments, pointing out that the Exodus is mentioned in connection with every single commandment. The reasoning behind this was that God redeemed Israel as his slaves to do his will (*Sifra* 57b; M&L, 117, for this and other examples). Since faithfulness to Torah is only doing that for which Israel was redeemed and chosen, the Rabbis could also add that one could take no credit for it (cf. *Pirke Aboth* 2:9). This teaching of the Rabbis is nicely summed up in the saying, "When you have done all that you have been commanded to do, say, 'We are unworthy servants; we have done no more than our duty' " (Lk. 17:10).

It is a fact that today many, perhaps the majority, of the people Israel are generally not faithful to Torah as the Rabbis of old would have wanted. It may be that a large number are not faithful to Torah in any sense. For all we know, however, this may have been the case in all ages. There is also a wide spectrum of views today, among Jews who do desire to remain faithful to Torah, as to how that should be done, ranging from the most liberal to the strictest interpretations of the rabbinic tradition. Formally speaking, the diversity within the Jewish people is comparable to that among Christians on matters of both teaching and practice, so that one could say that Jews have their own ecumenical problem just as Christians do. The comparison, however, is only formal, for the Jewish people, on the whole, have a remarkable sense of solidarity as a people which has no counterpart among Christians. The concern of American Jews for Israelis finds no comparable American Christian concern for Lebanese Christians, for example — a lack which Jews find hard to understand. Thus despite diversity of interpretation — ranging from that of Jewish secularists who reduce God's Torah to Jewish tradition and custom of ancient times, irrelevant for today except as evidence of developing Jewish values, to strict literalists of the oral Torah — the Jewish people manifest an identity still marked by its relationship to the Torah. Israel's witness of fidelity to Torah therefore continues, and the diversity of the forms that it takes is a reminder that the Torah has been given over to Israel, and that the keeping of it is Israel's human responsibility. How that responsibility is to be exercised can only be settled in the continuing history of the Jewish people in their covenant with the God of Israel.

3. COVENANTAL FREEDOM: "IT IS NOT IN THE HEAVENS"

i. *Israel, wrestler with God and man*

Israel's history has not been tranquil. From biblical times to Roman occupation, in exile under Christian and Muslim rulers, in the modern era, and now also in its partial return to the land, the history of the Jewish people has been a history of struggle. Israel has indeed lived up to the name given to its ancestor Jacob: "Your name shall no more be called Jacob, but Israel, for you have wrestled with God and with men, and have prevailed" (Gen. 32:28). The Jewish people has wrestled with God throughout its history with God, and it has wrestled with its neighbors, and these struggles continue today. How could it be otherwise with the people on whom God has placed his hand, the point of contact between the holy God and this unfinished creation?

The Jews have always been a contentious people, it is sometimes said. The people Israel acknowledge it with their name and by their history. They contend with God and with their Gentile neighbors. They always have and, until Messiah comes, they surely always will. How could it be otherwise, since God has elected this people to be in the world but not of it, called to be different?

There is a reason for the contentiousness or difference of Israel: the covenant. God did not make his covenant with angels, but with the Jewish people. That means that the covenant is to be lived out under worldly conditions, by a people of flesh and blood, no worse but also no better than other peoples. The covenant, then, has a history and is historical. In this sense too, the Torah is not in the heavens. It is on earth, in the not always pure hands of the people Israel. This, be it observed, is not due to an unfortunate earthliness of the Jews, as if they had dragged something heavenly down into the mire of this world. On the contrary, this was God's design. It was his idea to call Abraham and make this covenant in just this creaturely way with his creatures, the Jewish people.

Following the reading of the Torah in the Sabbath Morning Service, the reader recites the following benediction: "Blessed art thou, LORD our God, King of the Universe, who hast given us the Torah of truth, and hast planted everlasting life in our midst" (*P.B.* 370). God chose to plant his revelation in the mud of Israel's life and to give his Torah into the creaturely hands of this people. Were those muddy hands to be ignored, the gift of revelation could never be seen.

The apostle to the Gentiles, in speaking of God's extention of his covenant with the children of Sarah through Christ to include those Gentiles, wrote to them, "For freedom Christ has set us free" (Gal. 5:1). For Paul, entry into that ancient covenant was for Gentiles and entry into freedom, and this is one more evidence of Paul's faithfulness to Israel's tradition. As the Rabbis put it, "When Torah entered the world, freedom entered the world" (*Gen.R.*, Wayera, 53, 7; M&L, 128). The Torah, and therefore the covenant, confers freedom, freedom from service to idolatry, freedom for the service of the one God who will redeem his creation. The covenant and its Torah confront Israel with the one real choice: life or death. It calls Israel to freely cooperate with God.

The covenant, then, is and has been from the beginning a partnership of unequals. Israel has never confused the two partners and has always been careful to mark the utter difference between the Creator and his creatures, and between, more specifically, the LORD God of Israel and Israel. Even its mystical tradition has been cautious of speaking of a *union* of the mystic with God, preferring to speak of *communion* (on this see G. Scholem, *The Messianic Idea*, 203ff, esp. 213f). Nevertheless it is a partnership, and both of these unequal partners have obligations to the other and the freedom to challenge the other concerning the terms of the partnership. The partnership calls for the free participation of both God and Israel.

ii. The affirming argument with God

Israel wrestles with God—and prevails! The love affair between God and Israel must be the stormiest, if most intimate, on record. It begins with a calm little family discussion, most deferential on the part of the creaturely partner, in which Abraham evidently thought it in order to remind God that certain actions would hardly be fitting to the righteous God of the whole world. In a number of the Psalms, Israel asked, in a state of frustration bordering on despair, whether God really knew his business. There were times when, according to Israel's testimony, God had had enough of this and told Israel that it had no right to ask such questions (e.g., God's response to Job out of the whirlwind). But the whole stormy history of intimacy is perhaps best captured in a story told by Elie Wiesel of a pious Jew, one of the victims of the expulsion of the Jews from Spain in 1492.

The man (as I recall the story), was traveling with his beloved wife and two sons, along the coast of north Africa. As they ran out of food and water, they lay down to sleep on succeeding evenings, only to arise one less the following morning. Yet each morning, having buried the one who had died, the man said his prayers to God. First the sons died, then the beloved wife. The man then prayed to God and said that God had now done everything he could to cause the man to abandon trust and the covenant. "Nevertheless," he continued, "even if you kill me, yet I will show you that I am stronger than you, for I shall refuse to abandon you as you have abandoned me!"

Israel has often argued with God, sometimes bitterly, but the very argument affirms the God with whom Israel contends. So in *Night* (1969, p. 44), Wiesel swears that never will he forget those flames which consumed his faith forever, "even if I am condemned to live as long as God Himself!" It is as if Israel could not escape the covenant, no matter what they do. They will be God's elect witness no matter what they intend. As a result, there is what can only be called a spiritual character to Jewish atheism, in the sense that the Jew points to the covenant and the electing God even when he or she aims to point in just the opposite direction. A Jew without faith and disdainful of Torah is not a good Jew, but he or she remains a Jew.

I recall receiving a term paper from a Jewish student in a class in the philosophy of religion which contained a fairly sophisticated argument for the nonexistence of "G-d," as the student consistently spelled the word!

Given the character of freedom that has been Israel's in its covenant with God from the beginning, given the two-sided nature of that covenant, which has always required that Israel contribute to the definition of its further course, one should be hesitant to mark off sharply the present, post-Holocaust and post–founding-of-the-State-of-Israel terms of the covenant from those prevailing in the biblical and in the rabbinic periods. Since last raising this question, we have had to take note of the ambiguity of revelation in the biblical period as well as today, and now we have had to reflect on Israel's freedom in the covenant from the first. Undoubtedly there have been changes. Torah and the covenant are, after all, "not in the heavens" but on earth. They are historical and should be expected to reflect changing circumstances in Israel's life. I find it sounder to say, therefore, not that the terms of the covenant have changed, but that it has been given to some Jews to see more clearly to what extent God has invested himself in Israel and how much he has always meant his covenant with Israel to be a genuine partnership. The more Israel exercises covenantal freedom, and the more it argues with God, the more does it affirm Israel's LORD.

iii. The stubborn argument with the church

Through fidelity to Torah, Israel affirms God; it also says No to the church. It said No to the church in the first century and it has kept on saying No. The church has acknowledged Israel's written Torah, but it has given it its own interpretation, according to which the church is the true heir of the promises to Israel, and the church is now the true Israel of God. Israel says No. It contradicts the church simply by remaining faithful to Torah. More exactly, it contradicts the church's claim to be Israel and to be the sole custodian of the revelation of the God of Israel by continuing to be true to itself. The church is confronted by actual Israel in the stubborn, continuing life of the Jewish people.

In its argument with the church, Israel charges that the church has spiritualized and moralized God's election and promises to his people. Whereas God's Torah testifies to God's choice of an actual, physical people, and his promises to their biological descendants, the church has wanted to speak only of the spiritual descendants of Abraham and has turned his promises into spiritual gifts, as if God could not morally commit himself to anything so ambiguous as the contentious Jewish people. From Israel's point of view, the church has lacked the courage to confess God's genuine engagement with the creaturely world of physical birth and a people of flesh and blood. That the covenant of the holy God could be continued by an act so crude as circumcision has been thought impossible by a spiritualizing church. Yet on the testimony of God's Torah, this is just the measure of God's involvement in his creation. The God of Israel, whom the church claims to serve, is not above engaging himself to a historical people in the flesh and blood of their creaturely existence, for so, according to Torah, he created them, and that which he created is good. Israel raises the question for the church whether it really knows this God.

In its argument with the church, Israel also charges that the church has spiritualized and moralized God's commandments and therefore the service that God requires of his creatures. It has decided that only some of God's commandments, the ones it defines as "moral," are to be obeyed, whereas the others, which it defines as "ceremonial" may be ignored or given a spiritual — that is, symbolic — interpretation. Its arguments in defense of this distinction are all grounded in its pretention to having displaced the Jewish people as God's Israel. Having made that mistake, how else was it to acknowledge the authority of scriptural commandments that obviously referred to the Jewish people and its life in fidelity to Torah? But this was only to compound the mistake. In failing to see that Torah was given to *Israel*, not to the Gentiles, the church had to spiritualize and moralize the commandments so as to make them relevant to a Gentile church that correctly knew itself to have been called by God to serve him in a Gentile way. The result was a weakening of the commandments: as given to Israel, they demanded creaturely obedience in the totality of life; as interpreted selectively by the church, they served to enforce a division between religious and secular activity. The scope of God's claim was thereby restricted to the moral and spiritual areas of life.

In its argument with the church, Israel therefore bears a witness that concurs with that which was given to the church in Jesus Christ: God's word has truly been given into the hands of men, and God's servant is called to place his or her total existence into the service of that word. God's gracious commanding word is not in the heavens; it is here on earth. And that word asks for concrete, creaturely responsibility. In saying No to the church, Israel is in effect asking the church whether it really knows the One it confesses as the Son of God.

4. JESUS AND THE TORAH: INCARNATE COMMAND AND RESPONSE

i. Jesus and Torah

Faithfulness to Torah confronts the church not only in the witness of Israel, but also in that person who most centrally represents Israel to the Gentile church, the Jew Jesus of Nazareth. The attitude and practice of Jesus with respect to Torah are matters calling for some caution, for much of what the Gospels tell us explicitly about these matters is to be found in passages recounting controversies with "the Pharisees," or "the Scribes and Pharisees," and there is reason to wonder whether these may not come from a time when the Pharisees became the dominant force in Jewry and so the major competitors of the young church, namely after the destruction of the Temple in 70 C.E. Whether early or late, these passages provide conflicting testimony. Not one of them, however, suggests that Jesus was other than a Torah-faithful Jew of his time.

According to some passages, Jesus followed what could be called a liberal interpretation of the Torah, more liberal, that is, than those with whom he is reported to have debated. On the premise that the Sabbath was made for man (see M&L 711 for an argument that this teaching is older than its rabbinic and Markan sources), for example, Jesus reportedly permitted his disciples to gather food and also cured a man with a withered hand (Mk. 2:23ff; 3:1ff). In neither story nor in any other did the apostolic tradition preserve a memory of Jesus himself ever having violated a single commandment. Indeed he is sometimes reported as having been more strict than those with whom he was arguing, as for example on the permissibility of divorce (Mk. 10:2f). In every case, however, the sanctity and authority of the Torah is unquestioned. What is debated is its interpretation.

There are other passages in the Gospels according to which Jesus taught the importance of fidelity to Torah in terms fully compatible with the later Rabbis. To the young man asking what he should do to inherit eternal life, Jesus answers that he should keep the commandments (Mk. 10:17–19 and parallels). To the "lawyer" asking the same question, in Luke's version, Jesus asks what Torah teaches, and, receiving in reply the answer that one should love God and one's neighbor, is reported to have said, "Do this and you shall live" (Lk. 10:25–28). There is also the passage from the Sermon on the Mount which could have been attributed to any of the Tannaim: "Truly, I say to you, till heaven and earth pass away, not the smallest letter of Torah nor even the smallest part of a letter will pass away until it is all accomplished. Whoever then relaxes one of the least of these commandments and teaches men so, shall be called least in the kingdom of heaven; but he who does them and teaches them shall be called great in the kingdom of heaven" (Mt. 5:18–19).

On the basis of this uncertain evidence, we may cautiously conclude that Jesus, as we should in any case expect from a teacher of Israel, called his people to greater not less fidelity to the Torah of God. The interpretation of Torah was probably a more open question in Jesus' time than it was in the rabbinic period, and even then it was a matter of some discussion, as the Talmud makes unmistakably clear. The range of the spectrum of interpretation in the first century is none too clear, as is consequently our understanding of where Jesus stood within that spectrum. It seems evident, however, that he stood for the sanctity, validity, and authority of God's Torah for Israel. We may reasonably conclude that it was for him the word of God from which his people lived, and that until the realization of that for which the Torah had been given, the completion of God's unfinished creation, the coming of the reign of God, Torah would continue to be the lamp that guided Israel's path.

ii. *Righteousness of God apart from, not contrary to, Torah*

Beyond the question of Jesus' own attitude to Torah, there

lies the theological question of the relationship in God's design between Jesus and the Torah. The basis for the church's understanding here is the teaching of Paul, the apostle to the Gentiles. We take as central to Paul's teaching the two complementary confessions that in Christ the righteousness of God has now appeared apart from Torah, and that consequently Christ is the goal of the Torah (Rom. 3:21 and Rom. 10:4).

As was argued in Chapter IV (4, iii and iv), the righteousness of God that had now appeared was the fulfilling of the promise to Abraham that he would be the father of many nations (*goyim*, Gentiles, Gen. 17:5). This was taking place through the preaching of Paul to the Gentiles that God had laid claim upon them in Jesus Christ. God had done this as an act of sheer generosity, and the only appropriate response was for the Gentiles to accept the righteousness of Jesus Christ as God's way of reconciling them to himself. The word of their forgiveness, giving life to those who were dead in their sins, was to be trusted. From now on, they were to cling to the robe of this one Jew (Zech. 8:23) who was given for them as their way to the Father.

Thus had God's righteousness come to the Gentiles, not by way of the Torah, as it had for Israel, but quite apart from or without reference to the Torah. (Paul may reflect what seems to have been a conviction of the apostolic witness, that Jesus' obedience was, so to speak, first of all to God, and secondarily to Torah.) As a good Jew, however, Paul was sure that God is one, and therefore that he who had called Israel to the Torah was the same one who had called the Gentiles to Jesus Christ, and both as a means of calling all to himself. This new enactment of God's righteousness was therefore not contrary to the Torah. Indeed, it was announced in the Torah. So Paul could say that for the Gentiles — and he was called to be the apostle to the Gentiles — Christ was the goal toward which the Torah tended. That is to say, as the Torah was God's righteousness for Israel, fulfilling part of God's promise to Abraham, so Christ completed what had been begun with the gift of Torah, by fulfilling the rest of that promise. What was begun with the Torah reached its goal with Jesus Christ, that the whole world should come to the knowledge of God and within the sweep of God's mercy (Rom. 11:32).

Because Paul was obedient to his calling to preach to the Gentiles, we learn much from his letters about the consequences of the Torah for Gentiles, but practically nothing about its role for Israel. It would have been utterly out of keeping with his faithfulness to his calling had he shifted his attention to Israel's relationship to Torah and asserted, as many have translated him, that Christ is the end — as *finis* — of the Torah for Israel. The sentence in question (Rom. 10:4) comes in the context of Paul's agonizing over Israel because it refused to see and so acknowledge this new manifestation of God's righteousness in Jesus Christ, because, in other words, Israel did not recognize that God had now accepted (justified) the Gentiles whose only claim was Jesus Christ. Instead, they continued to think that only those in the covenant, their own covenant with God, were the recipients of God's mercy, not seeing that the goal of the covenant — and so of the Torah — was that all should be embraced by mercy. They failed to see that their own Torah pointed to the opening up of the covenant of God's mercy to all peoples. Christ could not have been the termination of a Torah which pointed, so Paul was convinced, to his coming. He could be and was the goal of that which began with Torah, the fulfilling of the promises of God to Abraham. Christ is the *telos* of the Torah because in him God has said Yes to all of those promises which the Torah contains (2 Cor. 1:20).

In attempting to understand how Paul saw the relationship between Jesus and the Torah, it is essential to keep clearly in mind that he was primarily addressing Gentile readers, those to whom he believed himself sent by God through Christ. We catch only glimpses of his understanding of the role of Torah for Israel, as when he listed the Torah as one of Israel's special gifts from God (Rom. 9:4), said it was binding upon every Jew (Rom. 2:23, 24), and claimed it was the Jew's great advantage over any Gentile (Rom. 3:1, 2). These positive assertions of the

Torah's place in Israel's life, it should be noted, were written over twenty-five years *after* Easter! That means that for Paul, the value of the Torah as God's gift to Israel had not been changed by the coming, death, and resurrection of Christ.

There may be some truth in Luke's story that Paul was *accused* of teaching "all the Jews who are among the Gentiles to forsake Moses, telling them not to circumcise their children or observe the customs" (Acts 21:21), but there is not a single verse of any of Paul's authentic letters to support the charge. The opponent(s) of the author of the Epistle of James clearly misunderstood Paul on another vital matter, and the author of the Second Epistle of Peter was disturbed about unspecified misunderstandings of Paul (2 Pet. 3:16). Acts 21:21 reflects another important misunderstanding of Paul that has lived on in the major exegetical tradition of the church.

Paul surely thought that Christ was God's confirmation of his promises to Israel (2 Cor. 2:20, Rom. 15:8), and that God's forgiveness and mercy in Christ would be effective for all the world, Israel included (Phil. 2:10, 11; 1 Cor. 15:22; Rom. 11:32). As the apostle to the *Gentiles*, however, Paul's interest was in what Christ had accomplished with respect to the grim consequences of the Torah for the seventy nations that, having rejected it when it was offered from Sinai, were consequently under its curse. Christ had removed that curse completely (Gal. 3:13) as well as the confinement and restraint of Torah's cosmic rule over the nations (Gal. 3:23). God had given life to dead Gentiles and made them heirs of Abraham, not by means of bringing them into the relationship to the Torah that was Israel's, but by means of Christ's death and resurrection for them (Rom. 3:21–25; 6:4–8).

The conclusion to which Paul leads us concerning the relationship between Jesus and the Torah is therefore a dual one. With respect to Israel, Jesus is God's confirmation of Torah, in all its holiness and goodness, and with all its promises. With respect to the Gentiles, Christ has died and been raised to free them from the curse of Torah as it works apart from the covenant, bringing them within God's covenantal love and mercy.

iii. *The incarnate word of command*

Israel's fidelity to Torah is a witness to the church of the incarnation of God's commanding word. "It is not in the heavens" (Deut. 30:12). God's commanding, life-giving, creative word is given into the hands of sinful men and women. It is given into the midst of and meets men and women in the smallest details of their daily life, laying God's sovereign claim upon the totality of their existence. God's word has been addressed to human beings, according to Israel's witness, in the language of human beings. The result is that they can hear it, understand it, and do it.

"The word is very near you" (Deut. 30:14). Torah is "from heaven," that is, from God himself, but it is all given through Moses. Torah is God's own word, but it is all in the words of Moses. There is therefore no need to seek out anything hidden or esoteric: "The secret things belong to the LORD our God; but the things that are revealed belong to us and to our children forever, that we may do all the words of this Torah" (Deut. 29:29). He who hears the words of Moses hears the words of God. The intimacy of God's commanding word, in justice and in mercy, is assured by the intimacy of God, Torah, and Israel. The nearness of the words of Torah are the sign of the nearness of God. No intermediary can come between, because God has made that unnecessary.

We have cited the midrashic parable of the king who begged to come live with the princely bridegroom to whom his only and beloved daughter was married and from whom he could not be separated. So God's intimacy with his beloved Torah assures his closeness to Israel. To this we may add another: "If a pupil is ill, and the teacher goes to visit him, the other pupils go before to announce the coming teacher. But when God went to visit Abraham, he went first, before the angels (Gen. 18:1, 2). Is there anyone more humble than he?" (*Tanh.*, Wayera, 2, f.31b; M&L, 30). The Torah, then, far from being an intermediary between God and Israel, binds them together.

The incarnation of God's commanding word, to which Israel's fidelity testifies, confirms God's primary witness to his Gentile church of this same reality in the Torah-true Jew, Jesus of Nazareth. This is the theme of the Prologue of the Gospel according to John: God's word which was with God and is God became flesh and dwelled among us. "The Torah was given through Moses, [and now God's] generosity [also for the Gentiles] and trustworthiness [to his promise to Abraham, testified to in that Torah] have happened in Jesus Christ" (John 1:17). The author of the Gospel according to Matthew has Jesus confirm the gift of Torah to Moses by having Jesus teach also from a mountain (5:1, 2), stressing the commandments of the Torah (5:19) and the necessity of doing the will of God (7:21), a will given in words that can be done (7:24). Israel's witness to the incarnate character of God's commanding word is therefore a reminder to the church of that which God has shown it in Jesus Christ: God's word is not in the heavens!

The Gentile church, however, has been called into existence by the word that has drawn near to them in Jesus of Nazareth. As God has bound himself and Israel together in his incarnate Torah, so he has bound the church to himself in Jesus, who is God's own commanding word to his church. As Israel has God very near to it by having God's Torah very near, so the church draws near to God by drawing near to the Torah-faithful Jew Jesus.

iv. *The incarnation of creaturely responsibility*

Israel's fidelity to Torah is a witness to the church of the incarnate character of creaturely responsibility. God is not primarily concerned with our religious life, whatever that may be — Israel knows no distinction between religion and life — but with the totality of our creaturely existence. If we know ourselves as God's creatures and God as our Creator, of course, then all our life will be lived in awareness of (with directedness, *kavvanah*, toward) God. But this has as much to do with our work and commerce, with war, politics, and social relationships, as it has to do with our prayers. In all that we human beings are and

do, in all of our flesh and blood existence, we are called to loving responsibility to God and to our neighbor. That is Israel's
witness.

Israel makes this witness to the creatureliness of responsibility to God by the mundaneness, so to speak, of its life in Torah.
From rising in the morning until retiring at night, the day is
punctuated by the cycle of Daily Prayers, which include blessings to be said while washing one's hands, going to the bathroom,
putting on clothes, and so on, in the morning, to prayers for
peace and a safe rest at night, all interspersed with Psalms and
passages from the Torah. The week in turn is marked off by
the celebration of the Sabbath, making a distinct break from the
pattern of the other six days, and the year in turn is punctuated
by the various festivals and fast days. Time and the cycles of
day, week, month, and year are thereby taken up into Torah-
shaped existence.

In addition, that most central aspect of creaturely existence,
eating, is totally shaped by the rules of *kashrut*, with its fine distinctions of what may and may not be eaten, and of what may and
may not be cooked and eaten with what. The church has tended
to sneer at this practice, but in doing so it misses Israel's witness
to God's concern for human responsibility in the concrete reality of our creaturely life. When the church's concern for obedience
to God in the actual continuity of daily life, when its righteousness
"exceeds that of the scribes and the Pharisees" (Matt. 5:20),
then — and not until then — will it be entitled to form an opinion
about the Jewish observance of *kashrut*. Until then, it might
ponder the words attributed to Rabbi Abba ben Yudan: "All
that God has declared to be unclean in animals he has pronounced desirable [*kasher*] in men. In animals he has declared
'blind or broken or maimed or having a blemish' to be unser-
viceable (Lev. 22:22), but in men he has declared the broken
and crushed heart to be desirable." To this Rabbi Alexandri
added, "If a private person uses broken vessels, it is a disgrace
to him, but God uses broken vessels, as it is said, 'The LORD

is near to the broken hearted' (Ps. 34:18)" (*Lev.R.*, Zaw, 7:2, M&L, 476).

Further, Jewish life has been shaped by the study of Torah, regarded as the highest form of service to God's revelation. Learning, meditating on, and discussing together the Torah of God has contributed markedly to the development of Torah-shaped Jewish lives. As the Rabbis taught, one who studies God's Torah will be concerned for justice and mercy, the primary attributes of Torah's author. Israel's life with Torah has thus helped to shape the Jewish people to God's command in the flesh of its creaturely existence.

The Gentile church has been called to the service of the God of Israel by the Spirit through Jesus Christ. The Spirit that has called them is the Spirit of the giver of the Torah, but he has called the Gentiles, not directly to Torah, but to the Torah-faithful Jew Jesus. The form of that call is therefore the command of Jesus, "Follow me." Consequently, the apostolic witness of the church has stressed the obedience of Jesus to the will of God, a theme that is basic for the Apostolic Writings. Jesus' faithfulness to God, which is often presented in the Gospels as having taken the form of explicit faithfulness to the Torah of God, is fundamental to the existence of the church, because Jesus is the way for the Gentiles into the covenant of the God of Abraham. The Gentile church has its relationship to Torah by means of holding onto Jesus Christ in his obedience to God and as the church's authoritative teacher (rabbi) who interprets God's commandments to them.

The relationships between Israel, Torah, Jesus, the church, and God, which have just been discussed, can be clarified by placing the varying terms in a series. Israel is called to obedience to Torah and therewith to God. Jesus was called to obedience to God and therewith to Torah. The church is called to obedience to Jesus and therewith to God. The church is therefore called to be attentive but not subject to Torah. Looking directly to Jesus, it should be casting a frequent glance over its shoulder, as it were, to God's Torah, which is of God as Jesus is of God.

Consequently, the church is called to let itself be shaped by Christ, even as Israel is called to let itself be shaped by the Torah. Christ-shaped life (Gal. 4:19; 1 Cor. 6:15, 12:13, 27; Phil. 2:1, 2, 5; Eph. 4:15) is God's will for his church, as Torah-shaped life is his will for Israel. Israel's fidelity to Torah reminds the church that this calling relates to all the details of its life, from giving a cup of cold water to one in need (Matt. 10:42) to visiting the sick and welcoming a stranger (Matt. 25:34–36). Israel's witness to the church is that God's concern for the totality of life is to be taken seriously in all its detail. Israel can therefore remind the church of that unity and intimacy of God's gracious commanding word and the creatureliness of human response which the church was first invited to see in Jesus.

CHAPTER EIGHT

Israel and Jesus

God's word to Israel of his involvement in his creation for its good is embodied for the Gentiles in the Jew Jesus of Nazareth. His way prepared and made possible by Israel's Sages and Pharisees, he proclaimed, was and is the word of God's ever new generosity to all his creatures. This word calls Israel to a renewal of its Torah-faithfulness. It calls the church to follow Jesus as the way into the service of God.

1. ISRAEL AS THE CONTEXT OF JESUS

i. *Israel of the first century*

As God is one, so his word is one. God's word to the Gentiles in Christ cannot therefore contradict his word to Israel of his involvement in his creation for its good. On the contrary, it can only confirm it. God's word is one, but it comes always concretely and particularly to each addressee. To Israel it first came and comes ever anew as Torah. To the church it first came and comes ever anew embodied in Jesus Christ, the Jew from Nazareth. The new expression of God's word in Jesus, however, is one with God's word to Israel, for Jesus is one with Israel.

Jesus' relationship to Israel consists first of all in the fact that he has it as his essential context, theologically as well as historically. For the church it will never be adequate to attempt to account for Jesus of Nazareth on historical grounds alone. The Jew Jesus was certainly the product of historical circumstances, as is every human being, but this Jew as the embodiment of God's word was there as an act of God. "In the beginning was the word, . . . and the word happened as flesh." In the beginning was the word that made history, not the history into which the word was spoken.

This is the profoundly important insight formulated in the doctrine of the enhypostatic character of the man Jesus. The doctrine stresses that the Jew Jesus appeared on the scene of history only because the divine word entered into and thereby made history, the history of this man. It is a standing warning from its patristic authors against beginning with a "Christology from below." As the event of Jesus began "from above," so should the church's reflection upon that event.

On the other hand, that God chose to speak his word in this Jew, whose life took shape in a particular time and place, must also receive its due share of attention. Fundamental to that shaping was the world of Judaism, the situation of Israel into which Jesus was born, for in this context God was pleased to begin the fulfillment of his promise to Abraham that he would become the father of many Gentiles. It is not sufficient, therefore, to stress that Jesus was born a Jew. We must be as specific as God was: Jesus was born a Jew in *eretz Yisrael* in the first century of the Common Era, a Jew of that time and of that Judaism which was taking shape under the guidance of Israel's Sages and Pharisees.

Politically, it was a bad time for Israel. It had lost effectively its independence to the power of Rome in 63 B.C.E., when Jerusalem was taken, and the city was again captured by Roman soldiers twenty-six years later. Then began forty years of relative but stern stability under Herod, acting as the Roman emperor's agent. During Herod's reign, the land was ruled as his private possession; the Torah had no standing in his eyes as the constitution of the state. Although Herod rebuilt the Temple to appease the people, he also placed the Roman eagle on its facade! In the sixth year of the Common Era, Rome stabilized the situation following Herod's death by making Judea into a province of the empire, governed by a Roman procurator, never fully independent of the Roman governor of Syria. Again, a relative stability lasted until the appointment in 26 C.E. of Pontius Pilate as procurator. For ten years, until Pilate's recall, oppression and resistance grew, sowing the seeds of the revolt that ended with the siege and destruction of Jerusalem and its Temple in the year 70. The historical context of Jesus was therefore one of political subjugation, Roman occupation, and the rise of resistence fighters — the Zealots.

It was a sign of the times that one of the Twelve [apostles] was called Simon *the Zealot*, and that two of the others were nicknamed "Sons of Thunder." It has also been speculated that Judas *Iscariot's* name may be a corruption of *sicarii*, the name given frequently to the Zealots. Finally, Jesus was reported to have been crucified between two *lestai*, "the official Greek designation for Zealots" (*E.J.*, 16, 949). Jesus could hardly have been a Jew of his time without having some contact with the Zealots. He was executed by the very power which the Zealots were fighting.

Israel was to survive this painful period of its history, including the traumatic defeats at the hand of the Romans in 70 and 135 C.E., primarily because of the work of the Sages and the Pharisees. With these terms we designate those individuals and schools of students of the Torah who carried through the reforms initiated by Ezra, who worked to establish the Torah in the daily lives of as many Jews as possible, not only in Jerusalem and Judea, but throughout the Diaspora. In spite of Herod and in spite of Roman occupation, there were those who were producing a Torah-true Israel in the first century of the Common Era, and their efforts obviously shaped the life of Jesus and those about him.

Outstanding among these shapers of Israel were Hillel and Shammai, the first of the Tannaim, and their schools. Outstanding among their institutions was the Synagogue, which brought the teaching and study of the Torah even to the small Galilean village of Nazareth. God chose as the context for the shaping of his incarnate word the developing Judaism of the Tannaim. He chose the context of the Judaism being shaped by the Pharisees.

ii. Jesus and the Pharisees

Given the fact that there is no scholarly consensus even on the definition of the Pharisees, Michael Cook (*J.E.S.*, 1978, 449) has concluded that we simply do not have the evidence to make a judgment about the historical relationship between Jesus and the Pharisees. The difficulty arises from the fact that the various sources are not in agreement, and each source is inconsistent. This clearly applies to the Gospels. The author of the Gospel according to Matthew was able to lump the Pharisees together with the chief priests (21:45; 27:62) and even with the Sadducees! The Gospel according to Mark says that the Pharisees, this time lumped together with the "Herodians" (whoever they may be supposed to have been), wanted to destroy Jesus, yet the Pharisees are not even mentioned in Mark's passion narrative. Luke, on the other hand, reports several incidents in which Pharisees appear as friends of Jesus. It seems a fair surmise that by the time the Gospels were written, the historical memory of the early church had lost track of the Jewish leadership in the time of Jesus. The vehement accusations of hypocrisy, primarily in Matthew 23, may well have had much more of a base in the developing conflict between the church and the Synagogue after 70 C.E., than it had in the life of Jesus.

Perhaps from Jesus, or at least from early in the life of the church, comes the judgment that the Pharisees "sit in the seat of Moses" (Matt. 23:2), meaning that they are to be accepted as authoritative teachers of the Torah. If such established figures as Hillel and Shammai could disagree about the interpretation of the Torah (our records refer primarily to halakhic judgments, admittedly), it seems perfectly conceivable that Jesus would have been in disagreement with at least some of his contemporaries. Nevertheless, similarities of some of Jesus' teaching and some of the later rabbinic teachings, suggests that he was not completely outside of the general movement for the reform of Israel which is associated with the Pharisees, but even so tentative a conclusion must remain hypothetical.

The problem of Jesus and the Pharisees resides in the fact that the polemics ascribed to him by the developing early tradition has been canonized in the text of the church's Gospels. When one recalls how minimally the results of over a century of biblical criticism have penetrated the minds of most Christians, one can scarcely expect a ready openness to the distinction between words ascribed to Jesus by the polemical concerns of the evangelists, and words which are more likely to have been those of Jesus himself. The church's leadership has a long and difficult task ahead of it to stimulate the sort of teaching and preaching that may someday shake the unreliable picture of the Pharisees which the Gospels, taken alone, inevitably produce. The only conclusion that is fair to the serious difficulties of historical reconstruction in this matter is that Jesus came into conflict with at least *some* Jews of *some* standing in Jerusalem. Just who they were and just what the issues were may never be known. In the end, in any case, it was Pilate who stepped in and settled the matter in a thoroughly Roman way.

iii. Jesus for Israel: the intention

We are on more solid historical grounds when we turn to the concern that Jesus had for his people. The texts are few, but they are consistent in reflecting an exclusive, positive concern for Israel and a negative view of the Gentiles. They would seem to be reliable, for a Gentile church would not have invented them, nor is it likely that the church would have preserved them had they not carried the authority of the earliest apostolic tradition.

The message of Jesus was for Israel — who else would have understood a proclamation that "the kingdom of God is at hand" or the call to "repent"? Jews knew that language; the Gentiles did not. Jesus spoke in the language of Israel, to Israel and about Israel. If that is not clear enough on the grounds of the most rudimentary linguistic analysis, it is made sharper in his instructions to the Twelve, as Matthew tells it: "Go nowhere to the gentiles, and do not enter a Samaritan town, but go instead to the lost sheep of the house of Israel" (10:5, 6). The intention here implied is made explicit in a saying reported in Matt. 15:24, according to which Jesus said, "I was sent only to the lost sheep of the house of Israel."

Jesus' concern for the lost sheep included a concern that they be accepted back by the rest of the flock, but it was never in conflict with his concern with the flock of faithful Israel. That is clearly the point of the last part of his parable of the Prodigal or Lost Son. To the elder son, who had "never disobeyed [the father's] command," the father said, "Son, you *are* with me, and all that *is* mine *is* yours." (Lk. 15:29, 32, 31. Cf. Peter von der Osten-Sacken, *Grundzüge*, 81.)

Further evidence of Jesus' intention to address his message to and work for the reform of Israel is provided by the story of his encounter with a Gentile woman seeking his help for her demonically possessed daughter (Mk. 7:25–30; Matt. 15:22–28). The response Jesus makes is that "It is not right to take the children's bread and throw it to the dogs." The children of Israel, and Gentile dogs! Luther's remarkable sermon on this text, for all its depth and power, fails to open up this distinction, so typical of the Jews of Jesus' day—*and of Jesus himself*! The bread that Jesus had to offer was for the children, not for dogs. It was perfectly consistent, then, that in one account of Jesus' eschateological vision, the Twelve would be seated on twelve thrones judging—that is, supervising, ruling—"the twelve tribes of Israel" (Matt. 19:28), with no mention of the Gentiles.

Finally, we may add Jesus' lament over Jerusalem, reported by Matthew and Luke (Matt. 23:37; Lk. 13:34): "How often have I yearned to gather your children, as a hen gathers her brood under her wings." No clearer expression is possible of an intention to recall Israel to its holy covenant with the God of Israel. Clearly, Jesus is presented in one of the oldest strata of the apostolic tradition as having Israel, and the world only by way of Israel, as the focus of his concern and mission. In this, he stood in the line of Israel's prophets, a Jew arguing with other Jews about what it means to be God's beloved people.

Jesus' self-understanding, as presented by Matthew, is reflected in other words of the evangelists. The Gospel of John has John the Baptist say that he came in order "that [Jesus] might be revealed to *Israel*" (1:31). The Gospel of Matthew quotes Micah 5:2 as a prophecy that the Messiah would be born in Bethlehem and would "govern my people Israel," which prophecy the evangelist saw fulfilled in Jesus (Matt. 2:6). To this may be added the evidence of the Gospels that Jesus was given the title "Messiah" by his early followers (all Jews, of course), the sense of which is precisely captured by the author of Luke-Acts when he has the disciples ask the risen Jesus (Acts 1:6), "Will you at this time restore the kingdom to Israel?" The question balances the hymns of praise at the beginning of Luke's story, in which Mary affirms that with the approaching birth of Jesus, God "has helped his servant *Israel*" (1:54), and Zechariah confesses that God "has visited and redeemed *his people*" (1:68). Jesus, according to Luke, was to be also "a light of revelation for the Gentiles," but only because he was first of all "for the glory of [God's] people Israel" (2:32).

The evidence is clear and coherent: as the Gospels present him, Jesus was sent by God, and understood himself to have been sent by God, and was remembered by the church as having been sent by God, to *Israel*. Judging by the intention of the sender and the sent, Jesus was for Israel. Only incidentally and as exceptions did the Gentiles have any place in this plan, for dogs *do* have their rights. So the Gentile church preserved a memory of Jesus — which it soon proceeded to forget.

iv. Jesus for the Gentiles: the consequence

What the church *has* remembered is Jesus as light for the Gentiles, the incarnate word of God's free generosity in opening to them the door of his heart by opening their hearts to trust in the faithfulness of Jesus. Despite his intentions to go only to the lost sheep of the house of Israel, Jesus' way led instead primarily to the Gentiles, "strangers to the covenant and its promise, without hope and without God in the world" (Eph. 2:12). During Jesus's life, of course, and for a short time after Easter, all his disciples and followers were Jews. The Jesus movement began as a wholly intra-Jewish affair. Before long, however, the mission to the Gentiles began and was to transform the movement into so fully a Gentile one that Jews within it became an oddity.

The turning point for this transformation was God's "revelation of Jesus Christ" to the Pharisee Shaul (or Saul, called Paul in Greek), with the commission "to preach him among the Gentiles" (Gal. 1:12, 16). It is possible that Barnabas, and perhaps others, preceded Paul in this work, but Paul marks the turn because he was recognized by the Jerusalem leadership as having a place in the Gentile mission comparable to Peter's standing in the Judean churches (Gal. 2:6–9). At the least, Paul made a mighty contribution to the transformation of the Jewish Jesus-movement into the Gentile church. The so-called "Great Commission" of the risen Jesus to his disciples, with which the Gospel according to Matthew ends (28:19–20), commanding them to go make disciples of all the Gentiles, must surely have come from a time when the Gentile mission was under way and accepted. From our limited sources, we would have to say that Paul, and his co-workers in the Gentile mission, were the first we know of to have received this particular commission!

In interpreting the significance of Jesus, or his own calling as the apostle to the Gentiles, Paul never referred to Jesus' self-understanding as having been sent only to the lost sheep of the house of Israel. In one letter he asserted that "Christ became a servant to the circumcised" (Rom. 15:8), an assertion which we shall examine with care in Chapter Eleven, but otherwise, his texts for understanding the purpose or intent of Jesus and of God are all drawn from the Jewish Scriptures. There is where he read of God's promise to Abraham that he would be the father of many Gentiles (Gen. 17:4, 5), and there he read of the servant of God to whom God said that he would be a light to lighten the Gentiles (Isa. 49:6). The transformation of which we have spoken and in which Paul played so large a role was, as Paul saw it, the unfolding of a purpose as old as the covenant with Abraham. Jesus was for the Gentiles because God had always planned to bring them into his covenant purpose. What was new in his day was the fact that this was beginning to happen, and Jesus was God's way of bringing this about.

v. Jesus, Israel, and the church

So, what shall we say to this? Did God change his mind? Did he send Jesus to restore Israel, as Jesus appears to have taught, and then decide instead to make him the righteousness of God for the Gentiles, as Paul said? Or did Jesus misunderstand his sending? Or are we to be instructed in a divine hermeneutics, to the effect that everything depends on the consequences and nothing on the intention? No, such naive questions arise from a too superficial grasp of the whole complex of Jesus, Israel, and the church. If we begin from a careful understanding of Paul, one that never forgets that he was a Jew to the core, I believe that the contradiction between the intention of Jesus to confine his ministry to Israel and the Pauline mission to the Gentiles can be shown to be one only in appearance.

According to Paul, as we have seen, God's whole purpose in Jesus Christ was to carry through the fullness of the promises to Abraham and the prophetic vision of the covenant of Deutero-Isaiah. In Christ God was opening up a tremendous enhancement of that which he had begun with Israel. It was therefore coherent that this opening to the Gentiles should take place from within the very heart of Israel. It was really not incidental to Paul's thinking that Jesus was a Jew (Rom. 9:5) and that he was "descended from David" (Rom. 1:3). The new righteousness of the God of Israel that was coming to the Gentiles came from the heart of the covenant and so from the heart of Israel.

The church depends, therefore, on the unqualified Jewishness of Jesus, that he was totally of and for his people. The church depends upon Jesus having been and being the heart of Israel, for by being bound to Christ by the Spirit, it is bound to Israel in its covenant of mercy with God. Jesus is Israel-for-the-church, the way God has summed up and presented for the Gentiles the visible aspect of his covenant. Only a Jesus, therefore, who was totally for his own people could also be God's way for the Gentile church.

These reflections throw light on Paul's assertion that Christ is the goal of Torah (Rom. 10:4). The Rabbis were to teach that Torah is for the sake of Israel, as we have seen. Their teaching was that Israel in its fullness and its obedience to God was the goal for the attainment of which the Torah was given. So Paul, who saw that, with the obedient death of Jesus, God had begun to make good on his promise to Abraham, could see in Jesus the Israel which was Torah's goal: Jesus as Israel is the goal, the *telos*, of the Torah, for he is Israel effectively enlightening the Gentiles, so that all those who trust this new righteousness of God may be accepted by God. No wonder the Gentile church should preserve the memory of Jesus being concerned only for the lost sheep of the house of Israel! It is a memory forgotten by the church at the peril of the loss of recognizing its own continuing foundation!

2. JESUS AS ISRAEL: THE WORD OF THE HUMILITY AND GENEROSITY OF GOD

i. *In Creation*

Israel's holiest word is, "Hear O Israel, the LORD is our God, the LORD is one." As God is one, so Israel testifies, God's word and work are coherent. The word to which the church testifies, which has been spoken so intimately and powerfully into the hearts of so many Gentiles in Jesus of Nazareth, the word which they have discovered to be embodied in this Jew, could not be contrary to God's word of Torah to Israel. Because Jesus stood with Israel and for Israel, he has been able to bring to the Gentiles God's word to Israel. He has re-presented to the Gentile church Israel as God's chosen witness to the humility and generosity of the Creator.

Israel's witness, re-presented in Jesus, is to the humility and generosity of God, not simply in being Creator, but also in the intimacy of God's involvement with that which he created. The God of Israel, whom Jesus, along with the Rabbis, called Father, is utterly different from the deity of the Deists, who wound up the clock, so to speak, and then left it to itself. On the contrary, the God of Israel and the Father of Jesus Christ is a God ever anew involved with his creation, doing in it again and again what he did to bring it into being.

Ever again the God of Israel has proved himself to be the one "who calls into being the things that are not" (Rom. 4:17), as he was "in the beginning." So from Abraham's old body "as good as dead" and "the barrenness of Sarah's womb" (Rom. 4:19) he brought forth the child of promise. He created a living people out of deadened slaves of the Egyptians. He is the one who from a valley of dry bones calls forth a mighty army (Ezek. 37), a prophecy of redemption the fulfillment of which Israel has experienced in varying degrees again and again. As Israel, Jesus was a notable case of the confirmation of the promise of redemption, in that once again, God gave new life to the crucified one. Finally, by binding Gentiles to this one risen Jew, God has confirmed the re-presentational identity of Jesus with his people Israel, confirming in him the election of Israel to be a light for the Gentiles, thereby bringing them from death into life. The God of Israel, according to Israel's testimony and confirmed by that of Jesus, is not merely concerned for his creatures; he is involved, committed to, and active within his creation for its good.

The creature Jesus of Nazareth could hardly, as a Jew, as Israel for the Gentiles, bear any other witness. The whole of creation is God's, and therefore nothing creaturely is foreign to him. Creaturely life is good, not only because the Creator made it, but also because that is where God is working out his purpose. Israel's witness, confirmed by that of Jesus, is to a Creator who is not above loving his creation and who is free enough to work generously within it and to leave it room to work with him. Such as been and is Israel's witness, rooted in its own life with the God who calls into genuine being things that are not. Jesus of Nazareth demonstrated his calling to be Israel by bearing just this witness to the humility and generosity of God the Creator.

ii. In the covenant with Israel

Jesus stood with and stands for his people also in bearing witness to the humility and generosity of God in his covenant with Israel. God commands, but he also listens. He judges, but he hears the complaints and petitions of Israel. He who is the King of the Universe is willing to be called the God of Israel. He is the living God as the God of the fathers, of Abraham, Isaac, and Jacob (cf. Matt. 22:32).

Israel, and therefore also Jesus as Israel, testify to the humility of God in graciously drawing near to Abraham, to Moses, to the prophets of Israel, indeed to every humble soul of this people, in order to draw them to himself. He is a God whose glory is to be close to the humble and meek, a theme recurring in the rabbinic line, "Is there any more humble than he?" (e.g. *Tanh.*, Wayera, 2, f.31b; *Tanh.B.*, Bereshit, 2a; M&L, 30, 474.) Such a God cares for every one of the lost sheep of the house of Israel (Matt. 18:10–14; Lk. 15:4–32).

The God of Israel and the Father of Jesus as Israel manifests his humility and generosity above all in his willingness to make his purposes dependent on Israel's participation and cooperation. That willingness is embedded in the covenant of Sinai. That covenant was and is God's invitation to Israel to take up the work of God, to share in his holiness, and so to help complete the unfinished creation. God may not need Israel's help; in his freedom, however, he has generously chosen to make Israel's help necessary to the accomplishment of his purpose for his creation. His generosity consists in giving Israel a task, the definition of which is his Torah. "This do and you will live" (Lk. 10:28; cf. Matt. 19:17b and par.). His humility consists in accepting Israel as his co-worker, and, along with Israel, also Gentiles bound to Jesus as Israel. The Jewish apostle to those Gentiles could therefore say, "Work out your own salvation with fear and trembling, for God is at work in you both to will and to work for his good pleasure" (Phil. 2:12–13). That could always have been said to Israel. Now Paul could say this to Gentiles, because God had made Jesus to be Israel for them.

iii. In Jesus Christ

If God was not too proud nor too niggardly to talk with Moses, "by far the meekest man on the face of the earth" (Num. 12:3), and that, "face to face as a man speaks with his friend" (Exod. 33:11; Deut. 34:10), then it was fitting of him to speak his mind in the birth, life, and death of one who was meek and lowly (Matt. 11:29). According to the witness of Israel, God has ever been close to those who were humble and lowly (Isa. 57:15; cf. Ps. 9:12; 10:17; 37:11; 147:6; Matt. 5:5; Phil. 2:8–9). God's work in Jesus Christ is of this same humility.

Because of his total obedience to God, Jesus would seem to have refused every title or ascription of honor (Mk. 10:18). It seems highly unlikely, therefore, that he would have understood himself as embodying the word of God, in any other sense than as being faithful to Israel's calling and consequently full of and living from the words of God as found in the Scriptures. Jesus as the embodied word of God had to have been a Gentile discovery of the post-Easter Gentile church. In the resurrection of Jesus, the Gentiles discovered that which Israel had learned in the Exodus/Sinai event: God was the One who gave life to the dead and called into existence the things which were not. Like Israel, moreover, they learned this in their own flesh, in that they themselves had been called from the death of paganism into a new life in the service of the living God. They therefore saw that this was God's word from "in the beginning." Now, "with the coming of the fullness of time" (Gal. 4:4), this creative word of God's willingness to involve himself with his creation, exemplified in his election of Israel as his people, was embodied in the risen one who had been awakened to new life from death on the cross. Nowhere was God's glory more clearly displayed for them than in the face of the one hanging from a Roman cross (2 Cor. 4:6). That is just "the likeness of God" which is "the glory of Christ" (4:4), that God's word in Jesus is of the humility and generosity of God. The oneness or closeness of Jesus and the one he called "Father," to which the theological tradition has referred in speaking of "the divinity" of Jesus, consists in this, that he bodied forth the humility and generosity of a God willing to share existence with his creation, and willing to share the work of completing that creation with his little people Israel.

Jesus Christ recapitulates and embodies Israel's reality, its relationship to God, and its calling to be a light for the Gentiles. So the Gospel according to Matthew has Jesus relive Israel's sojourn in Egypt to be called back to the land by God. And the theological tradition that saw in Jesus the re-presentation of Israel's prophets, priests, and kings, also was responding to this reality. Behind such witnesses stands the figure of Jesus-as-Israel, serving Israel in its mission to the Gentiles and being for them the place at which is seen the humility and the generosity of God. Just so is Jesus the *telos* of the Torah.

3. GOD'S WORD IN JESUS TO ISRAEL: TORAH-GENEROSITY

i. The lost sheep of the house of Israel

"I was sent only to the lost sheep of the house of Israel," Jesus is reported to have said (Matt. 15:24), and he instructed his disciples to leave the Gentile alone and to go instead "to the lost sheep of the house of Israel" (Matt. 10:6). From the parable of the lost sheep (Matt. 18:12–13; Lk. 15:4–6), as well as from common sense, it is clear what one does about lost sheep: one brings them home. The good shepherd goes looking for the strays and brings them back to the fold. The image of the Good Shepherd has become so familiar — and domesticated — for Christians that a Christian theology of the people Israel needs to rescue it from its generalized use in the church and return it to its setting in the ministry of Jesus. He was talking about lost *Jews* and said that he was sent to find them and lead them to be good Jews. The lost sheep for which he was concerned all belonged to and needed to be brought home to the house of *Israel*.

What shall we say, then, was God's word in Jesus Christ to Israel and to its lost sheep? The answer is evident enough. To Israel he said, "Open your hearts to receive back the strays. You are all Israel by the mercy and forgiveness of God, so take back the strays, welcome those that were lost, and rejoice with God over each lost sheep that was lost and is found again" (Lk. 15:3–7, 8–10, and 11–24, the parables of the lost sheep, the lost coin, and the prodigal son; cf. Matt. 18:23–35). And the word to the strays was, "Return, come home, for God dwells with him who is lowly and contrite. God wants to forgive and accept the sons and daughters of his people who return to him, for theirs is the reign of God that is coming and they shall inherit the earth" (Matt. 5:4–5; Jn. 8:3–11; Lk. 18:10–14).

Had not Israel heard this word before, both in the Torah of Moses and from its prophets? Of course it had, and it was to hear this same word from its Rabbis in the following centuries. The word of God that was embodied in Jesus for Israel was the same word of the One God from the beginning of all his ways with Israel: You shall be my people and I shall be your God. The commanding word of God to Israel that sounded from Sinai and was echoed by the prophets of Israel, was just that word which was taken up and repeated by the rabbi from Nazareth: be Israel!

ii. *Torah renewal in the heart*

Be Israel! That means to accept the dangerous but humbling fact of God's election. It also means *kavannah*, an inner directedness of the whole person toward God. And finally, it means fidelity to Torah. When those three things are added together, Torah renewal takes place and Israel becomes Israel, doing the will of the Father, loving him with all its heart and soul and mind, and loving and serving the neighbor. That was what Israel was called to be from the beginning, and by so being Israel, that was the way to cooperate with the Creator in the work of completing his unfinished creation.

At a dark moment in Israel's history, dark inwardly as well as externally, Jeremiah had been called to proclaim just this reality of Israel as central to God's future. God, spoke the prophet, announced that he would make "a new covenant with the house of Israel and the house of Judah" (Jer. 31:31). What was it that was to be new about it? Surely not a change of partners! The God of Sinai was the speaker, and God's election of Israel would stand: the new covenant would be between just those partners of the "old" covenant. "I will be their God and they shall be my people" (v. 33). It will therefore be not a different but a renewed covenant between these partners — nothing is even suggested about the Gentiles! Only this time — one might say, with this renewal or reformation — "I will put my Torah *within* them and I will write it on their hearts." Consequently, none will need to teach a neighbor, sister, or brother, "for they shall all know me" (v. 34), "and I will remember their sin no more" (v. 34). Note that this new covenant is not only with Israel, but that it is still a covenant and the Torah is still its center. There is an eschatological ring to this prophecy, but it leaves the impression that Jeremiah believed that this renewal of the Torah covenant could and would occur in time.

Prompted by his conviction that the reign of God was about to begin, Jesus called, here and now, for just such a renewal of the covenant as Jeremiah had proclaimed. In the following centuries, the Rabbis had the same goal in view, and with their houses of study and the Talmud as aids, they developed as near an approximation to putting the Torah within the Jewish people and writing it on their hearts as is possible to imagine in a preeschatological setting. Jesus, with his "Do this and live," stood clearly in the line, which ran from Jeremiah to the Rabbis, of concern for a reformation of Israel that would go to the heart and constitute a renewal of the Torah covenant between God and his people.

iii. Torah renewal from Ezra to Jesus

Jesus stood not only within the major line of workers for the renewal of the Jewish people; he is presented, at the least in the Gospel according to Matthew, as having stood on the stricter side (usally associated with the Pharisees) of that broad movement of reform which Ezra initiated and which came to flower in rabbinic Judaism. The evidence for this conclusion is the following:

1. On the matter of the Torah, Jesus is reported to have held that "till heaven and earth pass away, not the smallest letter of Torah nor even the smallest part of a letter will pass away until it is all accomplished. Whoever then relaxes one of the least of these commandments and teaches men so, shall be called least in the kingdom of heaven; but he who does them and teaches them shall be called great in the kingdom of heaven. For I tell you that unless your righeousness exceeds that of the scribes and Pharisees, you will never enter the kingdom of heaven" (Matt. 5:18–20).

2. In keeping with this view, Jesus is reported to have taken a stricter stand on divorce than the Torah itself (Matt. 5:32; cf. Deut. 24:1–4).

3. Jesus felt free to offer his own interpretation of Torah, much in the manner of the developing tradition of oral Torah in his time that was to become the Mishnah. Frequently his interpretations build "a fence around the law," as when he takes the prohibition to kill to include a prohibition against anger (Matt. 5:21–22), evidently on the basis of rabbinic logic: do not be angry and then you will not come near to killing. He is presented as having given a looser interpretation on other occasions, as in the story of his permitting his hungry disciples to pick and eat grain on a Sabbath (Matt. 12:1–7).

4. Jesus seems to have shared the negative view of Gentiles and followed the policy of Jewish separation from Gentile that was a feature of Ezra's reform movement. We have seen this in his reference to Gentiles as dogs in the story of the Syrophoenician woman. It is echoed in another saying: "Do not give what is holy to dogs, and do not throw your pearls before swine" (Matt. 7:6).

5. Finally, there is his call for an *imitatio Dei*: his disciples are to be perfect (or unlimited in goodness) as God is perfect.

The evidence places Jesus in the line that began with Ezra, passed through the Pharisees, and culminated in the rabbinic tradition embodied in the Talmud. God's word in Jesus to his people Israel was thus in fundamental accord with that of the written and the oral Torah.

iv. The messianic hope: Torah as God's generosity

Jesus' message began, according to Mark (1:15), "This is the time of fulfillment. The reign of God is at hand!" In an important sense, namely in the cosmic, apocalyptic sense which these words presumably had for most Jews of that day, he was wrong. The radical, cosmological transformation of the world, or even the messianic liberation of Israel from Roman domination, did not take place. Yet in another sense, Jesus' preaching of the kingdom or reign of God was fully consistent with Israel's trust in the generosity of God who had given Israel his beloved Torah. As God had chosen Israel and bestowed his Torah on it solely out of his generosity, so would he come to be its Redeemer.

The good news of the reign of God, as the Gospels present it, is of this same generosity in the coming redemption. The reign of God will be God's gift: "it is your Father's good pleasure to *give* you the kingdom" (Lk. 12:32). Messianic hope, for Israel and for Jesus along with his people, has been hope in a future that God would define. It would therefore be the future determined by the covenant and therefore bring the renewal of creation, making good all that was lacking in the present. It would also come as judgment, however, so it mattered in an ultimate sense what one did in the present. Hence the urgency of Jesus' preaching as expressed in many of the parables of the kingdom: the time to start living by God's generosity was right now!

In sum, God's word in Jesus to his people Israel was, "Be Israel better than you are being it in practice." Practice, not theory, was Jesus' concern. Of the two sons in the parable (Matt. 21:28–31), only he who actually did the will of his father is fit for the reign of God. A tree is known by its fruit (Matt. 12:33; cf. 7:20). Torah is a gift of God's generosity, a light for Israel's feet. Jesus knew this and Israel knew this, or should have known it on the basis of the teaching of the Torah itself. Jesus' word to Israel was, "Live by that generosity."

Jesus stood before and in the midst of his people as God's model of "being Israel." So he stands today and is recognized as at least *a* model by some Jews. By no means does he stand there in order to draw his fellow Jews away from being Jewish for the sake of some "goyish" enterprise called Christianity. On the contrary, Jesus' call to his people in his lifetime and to this day is rather that they be Jews as he was a Jew, that they be *God's* Jews.

"I tell you that Christ became a servant to the Jewish people in the cause of God's truthfulness, in order to confirm the promise made to the patriarchs *and* in order that the Gentiles might glorify God for his mercy" (Rom. 15:8–9). Jesus' service in his earthly ministry consisted above all in confirming the promises to the patriarchs that their descendants would forever be God's people, ever again renewed and reformed by him who was for ever their God. His life embodied the message that God is to be trusted. His risen ministry, as the apostle to the Gentiles discovered, was to open Gentile eyes to see that the one through whom they were called to serve the living God stood in just this faithful relationship to his people. Seeing this, realizing that the people of the Torah lived by God's mercy just as they did, the Gentiles would glorify God for his mercy to Israel as well as for his mercy to themselves. Thus *all* of God's promises to the patriarchs came to be confirmed by the Jew Jesus Christ. His servanthood was indeed in the cause of God's truthfulness.

4. GOD'S WORD IN JESUS TO THE CHURCH: JESUS-LIKE GENEROSITY

i. Conformation to Jesus

The church should be amazed that there was and is also a word of God in Jesus for the church, seeing that it became so soon the Gentile church. To his disciples, all fellow Jews, he said, "Follow me! Be God-obsessed Israelites; be the Israel to which God has committed himself. Ingest the Torah, so that it is written in your hearts." But what about the Gentile church? Are there any crumbs for the dogs?

There are not only crumbs; there is bread and wine! God had indeed a word to say in Jesus to the Gentile church, and its opening words are, "He is risen!" The church lives from that word, but why it is able to do so depends on the fact that he who was raised is the one who was crucified. The first step in understanding God's word in the risen Jesus to the church is therefore to understand his death.

Jesus was executed by Roman soldiers at the orders of the Roman procurator, Pontius Pilate, in an all-too-typical Jew–Gentile confrontation. Gentiles do not want to be bothered with Jews. Jews are uncomfortably different, for a reason that Gentiles do not understand: their election. From a Gentile persepective, the Jews, with their talk of being God's chosen people, simply presume too much. The Gentile world has and has always had its own agenda, and if the Jews will not adapt themselves to it (as Herod did quite well, Jesus not at all), then Gentiles tend to want to get rid of them. So it was with Jesus; he was crucified under Pontius Pilate.

The apostle to the Gentiles explained this to his Gentile readers in Rome by saying that Jesus was "handed over [to his executioners, or to death] for our falling away," or our missteps, or offenses (Rom. 4:25a). What was this falling away, these missteps or offenses, which led to the cross? The cross itself offers the answer. The cleft between the executioners and the condemned Jew puts into focus, first of all, the cleft between the Jews and the Roman world. That is to say, the cleft dramatized is that between the people of God and the rest of the world, between God's purpose, expressed concretely in his calling of Israel as his people, and God's incomplete and unenlightened creation. Jesus died because the world refuses to come to terms with God's purpose in calling Israel — except on its own violent, self-centered terms.

Paul claimed that in accepting this defeat, God was showing his love for the world (Rom. 5:8), for Jesus' death was God's way of reconciling the Gentile world to himself (5:10; cf. 2 Cor. 5:19). Paul's good news, however, does not end at that point, with the death that both brings into focus and challenges the split between God and his purposes on the one hand, and the corruption of God's good creation on the other. Jesus, he wrote, "was handed over for our offenses *and raised for our being-made-right*" (Rom. 4:25).

How does this happen? How is it that the world with its corruption was put to death in Christ's death and was made right by his resurrection? Paul's answer may be summed up in two words: *"in him,"* and here we are confronted with the heart of the mystery of Israel and of Jesus' role as Israel-for-the-Gentiles. God set Jesus in the world to be there for all the others by making him to be Israel in exemplary fashion. Jesus could be for all the others because Israel was and had always been for all the others. Abraham had been called for the sake of the world. Now in Jesus this calling of Israel had been put into effect for all the Gentiles. He is God's way for the Gentiles to come before him in praise and thanksgiving. This new Gentile reality takes place totally in him.

There are two sides to this "in him." On the one hand, Jesus confirms and exemplifies Israel's role of making God known in the world. He is given to the church as its way to see God, so that in seeing him they will see the Father (Jn. 14:9). In his face they may see the glory of God (2 Cor. 5:6). The Gentile church has really no grounds at all for speaking of "the divinity of Christ." What does it know of divinity that is worth knowing? Rather, the church is given to know Jesus as the Son of a God otherwise unknown to it, the God of Israel. Donald Baillie was at least correct in arguing (*God Was in Christ*, 1948, 66ff) that the church properly confesses that God is Jesus-like, rather than the reverse. The Gentile church knows the God of Israel only as the Father of Jesus-as-Israel.

On the other hand, Jesus is the way for the Gentiles to come to God, "the way, the truth and the life," the only way for those who were far from the God of Israel to come close to him (Jn. 14:6). The church is invited to see itself as God has decided to see it: its only identity is "in him." Hence the call to "put him on" (Rom. 13:14; Gal. 3:27), to desire only to be "found in him" (Phil. 2:9), for only in him have the Gentiles any part in God's purposes. Such is the mystery of Israel's election for the sake of the world, now exemplified for it in Jesus Christ.

Conformation to Jesus, therefore, is the secret life of the Gentile church. Nothing else it does or that happens to it matters other than that it discover and rediscover itself in him, that it allow God to shape it to him. That is the reality of the life of the church, lived in trust in the Jesus-like generosity of God who has made this possible. Such is God's word in Jesus to the Gentile church.

ii. Co-formation with Israel

By God's design, in Jesus the Gentiles are made fellow citizens with the holy people of God and so members of the household of God (Eph. 2:19), sharing in the promises of and knowing and serving the living God. All this is theirs in him who is their way to God. The God to whom Jesus is the way, however, is the God of Abraham, the God of Isaac, and the God of Jacob. He is the God who has bound himself to the Jewish people in an everlasting covenant. The Gentiles can never come into the company of this God, therefore, without finding themselves in the company of the Jewish people.

The historical manifestation of this theological reality has been on the whole unhappy, especially for the Jewish people. Since the church consists overwhelmingly of Gentiles who worship the God of Israel, its intimacy with the Jewish people is unavoidable. The church, however, has only grudgingly and negatively acknowledged this relationship, at least until most recent times, and the Jews have paid it only the slightest attention. With both sides resisting the reality of that which the God of Israel had done through Jesus Christ, it is not surprising that their relationship has proved over the centuries to have been so fruitless and often destructive.

The God of Israel, however, has destined the Gentile church to be conformed to the Israelite Jesus. That destiny, then, must entail the co-formation of the church along with the people Israel. We are beginning to see the signs of this co-formation taking place in the present. After centuries of ignoring or despising each other, both the church and the Jewish people are becoming aware of each other and beginning to recognize that their destinies are intertwined.

If it be the will of God that the formation and ever new reformation of the Gentile church and the Jewish people take place in harmony and in mutual interaction, it has barely begun to happen. The challenges which they should be facing together are still largely confronted separately. Here and there, however, Christians and Jews are beginning to see that they can learn from each other and help each other move ahead on the path that lies ahead. In reshaping their understandings and practices with respect to relations between the sexes, family life, political responsibility, and many other matters, the long-delayed calling of both to co-formation is at least beginning to be heard. One of the more difficult challenges which they will do well to face together is that of their understanding of the way in which the God of

Abraham, Isaac, and Jacob has been and is at work in the People of the Book (Islam), and in the peoples of many books (Hindus and Buddhists, and others).

Co-formation means growing together in two distinct senses. It means each partner growing alongside of the other, with each one maintaining all that makes it distinctive. But growing together also means coming closer. For the Gentile church and the Jewish people, this will mean growing closer in understanding and love, the love that confers freedom on the other to be its distinctive self. Paul concluded his most extended reflections on the relationship between the church and the Jewish people by seeing them united only in their disobedience to God and, more importantly, in God's overriding mercy (Rom. 11:32).

iii. *Israel's light and enlightened Gentiles*

God's light for the Gentiles has taken the form of Israel represented in the Jew Jesus Christ. The church has Israel in the person of Jesus. It does not follow, however, that the church has therefore no need of the Jewish people themselves, for Jesus is Israel for the church in the reality of his own identity with his people. Jesus is Israel for the church as a Jew and so as one of and one with his people. To this day, the church needs that people in order to have Jesus as he is, as a Jew, not a Gentile. Jesus is Israel by the will of his Father, but he bears this calling always as one who stands with his people in their covenant with God.

In the confessional statement of the Rhineland Synod of the Evangelical Church of Germany (1980, cf. above, pp. 12f), it is asserted that Jesus "as the Messiah of Israel . . . binds the peoples of the world to the people of God." We have certainly argued that Jesus binds the Gentiles to the Jewish people, but does he do so *as the Messiah of Israel?* Our answer is No. The Messiah of Israel, a figure concerning which we may learn from the Jewish tradition, has never been conceived to play such a role. If the synodal assertion was meant to depend upon a Christian rather than a Jewish definition of "Messiah," it would have been helpful to have made that explicit. It might have been said, then, that as the *church's* "Messiah," Jesus binds, and so on. This, however, breaks the evident intent of the authors of this statement, which was to insist that the very Jewishness of Jesus is essential to the church.

The confusion of the synodal assertion can be overcome by leaving out the ambiguous term "Messiah," focusing instead on the solidarity of Jesus with his people as reflected in his concern for the lost sheep of the house of Israel and his longing to draw Jerusalem into a movement of renewal. Therein lies the real link between the peoples of the world and the people of God. The solidarity between Jesus and his people, however, his identity with them — in a word, his Jewishness — does not rest, finally, on a presumed intention of Jesus for which the historical evidence is unsure. Jewishness in not primarily a matter of intention. The Jewishness of Jesus and his solidarity with his people depend first of all on his birth to a Jewish mother, and then on his circumcision according to the Torah. Jesus is one with his people and stands for them in the midst of the Gentile church, because by God's election, the word of the God of Israel became Jewish flesh, because in the Jew Jesus God was confirming all his promises to his people.

The light that enlightens the Gentiles was and is a Jewish light. To ignore the people of Jesus is to ignore the risen *Jew*. Or it is an attempt to have the risen one as something other than the crucified one that he is. For the Gentile church to turn its back on the Jewish people is to turn away from the word and work of God. It is a refusal to hear the gospel of God.

5. THE RABBI OF NAZARETH AND THE RABBIS OF JAVNEH

i. *The renewal of Israel: Jesus*

In an ultimate sense, as well as in the context of the situation of the church in Galatia in the first century, "what matters is neither circumcision nor uncircumcision, but a new creation"

(Gal. 6:15). Neither Israel nor the church are ends in themselves. They both exist for the sake of the renewal of God's threatened creation. Those who can receive this word can stand under the blessing which follows (v. 16): "Peace and mercy be upon all who walk by this rule *and* upon the Israel of God." The blessing is pronounced over a church that knows that it lives by God's act of mercy in Christ, and over the Israel of God that has always existed by God's mercy. Both stand in the service of creation's renewal.

Renewal, or repentance (turning about, turning back to God, *teshuvah*), was central to the life and message of Jesus. Even with the maximum renewal, we would be unworthy servants, he said, so that humility and penitence were in his eyes better than piety (Lk. 18:10–14, the parable of the tax collector and the pious man). As we have seen, Jesus was deeply concerned for the renewal of God's people Israel. Historically considered, however, Israel's renewal was to come by way of the work of other rabbis than the one from Nazareth. Conceivably, this may have been no surprise to God, if it may be put so. Israel was locked in a struggle with Rome that was hardly conducive to a movement of renewal, and the Jewish preoccupation with Roman oppression had the indirect result of allowing the Gentile Jesus-movement to get started. But once the Gentile church was on its way, a new means had to be found to reform Israel. That means arose out of the ashes of the Temple in the form of Rabbi Johanan ben Zakkai and his colleagues and successors, the Rabbis of Javneh.

If it is true that what matters is neither Israel nor the church but the renewal of creation, then renewal will be an unending need for both Israel and the church. If God's will is the renewal of his partners in the covenant so that they can be his co-workers in the renewal of his creation, it matters less how it comes about than that it come about. *Semper reformanda*, always to be reformed, always in need of reform, always being reformed by the power of God's mercy: that title should stand over Israel and the church. That is what their co-formation is about. It is needed today as it was needed in the first century. Jesus willed the renewal of Israel and brought about a new creation among the Gentiles. The renewal of Israel came about otherwise.

ii. The Renewal of Israel: the Rabbis of Javneh

Rabbi Johanan ben Zakkai escaped from the besieged Jerusalem and was permitted to establish the rabbinic school or academy in the town of Javneh. The work that he began led to a major reform of Israel which made it possible to live the covenant and serve God without the hitherto essential Temple, and even without access to Jerusalem and much of the Land. Perhaps more important, it led to a reform of the Jewish people which wrote the Torah in their hearts, or at least in their memories and in every detail of their daily existence. The Jewish people that the church has known for almost its whole existence is the product of that renewal.

If one attempts to define the spirit or heart of this re-formation of the Jewish people, what we might call the spirit of Javneh, one can see how closely it matches Jesus' call to renewal. To blow the Shofar in Javneh was to sound a new note in more than a literal sense. It was to grasp the moment as immediately subject to God. The rabbis of Javneh called for Israel to turn to God in a new way (the old way, in which the Shofar could only be sounded from the now-destroyed Temple, being blocked), and thus to turn back by stepping ahead. It was a call to dare, here and now, to discover new ways to live by God's election and to be Israel even in utterly new circumstances. In its own way, the reform begun at Javneh was at least as radical and as basic as that for which Jesus had called.

The Javneh reformation, which was to produce rabbinic Judaism, kept the Jewish people together and vital until well into the modern era. Compared to it, the so-called Reform movement of nineteenth-century German Jewry was modest, even superficial, in no way as radical theologically. The occurrence of the newer movement, however, as well as the Haskalah (Enlightenment) movement of eastern Europe, pointed to the fact that Israel was indeed moving into new circumstances. Time may show that the rise of Zionism was more important than either movement and more attuned to the new situation in which the Jewish people was to find itself in the twentieth century. Like the reformation of Javneh, it was built on old foundations, yet it challenged the Jewish people to discover new ways in which to be Israel. The existence of the state of Israel is evidence enough of its creativity, as it is a call to that same degree of creativity in the covenant which was exercised at Javneh.

The shape and substance of renewal in the present, however, is no clearer and no less evidently needed for Israel than it is for the church. A Zionism torn between secularism and religious nationalism strikes one as too much of the nineteenth century to be helpful for the present and future, whereas Orthodoxy (basically, the rabbinic Judaism arising from the Javneh reformation) seems, with rare exceptions, to have lost too much of its original creativity to grasp the new moment confronting Israel and the church together. Nevertheless, Israel remains the people of God, and if God has renewed and reformed his people before, he can do it again, and perhaps in our own time. For Israel has a special role to play in the awakening of the church, so recently begun and so tentative, to its relationship to the Jewish people. Its service to the renewal of the church may even contribute to Israel's own renewal.

CHAPTER NINE

The Witness of Israel's Rejection of Christianity

Jewish faithfulness to Torah involves a rejection of traditional Christianity and of the church's traditional understanding of Paul's gospel. Israel therewith witnesses before the church to the incarnate, temporal involvement of God in Creation, in his election of Israel, and in his call to both Israel and the church to work and pray that his reign of righteousness come and his will of justice and love be done on earth.

1. REJECTION OF CHRISTIANITY, NOT OF JESUS OR EASTER

i. Jesus and his contemporaries

One could come to the conclusion, from reading the writings of the church over the centuries, that the Jewish people as a whole had met, heard, turned their backs on, and rejected Jesus of Nazareth. Once expressed, however, the thought appears to be historically impossible. The vast majority of the Jewish people who were the contemporaries of Jesus could not possibly even have heard of him, since they lived dispersed around the Mediterranean in all parts of the Roman Empire. Even of those who lived in *eretz Yisrael*, only a small number would in all probability have heard of the Galilean preacher and healer.

Whatever historical reality may underlie Mark's story of the crowd stirred up by the chief priests to demand of the tyrannical Roman procurator that he crucify a fellow Jew, it is clearly the passion narratives of the Gospels, which we shall discuss shortly, that have fed the idea that the Jewish people as a whole rejected Jesus. The Gospels themselves, however, provide hints to the contrary. Jesus seems to have had a considerable following in Galilee and a remarkably large following, for a Galilean, in Judea and Jerusalem. There does not appear to be evidence to support a historical rejection of him by his people. The evidence points rather to a good number of followers and disciples, and then also to some enemies.

If a general rejection of Jesus by his contemporaries seems unfounded, so also does a general Jewish rejection of the Easter faith of the earliest community. On the contrary, what evidence we do have points to large numbers of Jews joining the post-Easter Jesus movement. It was clearly a small minority movement within the Jewish people, but it was nevertheless made up at first entirely of Jews. Had there been no Jewish believers in the resurrection of Jesus, there would have been no later church. The Jewish people did indeed come in time to reject Christianity—i.e., the Christian church and its faith and life in Jesus Christ—and it did so as a whole and officially. That cannot be said with respect either to Jesus himself or to the peculiarly Jewish message of his resurrection. With respect to both of these, Jews took different positions.

ii. *The trial and death* (cf. G. Sloyan, *Jesus on Trial,* 1973)

There is little room for historical doubt about how Jesus died: it was on a Roman cross under a Roman sentence. There is considerable room for doubt, however, about the role played by some Jews in the events leading up to his arrest and execution. It is difficult for one not in the field of New Testament scholarship to tell, but there seems to be some agreement that the story of a night trial of Jesus by Jewish authorities has many doubtful elements to it. The Sanhedran would not have met by night, and a charge of messianic claims would not have been one of blasphemy. The story may reflect a memory that Jesus did have enemies among influential Jews in Jerusalem, but who they were and what part they played is lost to us behind the theological constructions of the passion narratives by the Evangelists.

We are on more solid ground when we come to the death of Jesus. Crucifixion was a Roman form of execution especially appropriate for political crimes. If the story of the title affixed to the cross is based on fact, then the charge against Jesus was in effect that of treason, of leading a rebellious movement intent upon replacing Roman authority with a Jewish king over Judea. Although the charge seems wide of the presumed intentions of Jesus, it would have made sense in the context of much of Jewish messianic hope at the time. If Jesus was in fact arrested by night and crucified the next day, his trial or hearing could not have been thorough. Pilate did not have a reputation for scrupulous attention to justice. It would have been enough for him that this unlettered Galilean was the center of a movement with messianic overtones. It would have been characteristic of what we know of Pilate to act quickly and brutally before this new movement got out of hand.

The story of Jesus' arrest and of his trial before Pilate, as we have them in the Gospels, however, go out of their way to show that Jews were more responsible for the course of events than Pilate. Having been written some forty to sixty years after the event, their authors may have been reading back into Jesus' time the conflict which they were having with the Jewish authorities of their own day. They may also have wished to play down the role of the Roman procurator in the death of Jesus. For whatever motives, they have left the church with a story according to which Jesus went to his death because of the cries of a crowd (Mark), even of "the whole people" (Matthew), shouting, "Crucify him!" That Pilate would have bothered to consult such a crowd, much less allow the release of a murderer and rebel, Barabbas, seems utterly improbable.

iii. Easter, the Jesus-movement and Israel

If we have not yet found what it is that Israel rejected in the life and death of Jesus, we do not find it either in the Easter appearances of Jesus nor in the Jewish Jesus movement that resulted. Resurrection was a Jewish idea, a specifically Pharisaic belief. Unusual for Judaism in the early Easter faith of the Jerusalem community was the conviction that this had taken place in the case of Jesus alone, without inaugurating a total transformation of the world, or, minimally, the restoration of Jewish sovereignty in their land. Since the earliest community undoubtedly expected the appearance of the Risen One in glory to inaugurate the new age in the immediate future, however, this variation on Jewish belief could not have seemed radical to them.

In any case, Easter faith could not have been an insuperable hurdle to many Jews, for those believers are said to have continued as a vital and growing community in Jerusalem, free to worship in the Temple with their fellow Jews. Luke's figures may be exaggerated but his report of its rapid growth may have some basis in fact. At least in its beginning, in any case, what was to become the Christian church was a Jewish movement within the range of Jewish sects or tendencies possible in this period of numerous competing groups (on the period, see J. Neusner, *First Century Judaism in Crisis*, 1975). It should be remembered that the "Normative Judaism" of the Rabbis had not yet taken shape.

The Jewish No to the church, then, is not to be found in the origins of the church. That No came indeed to be spoken, but it was spoken on the basis of further developments both in the church and in Israel. In its origins, the church was too small and too much a part of the complex of early first-century Judaism to be a threat to it. As long as the church was made up of Jews who believed that Jesus would come to redeem Israel from foreign domination and inaugurate the new age of the sovereignty of the God of Israel, even that a decisive step toward that day had been made with his death and resurrection, other Jews might be skeptical, but there was no reason for conflict. Once the church began to make headway among Gentile God-fearers, however, beginning to reap the harvest of Pharisaic proselytizing efforts (on this, see G. Sloyan, *Face to Face*, IX, 1982, 14ff), and doing so on the basis of an understanding of Torah increasingly at odds with that which was developing in Pharisaic (and on its way to becoming rabbinic) Judaism, responsible Jews had to say No, for such a development threatened the existence of the Jewish people and its covenant with God.

2. REJECTION OUT OF FIDELITY TO TORAH

1. *Torah as the issue*

The first sign of a conflict between at least some Jews and the new Jewish Jesus-movement came at an early date. Paul said (Gal. 1:13) that before he received his calling "to preach [Christ] among the Gentiles," he "persecuted the church of God and tried to destroy it." Had he acted on his own, or was he acting with the backing of some Jewish authorities, as the author of Luke-Acts has it (Acts 9:1, 2), and as part of a larger persecution (Acts 8:1)? Paul does not say. If there was a larger persecution, why had it started? Again, we do not know. In neither case are we told the cause of this persecution. Perhaps Paul gives us a hint by adding that he was "extremely zealous for the traditions of my fathers" (Gal. 1:14). That could mean that, as an eager champion of the oral Torah, he had persecuted this new sect for its lax practice, but this is reading much out of a few words. The possibility that the account in Acts of larger and continuing persecution may be colored by the later conflict between the church and the synagogue is great enough to leave us in doubt about the nature and above all the cause of the early conflict.

Paul is also the source for our knowledge of further hostility, only this time Paul was on the receiving end of it. He tells us (2 Cor. 11:24f) that five times he had received "the forty lashes less one" (cf. Deut. 25:1–3) "at the hands of the Judeans (or Jews)," but he does not tell us what the disputes had been about. Three times, he said, he was beaten with rods, and once he was stoned. The last punishment could conceivably have been on a charge of enticing other Jews "to serve other gods" (Deut. 13:6ff), a sin of which Paul would surely have claimed he was innocent. Not only did he know of no other God than the God of Israel, but he had also made a pact with the leaders of the Jerusalem church to divide the work, Paul himself going to the Gentiles and Peter to the Jews. A more likely charge against Paul would have been that he had served other gods (Deut. 17:2ff), a charge arising from a misunderstanding of his view of Christ. Had he been trying to explain to some of his fellow Jews his calling or his mission to the Gentiles? Again we have questions with no clear answers.

Repeatedly, we have found Paul in the middle of conflicts between the new Jesus-movement and at least some other Jews. In each case, we have Jews in conflict with Jews, although in the later cases, the conflict may have had something to do with the involvement of Gentiles in the new movement. In order to discover the roots of the Jewish objection to and rejection of Christianity, we shall have to look more closely at what Paul called "his gospel."

Whatever else Paul believed, he was convinced that Jesus had died and been raised for "all," not just for Israel, and that now God had determined to lay claim upon the nations that were outside of the covenant. They were to be brought into the realm of God's mercy apart from the Torah, as Israel had been brought in by means of it. On this matter an agreement of toleration had been struck between Paul and the leaders of the Jerusalem church (Gal. 2:6–9); the Jewish Jesus-movement in Jerusalem was at least willing to go along with Paul.

In order to understand how the rest of the Jewish people, or its leaders, would have reacted to this development, however, we need to consider who these Gentiles were to whom Paul preached and among whom he found so many hearers. If we judge them by Paul's letters, we must assume that they were well grounded in the Septuagint, the Greek translation of the Scriptures, for Paul certainly appears to have assumed that background in his readers. Those most likely to have had such knowledge would have been the "God-fearers," devout Gentiles, frequenters of the synagogue and worshipers of the God of Israel, who had not become full proselytes. There were a great number of these "semiproselytes" around the empire. Luke presents us with one (perhaps idealized) in the figure of the centurion Cornelius, "a devout man who feared God with all his household, gave alms liberally to the people, and prayed constantly to God; . . . an upright and God-fearing man, who is well spoken of by the whole Jewish nation" (Acts 10:1-2, 22). Of such, we may well suppose, were many of Paul's Gentile "converts."

Contrary to Paul, some Gentile members of the church thought that they and all other Gentile believers ought to become full proselytes, i.e., full-fledged Jews, becoming circumcised and taking on the whole obligation of Israel, in order to be members of the church. Paul attacked their teaching in his letter to the churches of Galatia, and his position was to prevail. The result was that Jews lived, ate, and worshiped with Gentiles in the churches of the Diaspora (whatever the practice may have been in Jerusalem), a situation which, from the Jewish perspective, was an invitation to assimilation: Jews in the church were on their way to losing their Jewishness and their solidarity with the people Israel, the more so as the church became increasingly Gentile in membership. The church, therefore, was not only "stealing" potential converts to Judaism; it was weakening the Jewishness of its Jewish members. To such a movement responsible Jews had to say No. The integrity of Israel and its fidelity to Torah was at stake.

ii. *Mutual hostility*

The break between the church and Israel developed over a period of time from which we have only limited records. Paul's last letters come from the late 50s of the Common Era. Mark's Gospel may have been written at the time of or immediately after the siege of Jerusalem and the destruction of the Second Temple in the year 70. The Gospel according to Matthew and Luke-

Acts, at least as we have them now, may date from somewhere around 80 to 90. Somewhere around the year 85 it is thought that a curse against "the Nazareans" was inserted into the "Eighteen Benedictions," which had as its intended effect the exclusion of Jewish members of the Jesus-movement from formal synagogue worship. We may tentatively conclude that by around the year 85 the break was completed and negative views of each other were established which produced over eighteen centuries of hostility.

The church's view of the Jewish people can be established fairly easily from the Gospels written or edited around the time of the break. The Jewish people are those who refused the king's invitation to the marriage feast of his son (Matt. 22:2–10). They are the wicked tenants who killed the son of the owner of the vineyard (Mark 12:1–9 and parallels in Matthew and Luke), and who therefore should be destroyed; the vineyard was to be given to others. The Jews are those who had demanded of Pilate that Jesus be crucified, and who had said (Matt. 27:25), "His blood be upon us and on our children!" In short, at the time of the break, the church had a view of the Jewish people as the former people of God who had forfeited their election by rejecting their Messiah and who had now been displaced by the church as the true heir of the covenant.

Sources for the Jewish view of the church at that time are almost nonexistent. We have only the *Birkat ha-minim* (see *E.J.*, ad loc., 4, 1035f), "the benediction concerning heretics," which is generally thought to have been invoked under Gamaliel II against the Christians. From this we may gather that Christianity was considered a Jewish heresy. As we have suggested, however, there may also be some truth behind Luke's story that Paul was thought to have taught "all the Jews who are among the Gentiles to forsake Moses, telling them not to circumcise their children or observe the customs" (Acts 21:21). From such limited and indirect sources we may draw only the general conclusion that the rabbinic leadership judged the church among them as a danger to Jewish fidelity to Torah. Given the church's developing assessment of the Jews, that judgment would seem to have been correct.

iii. The church and the Jewish people

The result of the mutual hostility developed by the last quarter of the first century was that the church and the Jewish people entered upon a period of mutual growth and development without either one trying to understand the other, much less seeking any cooperation. The church looked at the Jews from its own position and saw only a stubborn refusal to accept what the church preached as the truth. It seems never to have crossed Christian minds that what the church called Jewish stubbornness was, from Israel's perspective, fidelity to Torah and Torah's Author. Israel's refusal to accept the church's view followed from its steadfast maintainance of its covenant with God. It seems never to have crossed Jewish minds that Torah's Author might do a new thing outside Torah. Neither side saw that Israel's No to the church was its Yes to the very God who had called the church into being.

What the Jewish people were taught by their Rabbis to deny was a church which taught that Israel's covenant with God had been superseded. The church was asking Israel to agree that its faithfulness to Torah had no longer any meaning, because God's faithfulness to his people had come to an end. For Israel to have accepted such a church would have been a betrayal of the covenant and a denial of the faithfulness of God!

The choice with which such a church confronted the Jews was quite different from that confronting those Jews who entered the early Jesus-movement. The latter came to belief in Jesus as the one appointed by God to come soon as *Israel's* Messiah. They joined a Jewish movement as Jews and, so far as we can tell, they remained in it as Jews. Fidelity to Torah was never in question for them. It was a quite different matter, two generations later, for those Jews confronted by the church in the last quarter of the first century. By then, the movement had become perhaps already predominantly Gentile in membership, and Jews who joined it had to turn their backs on the rest of their people. To use a single term, such as "Jewish Christians," for these radically different cases is to obsure the profound change that took place in the first fifty years of the life of the church.

The key to understanding that change is the Pauline corpus, especially the letters to the Galatians and to the Romans. Much may have been going on in other churches and under the leadership of other figures, but we have no record other than that provided by Paul's letters. Those letters, moreover, became the center of the collection of documents which became canonical for the church, so that, for better or worse, Paul became the pivotal figure around which the church came to its negative view of Israel and its fidelity to Torah. Whether the church understood Paul is therefore a question central to the church's reconsideration of its relationship to the Jewish people. It also underlies the further question, whether the church can hear and benefit from the witness of the Jewish rejection of Christianity.

3. PAUL'S GOSPEL, THEN AND NOW

i. His gospel: the opening to the Gentiles

Paul's good news always included the item that it was addressed to the Gentiles. It was, he believed, "the power of God for salvation," of course "for the Jew" — what would the God of Israel do that would not benefit his people? — but "also for the Greek" (Rom. 1:16). Promised long ago in the Scriptures of Israel, it concerned God's Son, who had made Paul an apostle "to bring about obedience to the faith among all the Gentiles" (Rom. 1:2–5). This good news was revealed to Paul, he tells us, in a revelation of Jesus Christ (Gal. 1:12), "in order that [he, Paul,] might preach Christ among the Gentiles" (Gal. 1:16). That the news was for the Gentiles was essential to its goodness.

What was this news that was good for the Jews because it was also good for the Gentiles? It was that in the death of Christ, God had dealt effectively with sin and death (Rom. 3:23–25;

5:15-19; 8:3-4), with all the weakness and bondage of this unfinished creation (Rom. 8:19-22). "In Christ God was reconciling the world to himself, not counting their trespasses against
them, and entrusting to [Paul] the message of reconciliation" (2
Cor. 5:19). Thereby God had made good on his promise and
"guaranteed it to *all* Abraham's descendants, *not only* to those who
have the Torah, but also to those who share Abraham's faith,
for he is the father of us all" (Rom. 4:16). Thus the news is good
for Israel because it is news that God has made good on his promises to the Patriarch. Abraham has indeed become the father
of many *goyim*, and by bringing many Gentiles to obedience to
the God of Israel, "in order that the just requirement of the Torah
might be fulfilled in [them] (Rom. 8:4), Torah has indeed found
its goal in Christ (Rom. 10:4)" of ruling over the creation that
had been made according to its pattern.

Did this new enactment of God's righteousness, of making his
creation right, annul his original covenant with Israel? God forbid, Paul cried! God is faithful in all his work, and his Torah
is good and holy. What God had done was to move one step
beyond Torah and the covenant with Israel and fulfill a tremen-
dously important promise contained in it, so that now Israel with
its Torah, and the Gentiles who had been under the alien dominion of Torah, were now all united under the unfathomable mercy
of God. Although Paul regretted deeply that most Jews were blind
to this demonstration of God's faithfulness to his promise to them
(Rom. 10:1-3), he had no doubt that God's mercy did in fact
now rule over all. He left it to God, however, as something
beyond human understanding, how the resulting unity of God's
children would show itself (Rom. 11:30-36).

Such we take to be Paul's gospel, the only one there is, he
said (Gal. 1:7). It can be heard if we let Paul be himself, a Jew
to the core, trained in the tradition of the oral Torah as well
as the Scriptures, but called by God to be the apostle to the Gentiles. It can be heard when we keep in mind, as any good Jew
of his background would have, the radical distinction between
Israel and the Gentiles. It can be heard, finally, if we share with

Paul Israel's faith in the absolute faithfulness of the God of Israel, whose gifts and call "are irrevocable" (Rom. 11:29). Given these premises, together with Paul's trust in Jesus Christ as the act and will of God, he could have arrived at no other good news than that which he preached, news that was good for Israel because it was also good for the Gentiles.

ii. The misunderstanding of Paul

If I am correct about Paul's gospel, then I must conclude that the church came to preach another gospel that is no gospel, at least in the important sense that it was not even intended to be good news for the Jewish people. This came about in large measure because the church lost all vital contact with Jewish teaching. You would never know from the writings of the Church Fathers that the reform of Javneh was taking hold in their own day, that the teaching of the oral Torah was codified and written down as the Mishnah by the beginning of the third and the Gemarah by the end of the fifth century of the Common Era. The church was not listening to Israel. It had never learned what Paul knew of Jewish teaching of his time, and it did not bother to learn the further development of that teaching that was taking place in the following centuries.

As a consequence, it missapplied Paul's words about the curse of Torah upon the seventy nations as if he had been speaking of its effect on Israel. *Torah* became *nomos* in the sense of *lex, Gesetz,* and *Law.* It was seen as Israel's burden rather than Israel's joy. It was thought to lead to the attempt to work one's way into God's favor, rather than as the gift of God's pure generosity. Paul was no longer the Jewish apostle to the Gentiles. He had become a Gentile himself, and an anti-Jewish one at that!

The result was that this "Gentile" Paul was heard to preach what was surely another gospel. This gospel was addressed universally to a world lost in an ocean of sins, utterly unable with Paul to "delight in the Torah of God" (Rom. 7:22) even when failing to live up to it. Into this world God had sent the church with the Law of God (which it had inherited from the

Jews) to condemn the world for failing to live up to its perfection. Once sufficiently humbled by this impossible task (its impossibility was part of this "good news"), the world was invited to fall on it knees and beg for divine mercy, which the church was authorized to proclaim on the basis of the suffering and death of Jesus. The church offered this new covenant, sealed with the blood of Jesus, as the successor to an old covenant which had only served to prepare the way for it.

According to this gospel and this reading of Paul, the Jews in their stubbornness had refused the mercy offered to them, killed the Christ, and so deserved the wrath of God and man. Trusting that by their careful performance of the commandments they would be able to earn God's love, they were doomed to fail and so must wander the earth an accursed people. Their only function was to be a living warning to good Christian souls of the evil consequences of the false pride of legalism and hypocritical Pharisaism. As a witness to the wrath of God they were to be kept alive, but as objects of God's wrath they were to be avoided as much as possible.

That, so the church believed, was Paul's gospel, good news for the church, but bad news for all those outside the church, "the Jew first of all," for Christ had brought an end, a terminus, to the Jewish Law (so Rom. 10:4 was read). Paul's blessing, "Peace and mercy be upon all who walk by this rule *and* upon God's Israel" (Gal. 6:16), was therefore edited, by omitting that last "and" — as e.g., in the *RSV*! — to read, "Peace and mercy be upon all who walk by this rule, upon the Israel (meaning of course "the new Israel," the church) of God." Paul's gospel of the reconciliation of the Jewish people and the Gentiles (and on its centrality, see Osten-Sacken, *Grundzüge*, 100ff) was thereby transformed into the grounds for centuries of hostility, persecution, and suffering.

iii. Which is the real Paul?

This "other" gospel of this "other" Paul had to be rejected by Israel. Such a Paul would have been not only a total apostate from Israel; he would be one who was completely ignorant of the oral Torah of his people. Luke's reports that Paul had studies under Gamaliel must be wrong, or else he must have been a hopeless student. Paul's own report, that "I advanced in Jewish observance far beyond most of my contemporaries, so extremely zealous was I for the traditions of my fathers" (Gal. 1:14), must be a lie. The picture of Israel drawn by such a Paul was not merely a caricature; it was completely false. To this whole construction the Jewish people had to say No.

In recent years, there have also appeared some Christians who, having learned something about Judaism and its teachings, and having assumed that Paul knew at least as much about it as they did, have also begun to reject the church's traditional picture of Paul and this traditional but other "gospel." Some have, but certainly not the majority. The church is presently engaged in a debate, conducted largely among biblical scholars and generally ignored by most of the church, as to which is the real Paul. Much is at stake in this debate, including ecclesiastical traditions, beloved teachers, and esteemed fathers. Indeed, the debate is ultimately about which is the real gospel!

It is unhappily the case that most of those Jews who know anything about Paul have also adopted the church's traditional reading of him. That is perhaps to be expected, for it would come from following the principle of letting another tradition define its own teachers. In the case of Paul, however, Jewish scholars could provide help by sharing their knowledge of the context of Jewish teaching which Paul brought to the definition of "his gospel." They could fairly raise the question whether the church has understood this Pharisee at all!

On the other hand, if Jewish scholarship were to reclaim Paul as a Jew, it would have to come to terms with what may have been his actual apostasy: Paul may have so identified with his Gentile converts as to have abandoned fidelity to Torah-living. At one point Paul wrote to them, "Become as I am, for I have become as you are" (Gal. 4:12). At another he wrote, "If, in our endeavor to be justified in Christ, we ourselves were found to

be (Gentile) sinners, is Christ then an agent of sin? Certainly
not! For since I build up again the things (i.e., the churches)
which I tore down (before his calling), then I prove myself an
apostate. For I through the Torah have died to the Torah, that
I might live to God" (Gal. 2:17–19, following Lloyd Gaston's
translation). If Gaston's careful argument is accepted, these passages suggest that Paul may have become an apostate in the service of his mission to the Gentiles.

More challenging to a Jewish effort to come to terms with
Paul's actual gospel is the fact that, although directed primarily
to the Gentiles and having primarily to do with them, it was
also for "the Jew first." What Paul would have said or did say
to his fellow Jews we do not know, but he was convinced that
Christ died for all and that in him God had acted apart from
the Torah to accomplish the very goal which he had revealed
in it, not only for Israel, but also for the Gentiles. The distinction between Jews and Gentiles was therefore subsumed under
and reduced to secondary importance by the one overarching
mercy of the one God. Jews would have to ask themselves how
they stood with respect to that gospel.

iv. Is "Paul" final?

The apostle to the Gentiles has a special place in the Gentile
church, and not just in the Lutheran churches. The teaching
of justification by grace alone to be received by faith, the emphasis on faith, in contrast to works, the distinction between Law
and Gospel, the importance of the preaching of the cross, and
the conception of the church as the body of Christ, all this and
much more has its grounding in the church's reading of Paul's
letters. Those letters, moreover, form an important part of the
church's Canon of Sacred Scripture. Much therefore turns on
the interpretation of Paul.

We must ask, however, whether Paul can provide even the
church with the last word on the relationship between the church

and the Jewish people. The church today has to decide now whether it recognizes the Israel of God in the present Jewish people, whether the covenant between God and Israel, which Paul believed to be irrevocable in his day, is still in force. I believe that Paul, especially when understood on his own terms as a Jew and a Pharisee, can nourish the church's efforts to turn toward the Jewish people in a spirit of reconciliation and cooperation. Paul's words can stimulate the words that need to be spoken today. Paul, however, cannot be the last word, not only because he himself insisted that God would be his own last word, on this as on every other matter (Rom. 11:33–36; 1 Cor. 15:28), but also because God requires of his church its own living response to Paul and the rest of the apostolic witness. Long after Paul's words were written, the history of the Jewish people and the Gentile church has gone on. Between Paul and the present lies the long journey which God and the Jewish people have made together and which the church has to take into consideration when responding to Paul, for that journey was made in the face of the long, bloody history of the church's anti-Judaism. As the church stumbles toward a better relationship to the good tree onto which it was grafted, it will need to find words of repentance for the suffering it has caused the Jews, words which it will not find in Paul's letters because he had no need of them.

As the church may recover the real Paul by coming to understand the Jewish teaching of his time, so it may learn to find the words it needs today by listening and learning from the Jewish people of this time. Israel is set in the world as a light for the Gentiles, a light for the way into a world of justice and peace. The light shines in the darkness and the darkness has not overcome it. If the church can heed that light and learn to listen to the witness of the Jewish rejection of its other Paul and that other gospel, it may be led into a better service of the one God.

4. THE JEWISH DIAGNOSIS OF CHRISTIANITY: SPIRITUALIZATION

i. *Law versus gospel*

The Jewish theologian Franz Rosenzweig, no enemy of the church, diagnosed Christianity as being subject to three inescapable dangers, three threatening lapses back into the paganism out of which it had been drawn. They were the temptation to believe in "a God that was only Spirit, no longer the Creator who gave his Law to the Jew, a Christ that was only Christ, no longer Jesus, and a world that was only totality, that no longer had the Holy Land as its center" (*Der Stern der Erlösung*, 460; cf. 447; E.T. 414, 402). How shall we sum up this danger? A tendency toward generalization and away from the specific? A tendency to abstraction and away from the concrete? A flight from the historical, from the mundane? We shall call it the temptation of and fall into spiritualization. It is Israel's diagnosis of the fundamental illness of the church. We can see it at work in several dichotomies which the church has developed, the first of which is that between Law and Gospel.

Most explicit and sharp in the Lutheran tradition, the dichotomy of Law and Gospel was developed by Augustine and therefore marks the whole of western Christianity. "Law" refers to God's commandments for righteous action: thou shalt do certain things and thou shalt not do other things. As the revealed will of God, it is holy and good, but for sinful human beings it is a disaster, for it holds up before them a standard of behavior they can never fulfill. "Gospel" refers to God's unmerited, gracious mercy. It is the good news that, in Christ, God has rescued sinful humanity from the consequences of its sin and offered it a way back to his love.

There are several unfortunate consequences to this teaching Israel must reject and against which it stands as a warning to the church. God's Torah does indeed reveal God's will, according to Israel's witness, but it does so in the context of the covenant. It reveals God's will for Israel, and it does so in the context of and because of God's merciful love for Israel. The righteousness that God wills of his people and the mercy which he shows to them are not contraries and not in opposition. The church's dichotomy is the fruit of blindness to the fact that the Torah is the best of good news, because it provides Israel with concrete instruction in how to walk in thankful response to God's mercy. The "good news" which the church has to offer is, in Israel's judgment, divorced from God's concern for righteousness; it can be offered far too easily without the call to holiness upon which the Torah insists.

Without saying a word, Israel by its mere existence stands before the church as a witness that God's people are the recipients of the Torah, just as God's church is the recipient of the gospel. As God is one, so these two cannot be contrary. The Torah is God's gospel for Israel. Israel's existence in fidelity to Torah puts the question to the church whether it has heard the part of Paul's gospel that concerns "the *law* of the Spirit of life in Christ Jesus" (Rom. 8:2). The Jewish rejection of Christianity entails the judgment that the church, with its negative view of the Torah and its gospel of a grace that makes too little of the gift of God's guidance, is suffering from the sickness of spiritualization.

ii. Works versus faith

The dichotomy of Law and gospel has also found expression in the split between works and faith. This secondary dichotomy has been developed in the context of "the introspective conscience of the west," with its anxious question, "What must I do to be saved?" The answer of the church has been, Believe in the gospel. Trust in Christ. In Luther's terminology, the gospel announces God's promise; the corresponding act from the human side can therefore only be to trust in that promise. To put one's trust in how one lived or behaved would be a denial that God approaches human beings with a promise. The gospel is the announcement of God's promise freely offered, to be received by faith, by believing that the promise is valid and that God is trustworthy. On this basis, God accepts the sinner, and on this basis the tree, now pronounced good, will bring forth good fruit. Being set free in Christ, the Christian will then become a "little Christ" to his neighbor.

The Jewish witness in rejecting Christianity raises a question about this teaching. Israel already knows about God's mercy and the fact that every human being, certainly including the Jew, can stand before the righteous God only because God is also merciful. It does not need the church in order to learn of the necessity of divine mercy, for that is central to the teaching of Moses, the Prophets, and especially of the Rabbis. Israel knows of this because the very covenant in which it lives and the Torah by which it lives are all the gift of God's unmerited generosity. But Israel must raise the question, how do you actually live, day by day, on the basis of God's mercy? It is all very well to say that a good tree brings forth good fruit, but is not a tree that produces good fruit just what we mean by a good tree? Is it not by the fruit that we know the worth of a fruit tree (Matt. 7:20; Lk. 6:44)?

From Israel's perspective, the doctrine of justification by faith alone sounds too spiritual for flesh-and-blood human beings. Its development out of the stricken conscience tends to result in a concentration of attention upon that interior, personal context. It does not look to the world of human interaction or the broader world of God's creation. Its God is too spiritual, its concern too interior. It leaves creation and the social world to fend for themselves. Above all, it asks too little of the human partners of God's covenant. Israel stands before the church in fidelity to Torah and asks whether the church cares for created life in God's creation. It asks, ultimately, whether the church cares for that which is incarnate, and it asks whether the church thinks that God's grace does not demand the human response of taking on responsibility for God's creation. The church at its best is aware of these dangers and from time to time has expressed this awareness (e.g., Bonhoeffer's *The Cost of Discipleship*, with its denunciation of "cheap grace"). By its very existence, Israel holds this issue up to the church daily.

iii. *Redemption, real or in principle?*

Israel's No to the church is loudest and clearest in its rejection of the Christian belief that Christ is the Redeemer and that redemption has been accomplished already with his death and resurrection. The Jewish people know something about redemption. They learned about it in the Exodus and introduced the concept into the world on the basis of this experience. The Jewish people also know in their flesh that the redemption which God has promised has not come. They know from their own firsthand experience that they live in an unredeemed world. How then could Jesus be the redeemer? He could not even have been the Messiah for which Israel hopes, for he did not even redeem Israel from Roman occupation.

The church has tried to meet this challenge by saying that the redemption accomplished in Jesus Christ is spiritual, or that it is proleptic, or that it is a redemption-in-principle. The first would mean that redemption touches the soul or spirit, not the body; the second would say that the decisive battle over sin and death has been won, anticipating the final victory, which will come with Christ's return; the third would say the same thing in nontemporal terms. Each of these moves is an attempt to hold onto the claim of redemption accomplished, in a world that admittedly does not appear to have been redeemed. In each case, the world as it appears — the real world? — takes second place at best to an invisible "reality."

From Israel's perspective, however, none of these moves meets the central problem that the church's teaching, however qualified, splits open the unity of the one God. It fails to do justice to the biblical witness that the Redeemer is the Creator and that the whole creation is in need of and has been promised redemption. A so-called redemption of the spirit is simply not redemption. An anticipation of redemption is still only an anticipation.

Israel knows about tokens of redemption. It first learned about redemption in the mind-bodied experience of the Exodus. That was a real but limited redemption, a protoredemption as we called it. Actual slaves were set free, but that was not the redemption of creation. Every Sabbath is celebrated by Israel as a tiny proleptic taste of redemption, but every Sabbath comes to an end and the week begins again. The state of Israel can be celebrated as marking the dawn of deliverance, but no state in the Middle East has yet beat its spears into pruning hooks. The Jewish people know and value the tokens of redemption that it has been given from time to time, or which it may celebrate again and again, but it has never confused the tokens with that of which they are but the sign. From the Jewish perspective, the church lives in just this confusion.

Israel's charge against the church is a serious one. It charges the church with having spiritualized both God and his creation. It charges the church with having settled for and preaching a redemption which is no redemption, which leaves creation, and therefore also its Creator, as failures! Israel makes this witness simply by existing, by refusing to accept the church as its successor or replacement. It makes its witness by rejecting Christianity. In doing so, it bears witness to the incarnate, temporal involvement of God in his creation and his call to his creatures to work and pray for the completion of his beloved creation in his reign of righteousness.

5. THE PRAYER OF JESUS

Israel's critical witness to the church can be brought into focus by looking at the prayer of that Jew from whom the Gentile church learned how to pray, the prayer of Jesus known as "The Lord's Prayer." We will examine this prayer and try to hear and learn from it as it was originally intended—instruction by one Jew for other Jews—rather than as a part of the church's tradition, which is how it is usually seen. We shall follow both the

Matthean version (6:9–13) that became the liturgical prayer of the church, and also the tighter Lukan version (11:2–4).

The address in Luke's version could not be more simple or more Jewish. It is simply, "Father." Although the opening is more elaborate in Matthew, it is introduced by a recommendation to make one's prayer simple: "not like the Gentiles, who think they will be heard for their many words." Here too, the "Our Father who art in the heavens," is a typical Jewish liturgical formula. Israel is God's son and God is Israel's Father; this familiarity is the fruit of the covenant between them. The Gentile church can only recite this prayer as those invited to hold onto that one Jew and repeat his words after him.

The first thing for which Israel prays, which the Gentiles have to learn about from Israel and learn that it comes first, is that God's name be sanctified, set off from everything else, revered as holy. Israel exists to sanctify God's name, for that name is Israel's foundation. The prayer opens, therefore, with an acknowledgment of the context which makes prayer possible at all.

The *name* of God is a weighty concept in the Scriptures. God *chooses* to make his name to *dwell* among his people, above all in the Temple, which is "the house for God's name" (1 Kings 8:44, 48). The place where God chooses to make his name dwell is where God is remembered and called upon, and the place where sacrifice is to be offered (Deut. 12:11; 16:2, 6; 26:2). God promised that "in every place where I cause my name to be remembered I will come to you and bless you" (Ex. 20:24). "The name of God", then, means God himself present to his people. In a word, it is the presence of God. To call on the name is to appeal to God's covenantal presence among his people. Israel can "trust in his holy name" (Ps. 33:21), for that is to trust that God is with Israel, that the covenant endures. It is therefore fitting that Israel asks God for pardon and guidance "for your name's sake" (Ps. 25:11; 31:3), since these blessings come on the basis of God's having drawn near to his elect people in making his covenant with them. In sum, "the name of God" stands for God in his covenantal presence with his people. Prayer is possible on this basis and on this basis only. No wonder that Israel's first concern is the holiness of the name of God.

If the name of God is basic in Israel's Scripture, it is the holy center of Israel's mystical tradition. According to kabbalistic doctrine, "all things exist only by virture of their degree of participation in the great Name of God" (G. Scholem, *Major Trends in Jewish Mysticism*, 133), and the author of the *Zohar* stressed that "the whole of the Torah . . . is nothing but the one great and holy Name of God" (210). God's holy name unfolds, as it were, in God's revelation and sustains the whole of creation. To sanctify the name of God is therefore to acknowledge all that God is and does.

Only Israel's prayer could begin in this way, and Israel's prayer could begin in no other way. Prayer, the conversation of human beings with their Creator, is possible and necessary because God has drawn near and bound them to himself in an eternal covenant. Prayer is the act of those human beings, the people Israel, to whom this has happened. It is an act based upon and itself a part of the covenantal relationship. Its focus is on God's having drawn near, but just as clearly, it is Israel's act. It is based on what God has done, but it is something which Israel may and must do. Prayer is therefore itself a covenantal act. It is Israel's proper act; the Gentiles have to learn this from Israel. Because by the Spirit, God has claimed the Gentiles as the younger brothers of the Jew who prayed Israel's prayer, they may make bold to say with him, "Our Father, hallowed be thy name."

On the basis of the covenant, Israel makes its first petition: "May your kingdom come!" May god's promised reign over his creation begin! Matthew adds the clarifying paraphrase, "May your will be done on earth!" Incredible as it may seem to Gentile minds, Israel's first petition consists of begging God to triumph! Israel petitions God to be God, which he wills not to be, so to speak, without Israel's participation. The Rabbis could even say that Israel's sin weakens God's power (*Sifre Deut.*, §319, cited in Moore I, 472)! The first petition of Israel's prayer points to the self-determination of God in having made his covenant with Israel: the completion of this threatened creation will not come without Israel's cooperation. It is Israel's privilege and responsibility to beg that God's reign come soon.

The kingdom or reign of God, as the Matthean addition underscores, is to occur on this earth, for the Redeemer is the Creator and his redemption will be of this creation. God's kingdom is for this world, not for the heavens. The heavens are doing all right: God's will is already being done there by the angels, God's holy messengers. Israel does not have to worry about any invisible powers in the heavenly places, for they do already the will of their Creator. The problem is here on earth. so Israel (accompanied by those Gentiles who have been taught and led by Israel) prays, "Thy will be done on earth."

Jesus taught his Jewish disciples to pray for the reign of God to come, and for God's righteous will to be done, here and now on earth. The Gentile church has believed that that teaching was also to be its guide in prayer. Yet the church has prayed primarily for a safe passage out of this world into a "kingdom of God" thought to be in the heavens. One must wonder where the church learned to pray for such a thing! Surely not from Israel. Surely not from the Jew who is Israel for the church. Jesus bears the witness of Israel to the church that it has not learned well how to pray. It has not learned well from Jesus what it is to pray for the coming of God's reign on earth. In order to learn from him, it will have to unlearn its gnostic ideas about an "other world." Israel calls the church to pray instead for God's world.

Having prayed for the coming of God's victory, Israel then asks of its Creator that he provide the minimum necessary for Israel's life in the covenant. Once again, the covenantal note is sounded: the prayer is for a necessity which is produced by the cooperation of God and human beings: bread. "Give us today (or 'each day'— Luke) our daily bread," perhaps, "our ration of bread" (the term is unusual and occurs nowhere else in the Apostolic Writings). The gift of manna in the wilderness, one day's supply at a time, underlies the petition. Bread for today is all that is asked for, one day at a time. With that, Israel can carry on. With that, the covenant can continue. It is sufficient for Israel, and the Gentiles may learn from Israel that it is also sufficient for them.

Having set prayer in the context of the covenant, with Israel hallowing God's name, having asked that God triumph in his creative, redemptive purpose, and that he provide the bare minimum for Israel to survive, Israel then acknowledges that, although it is God's covenanted partner, and although it is invited by God to become his co-worker, Israel never does its full share and therefore always needs God's forgiveness. "Forgive us our sins (or, with Matthew, 'debts')."

The petition for forgiveness is essential, but it is neither primary nor the whole matter of Israel's prayer. It has been said that one may distinguish the two great theologians of the Protestant Reformation by reference to the petitions of the Lord's Prayer, Luther focusing on "Forgive us our sins," and Calvin on "Thy will be done." Insofar as that is accurate, Calvin must rate as the better exegete. Israel's witness is that it stands ever in need of God's forgiveness. How could it be other for a people that knows that it stands before the Holy One of Israel? God's forgiveness of Israel's failings, however, is itself a moment in the larger reality of the covenant between them. It finds its place within Israel's life in the covenant. Consequently, a clause is coupled to the petition for forgiveness, recalling that life: "for we ourselves forgive all who are indebted to us" (Luke), or "as we also have forgiven our debtors" (Matthew). Forgiveness is not just God's business, contrary to Voltaire's cynical remark ("*Dieu pardonnera; c'est son métier*"). God's forgiveness is for those whom he has taught also to forgive each other. How could they ask for forgiveness if they did not live by that forgiveness? If they did not forgive each other, they would have ceased to sanctify God's holy name. The forgiveness of sins is a reality within the larger reality of the covenant between Israel and God, and the

Gentile in search of God's forgiveness will find it only because he or she has been granted a way into the framework of that covenant and so has learned from Israel that forgiveness entails human responsibility.

Israel's prayer ends with a recognition of creatureliness: "Lead us not into the trial," to which Matthew adds, "but deliver us from the evil (one)." The Matthean expansion suggests that our modern use of the term "temptation" is too mild a word for the trial-by-fire, as it were, of creation in the day of its redemption. The last petition connects with the first: Thy kingdom come, but rescue us from the catastrophic aspect of its coming.

Israel has never tolerated the idea of a second power in competition with the One God. The Rabbis were uncompromising on this point. But Israel has always known that we live in an unredeemed world. Satan, the evil one, is no match for God, but the powers of darkness can put up a dangerous struggle. Human beings are surely actors in this world, but they are also acted upon. Israel's prayer recognizes this and begs of God that the trauma of creation's completion not be more than poor creatures can handle. The ending is thus a fitting acknowledgment that the Redeemer is the Creator who knows the limits of his creatures.

The prayer of Jesus is Israel's prayer and the Gentile church does well to hear it and learn it as such. Prayer, as the church would know it, is after all a peculiarly Jewish activity, for it was born in the context of God's election of this people and grew up in Israel's life in the covenant. When the Gentile church first dared to pray, it was attempting a work long practiced by Israel. It was surely not trying to do what the Gentile world had essayed in a thousand forms, addressed to as many idols and dreams. When the church began to pray, it intended to follow in just that activity in which Abraham, Issac, and Jacob had shown the way. It had David and Solomon as examples and Israel's prophets and psalmists as guides. Above all, it had the Jew from Nazareth as Teacher. From him it has learned its central prayer.

That prayer, however, is Israel's, and to hear it otherwise is to misunderstand it and so to misuse it. The Gentile church prays in its own proper Gentile way when it learns to pray with Israel. The "Our" of "Our Father" belongs to Israel first, but the church may say that word legitimately when it remembers that fact and gives thanks that it has been called by God to add its pinfeathers to the wings of Israel's prayer, which soars in the strength of the covenant to the LORD God of Israel.

CHAPTER TEN

Israel's Mission

Elected to be the vanguard in the completion of creation, Israel bears witness, in the face of the church's "once-for-all," to the living God and so to a living covenant. By living the tension of its calling, therefore, the Jewish people testifies not only to the incompleteness of creation, but also to the need for, the limitations to, and the possibility of creaturely cooperation in working for God's future for his creation.

1. THE LIVING COVENANT OF THE LIVING GOD

i. The covenant of partnership

Israel trusts in God as the living God, the Creator who has given his Torah to his people, who has been with them in mercy and judgment throughout their history, and who has promised to redeem Israel and his whole creation. Insofar as Israel lives from its written Torah, it lives out a story not yet finished. Insofar as it lives from its oral Torah, it lives out a covenant or contract with God. By living out this story and this covenant, Israel walks a path through history with the living God. Morning by morning, year after year, century after century, Israel blesses the LORD who "renews the creation every day, constantly" (*P.B.*, 74). Of course Israel looks back to certain sacred moments, especially to Sinai, but it walks ahead in history with the living God in a living covenant toward the time of creation's redemption.

Israel has made and makes this witness in the face of a church which has often made much of the *"ephapax"* ("once-for-all") of a few verses of the Apostolic Writings (Rom. 6:10; Hebr. 9:12, 10:10), where it refers to Christ's death as the unrepeatable and sufficient ground for the church's confidence in God's mercy. The church, however, has enlarged this claim to encompass the totality of God's work, as if the whole story of redemption were contained in that single act, as if, contrary to the apostle to the Gentiles, the church did not have to hope for what has not yet come. Israel's steadfast witness is a reminder to the church that God lives and that the story is not yet over. Confronted with living Israel, the church is confronted with its continuing covenant with the living God.

The covenant between God and Israel, according to Israel's testimony, entails God's commitment to the Jewish people, and therefore also to the whole creation (or God's commitment to the Jews is the pledge of his commitment to creation — Israel can say this either way), as well as Israel's commitment to God. This covenant created a genuine partnership, however unequal the partners. So it was from the beginning at Sinai, and so it continued in a fresh way for rabbinic Judaism, beginning from Javneh.

Israel has trusted, sometimes in the face of an appalling weight of evidence to the contrary, that God would redeem Israel. From the Book of Job to the present, Israel has often been at a loss to fathom God's way of fulfilling his side of the partnership as Israel's shepherd and guardian. On the other hand, Israel has been quite clear about how it was to carry out its obligations as a partner in the covenant. The answer has been, in a word, halakhah: careful observance of the written and especially the oral Torah.

We have noted the argument that the terms of the covenant were amended around the time of the destruction of the Second Temple and the founding of the academy of Javneh, but we have also remarked that it can equally well be argued that continuity has been more evident than change. The production and redaction of the Canon of Torah, for example, was no less daring an innovation than the development and codification of the Mishnah. The covenant has always required Israel's active participation as a full partner in God's covenantal purpose.

On the other hand, the covenant has been and is lived in time, and Torah is "not in the heavens," so some degree of change is to be expected. It could be that an inclination to see change predominating is a reflection of our modern difficulty in singing unto the LORD a new song, together with our near inability to sing the old song as we think it used to be sung. That is to say, we seem to find it foreign to speak of God's mighty arm at work when human beings engage in battle, but the fact remains that when Israel of old spoke that way, it did so after a no less human battle than any we may have seen in our time. Only we have lost the knack of singing a new song about it. Is it then the terms of the covenant that have changed, with Israel taking a more active role and God a more hidden one than formerly, or is it a shift in our perception or in our use of language?

There is at least one point at which we can speak of a change in Israel's conception of the covenantal partnership, and this occurred in the kabbalistic response to the horrors of the expulsion of the Jews from Spain in 1492, some of which we discussed in connection with Isaac Luria's conception of the divine contraction in Creation. In Lurianic kabbalism, according to Scholem, the doctrine of *Tikkun*, restitution, incorporated the total life of the Jewish people into the redemptive process, so that every good deed and the fulfillment of each commandment added its bit to the restoration of this broken creation. "The doctrine of *Tikkun* raised every Jew to the rank of a protagonist in the great process of restitution, in a manner never heard of before" (*Major Trends*, 284).

Whatever the future of this line of thinking may be, there is in any case no doubt that the Holocaust had put a heavy burden on Israel's confidence in its covenant Partner. No consensus has yet emerged on God's apparent withdrawal from his responsibility to protect his people in their hour of desperate need. How or in what way God abided by the terms of the partnership of the covenant in the Holocaust remains a painful mystery. What is clear is that a large part of the Jewish people held to their commitment, living by Torah at the risk of earlier rather than later death, faithful to God and the covenant to the end. Israel's living witness in that extremity was still to the covenant of partnership.

ii. *The covenant of responsibility*

The partnership of the covenant entails the responsibility of each partner to the other and to the terms of the agreement. The LORD is to be Israel's God and Israel is to be God's people. Israel has to trust that God is standing by his covenant — even when it seems that he has forgotten it, as many a Psalm testifies — and Israel has to be faithful to Torah. The witness of Israel through the ages has centered quite properly on Israel's responsibility, and it is here that we are most apt to see the element of change or development in Israel's understanding of its covenant with God.

As we saw already in the doctine of *Tikkun*, the direction of change is toward Israel being called to increasing responsibility, and for God to place more and more of the burden of creation's completion or restoration on Israel's shoulders. As we have said, the other side of this could be argued by underscoring the extent to which the biblical understanding of the covenant already presented it as a genuine partnership. Nevertheless, as we come into the more recent history of the covenant, especially in the last century or so, we can begin to see the impact on the Jewish people of the sense of Israel's responsibility for the outcome of this world.

An obvious and important example of this tradition of covenantal responsibility, appearing in a secular — but not always secular! — form, is the rise of Jewish socialism and the disproportionate Jewish involvement in socialist movements in the nineteenth century as well as in other movements of social, economic, and political reform on into the present. Jewish involvement in these movements has been variously motivated, some Jews taking part in the hope of solving "the Jewish question" (i.e., anti-semitism), others as a way out of Judaism altogether; but the tradition of Jewish recognition of human responsibility for the future of creation cannot be discounted. (For a useful survey, see the articles on *Socialism* and *Jewish Socialism* in *E.J.* 15, 24–52.)

More influential among the Jewish people and on the course of the covenant has been the Zionist movement, representing as it does the clearest evidence for a shift in the character of Israel's responsibility for the future of the covenant. Zionism, at its center, was and is a movement to return the Jewish people to, and restore Jewish sovereignty in, *eretz Yisrael*. This return and restoration was previously undreamed of apart from the coming of the messianic age, yet its partial realization is now blessed by devout Jews, as we have heard, as "marking the dawn of Israel's redemption." Its realization has been partial, for the great majority of Jews have not returned to their land, and Jewish sovereignty, though real, has yet to produce a day of peace with most of its neighbors. Zionist accomplishments, however, have, in the eyes of some, opened a new chapter in the history of the covenant, for they have been achieved, at least as far as the human eye can see, by Jews acting on their own.

Without denying for a moment the human effort that went into the realization of the Zionist agenda, the question may still be asked whether this represents a new stage of the covenant, for such a judgment tends to ignore the qualification "as far as the eye can see." Once more we need to ask what the human eye could see of the Exodus, of the conquest of the land under Joshua and the Judges, of David's conquest of Jerusalem, or of the return of the Exiles from Babylonia. Was human action ever accompanied *visibly* by the hand of God? Has not the continuation of the covenant always required action on the part of Jews? What from one perspective may be called a shift in the terms of the covenant, may from another perspective be defined as a shift in our way of speaking of God. The question, at the deepest theological level, concerns the place of freedom, God's and Israel's, in the covenant.

iii. The covenant of freedom

God's love confers freedom. God's love for Israel, according to Israel's testimony, has always been a liberating love, and his acts of love for Israel have given Israel its freedom. This happened in the Exodus, and it happened again in the giving of the Torah from Sinai. It recurred in the gift of the oral Torah, and in the mystical insights of the Kabbalists. In each case, a further gift of God's love has bestowed a further freedom on Israel.

The covenant between God and Israel is not only grounded in God's freedom; it is a covenant in which God remains fully free. It came about by a free decision of God to have this people as his own, and it continues in God's freedom to be forever the God of this people. He retains his freedom to punish Israel when it falls away from him, and he retains his freedom to welcome Israel back when it repents. As he was free to determine himself as the God of Israel, so he is free to stand by his covenant and not give up on Israel.

The covenant between God and Israel depends also on Israel's freedom. It could not have come into being without Israel's free agreement, and it requires Israel's free renewal on every Day of Atonement. With this covenant Israel was given freedom. As Rabbi Soleveitchik is said to have taught, "Bondage to God is all encompassing and by definition releases man from all other bonds" (P. Peli, *On Repentance*, 241). The covenant of freedom invites the Jewish people into the unending risk of interpreting Torah and the will of God, the fruit of which is the rich halakhic tradition of the Rabbis which continues and grows to this day. Israel is free to decide, to make up its own mind, not waiting for a voice from heaven.

The covenant of freedom is therefore open-ended on both sides, that of God and that of Israel. God is free to do a new thing out of his love for his people, and they are free to interpret God's will in new ways. A repentant Israel could conceivably discover new patterns of faithfulness to Torah that would not fit into the old dichotomy of Orthodoxy/Reform, not to speak of the rather un-Jewish dichotomy of religious/secular. Rav Kook was surely feeling his way into such new paths as Israel was on the threshold of its present strange new condition of living the next stage of the covenant partly once more in its own land, and partly in a Diaspora-by-choice. A future for that covenant is promised, but how it may look in the future is far from clear, for it is a covenant of freedom.

2. THE WITNESS TO THE NEED TO WORK FOR GOD'S FUTURE

i. *Creation's vanguard*

Israel's election to be a kingdom of priests and a holy nation (Ex. 19:6) places it uncomfortably in the vanguard of creation's struggle for completion. Israel stands at the point of contact between God and this unfinished world, for God's Presence is with his people and his people exist in the midst of the nations. It is the humbling glory but also the painful burden of Israel's calling to live at the point of tension where the Holy One of Israel, he who wills the renewal of his creation, touches most intimately the as yet unredeemed world.

As a lamp set to cast light for the unenlightened Gentiles, Israel shines in the midst of darkness. By its light, darkness may be seen to be darkness. The church talks much of a fallen or unredeemed world. Israel, simply by existing, reveals the unfinished condition of creation.

Israel's witness, however, is not simply *that* the world is in need of redemption. Israel lives out a witness that God wants a creaturely cooperation in achieving his purpose for his creation. Israel's witness is not at all to any Promethean ability of human beings to save either themselves or the world, but it is also not to a God who accomplishes his purpose without drawing his creatures into his purpose. The God to whom Israel bears witness is one who has graciously determined that his creatures may and can be his co-workers in the renewal of the world. The covenant of partnership, responsibility, and freedom is Israel's grounds for this witness.

Israel makes this witness by the very fact of its life in the covenant. Its life of a call to holiness in an unredeemed world is inevitably one of tension. It puts Israel in a state of tension with the other nations, and it awakens tensions within Israel's own life. Both of these conflicts, unavoidable for a people called to be creation's vanguard, reveal the unfinished character of creation and also the call to work for God's future for it.

ii. Conflict with the nations

Were the creation in a right relationship with its Creator, it could only accept with joy and thanksgiving the presence in its midst of God's elect people as a light, guide, and blessing, the sure sign of God's loving commitment to its completion. Such is clearly not the case. On the contrary, Israel has been from its beginning until today in conflict with the nations. The nations have called this conflict and its cause by various names; the best known of them in this century is "The Jewish Question." (Pseudoscientific racial theorists of the last century coined the term "antisemitism" for the problem. Dr. James Parkes used to argue that it is only misleadingly spelled "anti-Semitism," as if there were such a thing as "Semitism," as if the issue had to do with a recognized and established racial category rather than with Israel, with the Jews themselves. A more accurate term for the phenomenon would therefore be "anti-Jewism.").

The term "The Jewish Question" reveals the blindness of the nations to the problem itself. What is in question is not the Jews but the nations, indeed the whole order of creation. The question that calls for an answer is that of the Psalmist (Ps. 2:1, 2): "Why do the nations (*goyim*) rage and the peoples utter folly . . . against the LORD and his anointed?" It should more properly be called "The Gentile Question." The conflict referred to by these terms is that between an unredeemed world and the agents whom God has chosen to bring closer the day of his redemption.

The more recent form of this same confusion of the issue appears in the term "The Palestinian Question." This phrase, as used by the world, refers to Israel's assumed obligation to do something about the Arabs of Palestine, of *eretz Yisrael*, in order to provide for them a land and a sovereign state. The state of Israel is supposed to provide an answer to "The Palestinian Question." This ignores, however, that the flight of the Arabs in question and their resulting refugee status were the direct result of the war of annihilation which the surrounding Arab states began in 1948, the moment the state of Israel was born. The Arabs persuaded the Palestinians to flee and have kept them in a refugee status ever since. In nineteen years of military occupation of "the West Bank" (a designation which makes sense only from a Jordanian expansionist perspective), Jordan did nothing to help create a Palestinian state. To this day, Egypt is the only neighboring state that has been willing to make peace with Israel. The so-called Palestinian Question is in fact a question to the Arab states as to when they will make peace with Israel. The heart of the question is when these states will ever come to recognize and accept the existence of the state of Israel.

Israel has never been in doubt that it is itself a part of the unredeemed world, and therefore there has been considerable Jewish and Israeli resentment at the world's employment of what has been called a "double standard," asking of the state of Israel a level of moral behavior in both internal and external affairs that it demands of no other state, least of all of Israel's immediate neighbors. The resentment is understandable but it is out of place: the so-called double standard, which is in fact a single standard for Israel and practically no standard for other nations, is evidence that Israel's witness has been seen at least dimly by the world. As the elect witness to the righteousness of God and of his righteous will for his creatures, Israel has introduced into the world at least a faint awareness of the Creator's demand for justice. When Israel is in question, that awareness surfaces in a way that does not occur when the conduct of other nations is being considered. Israel is carrying out its divine mandate when it asks of the world that it apply just that one standard of conduct also to the actions of every other nation. It can hardly object that its own behavior be measured by that standard. The tension that arises in this matter is again evidence of the stresses inherent in Israel's election as the vanguard of creation's struggle for completion.

iii. Israel's inner conflicts

The Jewish people bear witness to the need to work for the renewal of creation by their long history of internal struggle to be Israel. Is there another people on earth who for more than three millennia have wrestled so persistently with themselves over the meaning and form of their life? What is it to be a Jew? What is it to be God's elect people? From the conflict between its kings and prophets in biblical times, through clashes between Pharisees and Sadducees at the end of the Second Temple Period, on through the tensions between halakhic and mystical tendencies, to more recent conflicts between Orthodox and Reform, Bundist and Zionist, secularist and religionist, and present tensions between the state of Israel and the Diaspora, Israel's history has been one of wrestling over the question of how to fulfill its calling to cooperate with the Creator's concern for his creation. Debate over whether the state of Israel could remain a Jewish state if it were to annex the binational areas of Judea and Samaria is only the latest form of the inner tension that has marked the history of this people.

Nothing reveals this internal struggle more than the central place which Judaism has always given to the concept of *teshuvah*, return, "repentance." To turn back or return implies that there was and is a condition from which one has lapsed or fallen away, and that one can once more realize that earlier and better state, one that was established by God in his generosity. It implies that this is something which the penitent can and must do him- or herself. There is no passive form of the verb to repent. It is the responsibility, the exclusive responsibility, of each and every Jew to make this move, both individually and collectively, and, according to Israel's testimony, heaven waits upon this human act. "All is in the hands of heaven except the fear of heaven."

The need for human cooperation in the work of creation's completion is testified to today by two major struggles in which the Jewish people are involved. In the Diaspora, the struggle is for the survival of the Jewish people, not in the face of traditional anti-Judaism and persecution, for in most lands of the Diaspora, Jews have generally been granted full status as citizens and full protection of the laws. The threat is not that of being killed; it is rather that of assimilation, of forgetting about and losing their identity as Jews and so of giving up on the struggle entrusted to Israel of being the vanguard of creation's completion. Return and renewal would be Israel's ancient answer to this problem, centering as it does on the promise of the God of Israel to preserve his people. A more usual contemporary answer with less solid roots is to devise strategies for preserving Jewishness which evade the question whether Jewishness makes any sense apart from Israel's divine election. Such strategies fall under the judgment of Rosenzweig's essay, *"Atheistishe Theologie."* The hard question that stands before the Diaspora is, what is it that matters to both God *and* Israel: the number of Jews who call themselves Jews in one sense or another, or the way in which those Jews who so call themselves, however few, understand and live out their identity?

The other major struggle is over the future of the state of Israel, over the shape of renewal and return in the land. Here too the threat is no longer that of physical annihilation at the hands of its anti-Jewish neighbors, for Israel has, at great material and psychic cost, made itself militarily superior to any combination of neighboring armies, and it has had the generous support of the Diaspora and also of the United States government. The struggle is rather an internal one, over the character and quality of life of the Jewish state.

This struggle has taken and takes many forms, but one of the more fundamental is that of two tendencies from within the Zionist movement, the one working for a Jewish state, the other for the recovery for the Jews of the biblical Land of Israel. Gentiles should be aware that if they take either side, they are joining some Jews against other Jews. Gentile Christians, therefore, would do well to move with great circumspection when considering this issue, remembering above all that this conflict within the Jewish people is a reflection of Israel's place in the vanguard of creation as it wrestles with God's demand upon it to be his co-worker in the restoration and completion of creation.

iv. Israel for the Enlightenment

The remarkably central role of Jews in the movements of modernity that began with the Enlightenment is a part of Israel's witness to the need to work for the completion of creation, not less when it has come in totally secularized forms. Two hundred years ago there began the Emancipation of the Jewish people from the restrictions placed upon them by the governments of Christendom. They were given equal status before the law in the new United States and the doctrine of equality of the French Revolution soon spread across Europe. Emancipation opened the doors of the ghetto, and Jews threw themselves into every line of work and cause for social betterment thus opened to them for the first time since the Christian church came to power in the Roman Empire. The participation of Jews in the work of every field of human learning and service soon grew out of all proportion to their numbers. In the sciences and the humanities, in medicine, music and the arts, in government and public service, Jews have made outstanding contributions.

At the beginning of this development, Moses Mendelssohn showed himself to be a champion of the Enlightenment by arguing that the teachings of true religion were to be found by reason alone. For him the God of reason and the God of Sinai were one. Judaism, therefore, was not a revealed religion; it was a revealed law. The God of reason revealed his Torah as the way for the Jews. Gentiles were in no way obligated to follow this path. Consequently, there was for him no conflict whatsoever between utter fidelity to Torah, the Jewish pattern of life, and full participation in the Enlightenment. Indeed, he thought that the improvement of the conditions under which Jews lived was fully consistent with human progress, in effect, that the Emancipation of the Jews was a natural consequence of the Enlightenment.

As the reign of the Enlightenment came to an end with the First World War, the famous Marburg philosopher, Hermann Cohen, could still write a book entitled *Die Religion der Vernunft aus der Quellen des Judentums*! True, by this time, God had become for Cohen more than an idea, a postulate of reason, but Cohen was still convinced that there was no conflict between enlightened rationalism and enlightened Judaism. The future of Jewish hope was identical with the future of humanity, for human beings were co-workers in the renewal of creation, with the responsibility to bring about the messianic era. Once more we hear Israel's persistent witness to the need to work for the completion of creation, even when that witness came perilously close to losing itself in the optimism of the Enlightenment.

3. THE WITNESS TO CREATURELY LIMITS

i. Assimilation

Israel's witness to human responsibility in God's purposes is tempered by its further witness to the fact that human beings are creatures who cannot do the work of God except as his co-workers. The covenant testifies to God's desire that he have human partners in the work of renewing creation, but the partnership is of unequals. The human component is essential, but it is so because God has graciously taken it up and assigned a place to it in his plans. Faithful Israel knows that its Redeemer is the LORD. Humanity has a role to play, but what it can accomplish is limited.

Evidence of the limitations of creaturely solutions to creation's problems may be seen in the erosion of the great hopes awakened by the Emancipation when it was discovered that Emancipation was intended to be on the Gentiles' terms. If a Moses Mendelssohn could embrace the Enlightenment, said his Gentile critics, then he should leave his narrow Jewish ways behind and become a good Christian "like the rest of us." What went by the name of Emancipation was in fact intended by the powers that be — and was accepted by many Jews — as an invitation to assimilation. Conservatives had feared just this consequence of the course that Mendelssohn advocated, and this fear underlies the Orthodox disdain of Reform Judaism. The Orthodox objection should not be dismissed as reactionary; they feared for the future of the Jewish people, and their fears were not absurd. For untold numbers of Jews, the door out of the ghetto became the way out of Jewishness.

Emancipation was greeted by many Jews as freedom to be openly Jewish, but for many others it presented a "freedom" to leave their people. The pressures leading to this eventuality were not only external. The pattern of Jewish life had been developed with a realistic view of the hostility of the enveloping Christendom. To live Jewishly in an open society, that of the United States, for example, has proved to be too much of a bother for many, with the result that within several generations in this new environment, about one in three Jews "opts out" (A. Hertzberg, "The Emancipation: a Reassessment after Two Centuries," *Modern Judaism*, 1, 1981, 48). If the remaining two were to marry, they would have to raise on average three children as Jews simply to maintain present numbers.

Zionism, which was supposed to have been the solution to both anti-Jewism and assimilation, has also shown mixed results. It has drawn only a minority of Jews to the land of Israel, and it has offered the world an additional target for anti-Jewish hostility. Part of this failure was due perhaps to the fact that as a European movement, Zionism never took sufficiently into consideration the Jewish experience in America, where assimilation rather than anti-Jewism was becoming the larger problem. More serious is the fact that the great dream of a Jewish state as a haven from hatred has proved hard to realize, if one listens to Israeli critics of their own society. The hostility of neighboring Arab states has made of Israel a major military power, which was not exactly the Zionist dream.

The state of Israel provides ample evidence of the limitations inherent in the execution of the best of human intentions. The state that was to have ended anti-Jewism now finds itself stirring up hatred for all Jews, even in countries where almost none live. Geoffrey Wigoder, in an article surveying "The Jewish Scene in 5742," the year ending in September 1982 (*The Jerusalem Post*, International Edition, No. 1, 141, 16), listed the synagogue bombings and other acts of terrorism to which the Jews of the Diaspora had been subjected during the year and argued that most of this had come with a rising tide of anti-Israel feelings, much increased by the war in Lebanon and the way in which it was presented by the media. Then came a period of intense debate in the Knesset and throughout the country over the massacre of civilians in the Palestinian refugee camps, not fully stopped by the appointment of an official commission of inquiry. It is a little-considered irony that, although none deny that it was *Christians* who did the killing, the argument centered entirely on the extent of *Jewish* responsibility for this tragic affair. That is a minor point, but it reflects both the difficulties that Israel has had in achieving its own goals, and also its dedication to those goals.

The one thing that seems clear in all this is that a Gentile church that wishes to hear Israel's witness will do well to listen to all sides and attend to many Jewish voices. If it does so, it will hear not only of the pressing need to work for the renewal of creation, but also of the limits of all that human beings can accomplish. It will above all be given grounds to stand in amazement that God should be so daring as to have called his weak and erring creatures to be his partners and co-workers.

ii. Israel against the Enlightenment

We have heard Israel's voice in support of the Enlightenment;

we should also hear its voice in opposition to the Enlightenment. No one is more worth listening to on this score than Franz Rosenzweig, precisely because he was himself such a product of enlightened reason and became so thoroughly assimilated to the world of the German intellectual. Shaken in his relativism as a result of arguments with Eugen Rosenstock-Huessy, and on the brink of becoming a Christian, Rosenzweig discovered the immediacy and intimacy of the relationship between God and his people, and that, in returning to God, he was already at home and had no need to journey elsewhere.

What Rosenzweig "discovered" was God, not his Jewishness. His Jewishness mattered to him greatly, but that was because of his belief in God's election of the Jewish people. The turning point of his thought was not the uniqueness of his people nor a mess of potage labeled "Jewish values"; the turning point was what he called "the offensive idea of revelation." To Rosenzweig's Enlightenment-formed mind, the thought was indeed offensive, and, as he argued in his essay *"Atheistishe Theologie,"* it was offensive to the whole period, especially to a German intellectual. Nevertheless, that became his starting point for a whole "new thinking," as he called his theology.

Rosenzweig's voice is an important part of the witness of Israel to the priority of God in the redemption of the world. In his *Der Stern der Erlösung*, he gave an important place to the role of the creature as God's partner, in the Introduction to the Third Part the theme treated is "the Possibility of Obtaining the Kingdom by Prayer" (*das Reich zu Erbeten*). The role assigned to human beings is prayer. A more anti-Enlightenment conception of human responsibility for the future of the world would be hard to imagine. Rosenzweig, it need scarcely be added, was no Zionist, but this side of Israel's witness is also to be heard.

iii. Diaspora-by-choice

A third element in Israel's witness to the limitations inherent in the human contribution to God's purposes is the new fact,

which cannot be hidden, of Diaspora-by-choice. No less ambiguous than any other part of Israel's life and witness, from
its beginning to today, this new fact is one that can be interpreted in many ways. It is understandable that Israelis see
Diaspora-by-choice as a falling away from Jewish identity. It
was one thing to be in the Diaspora when there was no alternative, but now the Jewish state exists and programs are in place
to facilitate the transition for those who make *aliyah*. To decide
to remain in the Diaspora as a matter of choice is regarded as
self-contradictory behavior.

On the other hand, it can be argued that the Diaspora
represents an important form of Jewish existence and witness.
As leaven spread through the Gentile world, Jews slowly help
bring the day when all the world will acknowledge God and live
according to his will. It is therefore a messianic obligation to
remain where one lives. There are of course any number of
economic and secular reasons for Jews to remain, for example,
in the United States, or for three times the number of Jewish
emigrants from the Soviet Union to go to America as go to Israel,
but there are also religious arguments offered for as well as against
Diaspora-by-choice.

There is a further witness which the Jewish people are making by this divided identity and location, and that is to the inadequacy of any arrangement to bring the day of redemption.
Jews who have chosen to go to Israel bear witness to the evils
from which they fled and to their new/old nation as marking
the dawn of redemption. They point to both the unredeemed
character of the world, and yet to the possibility and hope for
its redemption. Jews who have chosen to remain in the Diaspora
bear witness to the fact that redemption concerns the whole world
and that the state of Israel is only a part, if assuredly the central
part, of God's creation. They point both to the world that God
will redeem, and also to the fact that the state of Israel may well
be a sign, even if it is not more than a sign, of the dawn of that
redemption.

iv. Hidden light for the world

One of the more interesting but little-known examples of Israel's actual exercise of its calling to be a light to the nations, carried out within the framework of secular nationhood, is its program of international assistance to developing countries, especially in Africa and Latin America. Following several earlier initiatives, the program was formally established in 1958, only ten years after the birth of the state, as the Division for International Cooperation within the Ministry of Foreign Affairs (*E.J.*, 9, 435ff). Being a small country with little capital resources, Israel concentrated on people, sending out experts in agriculture, education, medicine, community development, and public administration, and bringing in people from developing countries for intensive training in Israeli institutions. By the end of its first decade, Israel had sent out 2,562 experts to 64 Third World countries and had trained 10,569 men and women from 82. By 1972 the figures had reached 4,362 and 15,374 respectively (*E.J.*, 1973 Yearbook, 238). Although formal diplomatic relations with Israel were broken off by many African states benefiting from this service, following the Yom Kippur War of 1973, in most cases means were found to continue the work—and it is still going on: by 1981, the number of experts sent abroad had reached 8,190; the number of trainees, 25,796!

The numbers are impressive for a small country, but the figures do not tell the whole story. The slogan under which this program of international assistance has been conducted is "Serve, teach, leave." That is to say, the policy of Israeli experts abroad is to initiate the program of assistance, train the local people to continue it themselves, and then depart just as soon as it can be carried on without Israeli help. This means that Israel's international assistance experts working in developing countries abroad are constantly initiating new projects and turning them over to be run by trained citizens of the benefiting countries.

Unquestionably Israel has been seeking to make friends beyond its encircling hostile neighbors with its program of international assistance, and friendly relations lead to economic relations. Nevertheless, in this "secular" form, Israel is proving faithful to its calling to be a light and a blessing to the nations of the world, especially to those nations that, like Israel, have relatively recently won independence and are learning how to stand on their own feet.

4. THE POSSIBILITY OF CREATURELY COOPERATION WITH GOD

i. Holy worldliness

By living its covenantal relation with God, Israel is God's witness in the world that he has made possible creaturely cooperation with his redemptive purpose. Israel bears this witness by its practice of a holy worldliness and a worldly holiness. With the first expression we refer to the Jewish way of claiming the totality of life as the realm for fidelity to God. With the second we refer to the consequent indivisibility of Jewish life.

Jewish fidelity to God involves the whole person in the totality of his or her life, in the context of the total Jewish people. (It may be that fidelity to God is a concern of but one-tenth of all Jews. If so, we shall speak now of that one-tenth, the remnant, and then take up the others nine-tenths under the heading of the indivisibility of Jewish life.) Fidelity to God means turning back to God, or repentance. Although there is a special time of repentance in the Jewish year, the High Holy Days, with their climax in the Day of Atonement, *Yom Kippur*, Jewish existence is in every moment and in every situation a continuing turning back to God. From the biblical authors, through the Tannaim, through the great teacher Maimonides and up to such contemporary sages as Rabbi Soleveitchik, turning—repentance—has been seen as the decisive mark of Jewish life, *all* of Jewish life. To live Jewishly is to live in this constant renewal, from birth to death.

This gives to Jewish life its vitality, for there is no moment when the faithful Jew is not humbly picking him- or herself up, as it were, and setting out once more on the ever new path which

God has provided. When faithful Jews doodle in a dull moment, it is with the holy alphabet that they play, and when anything at all occurs, they have a blessing appropriate to the occasion. Their hours, days, weeks, and years are set in a rhythm of Jewish fidelity, so that in all they do, they can do it Jewishly.

The cycle of the day is marked by prayers on arising, so that there is a blessing to say for every act of preparing oneself for the coming day. Thrice daily come the regular prayers and blessings, but there are also blessings said for quite normal occurrences, such as how the weather turns out, and also for unanticipated events, such as the arrival of a guest, meeting an admirable stranger (Gentile as well as Jew—each is accorded an appropriate blessing), or the receipt of bad news. There is a grace to be said before meals and another after meals, but there are also individual blessings to be said over every manner of nourishment. There is even a blessing for the occasion of seeing a person of abnormal appearance: "Blessed art thou, LORD our God, King of the Universe, who dost vary the aspect of thy creatures" (*P.B.*, 778).

The totality of time is taken up into Jewish life as well by the weekly cycle based on Shabbat, which crowns the week and to which the whole week tends, and again by the cycle of the Jewish calendar, with its months and festivals. The result is that at any moment of the day, and in any day in the year, the Jew lives in Jewish time. Not a moment falls outside of this time.

Jewish existence is not only within Jewish time; it is made up of Jewish activity, for all activity for the faithful Jew is Jewish. This includes, second only to the study of Torah, one's relationships with others, beginning with the family. Most of what Gentiles would call "religion" is for Jews the life of the Jewish family— its life, that is, not just its praying and blessings, but also how it buys, cooks, and eats its food; its topics of conversation, and its loving and making love. Nowhere, according to rabbinic tradition, is the Presence of God (the *Shekhinah*) more certain than when a husband and wife make love together! The day-in-day-out life of the family is where Jewish existence happens.

Jewish existence sanctifies time and makes it Jewish through observation of the *Mitzvot*, the commandments, the broadest of which is the commandment to perform deeds of loving kindness. Such deeds relate first of all to human beings, but they also include how one treats animals, any living creature, and even nature. The *Mitzvot* of Torah, however, cover every realm of life, one's business dealings as well as holiday observance, conduct in war as well as helping the poor. The great halakhic tradition provides guidance in all areas of life; whether one adheres to it strictly or more flexibly, it stands as the sign that no area or aspect of life falls outside of the covenantal relationship to God.

And now, for the first time again after two millennia, Jews have been able to include the full range of political activity within the realm of fidelity to God. Jews of course have been active in politics and public affairs in the Diaspora to the extent that this has been possible for them in open societies, but the state of Israel is their own and there they have the full responsibility once more for the complex act of political fidelity to God. Here the halakhic tradition is less helpful, having been developed under conditions of the Galut, when Jews had little or no political responsibility or power. Nevertheless, the whole of Jewish tradition, from the biblical to the present time, makes impossible the exclusion of this area of life from the realm of fidelity to God.

We have seen that landed life for Israel is central to the covenant. Landed life entails political responsibility and power, and a good deal of the Scriptures is devoted to how fidelity to God is to be lived politically. The books of Joshua and Judges, Kings and Chronicles, and much of the prophetic corpus remind us that this has been an area of the most acute tension in Israel's life in the covenant. Jews have always disagreed about politics, but there have been few Jews who have ever thought that politics did not matter. So in the state of Israel today, but scarcely less in the Diaspora, Jews argue passionately over the right political and social course of that small country. The political debate in the Jewish community today over the policies of the Israeli government have all the intensity of a battle for the soul of the

Jewish people, and that is because nothing less than this is at stake. Thus Israel bears witness to the totality of life as the realm in which fidelity to God is to be lived. Gentiles would do well to listen and learn that lesson with as much or more attention as they devote to giving Jews advice about how they should proceed.

ii. Worldly holiness

We turn now to the consequence of Israel's holy worldliness, to its worldly holiness, or the indivisibility of the Jewish people, *klal Yisrael*. What we have described of Jewish existence is, we pointed out, one that may in actual practice be lived consciously and conscientiously by perhaps but a tenth of the people. What about the others, who make up the vast majority of the Jewish people? Here the Gentiles need to be especially attentive to Israel's witness if it is to be heard at all. Indeed, if the Gentile church does not hear Israel's witness at this point, it will misunderstand everything else in it. It is therefore incumbent on a Christian theology of the people Israel to make clear that God did not choose for himself a religion; he chose a people in all its worldly, irreligious reality. The holiness of this people is precisely its distinctive in-the-world existence as a whole people.

Israel has what may be called an inner as well as an outer unity. It knows no distinction between a religious and a secular sphere. It is all one, all God's creation. This unity arises from Israel's conviction of the unity and uniqueness of God. Everything else is creation. To separate out a religious part of creation is to start down the road to idolatry, and idolatry has always been for Israel *the* transgression. Neither the so-called "religious" Jew nor the so-called "secular" Jew has any brief to make for religion. They may argue and even come to blows, or at least stone-throwing, over Torah observance, but not over religion.

Israel's inner unity is grounded not only in the otherness of God but also in the nearness of God, a God whose reality is often more of a problem than a joy. The secular Jew may be sure God does not exist and yet spell the word with care, as we have seen, or wish that the nonexistent God would stop bothering the Jewish people. As someone once said of a quite nonreligious Jew, "She has this guest in the attic who won't go away." That "Guest in the attic" is part of the unifying destiny, whether wanted or not, of every Jew.

Israel's unity, however, is most evident in its outer form, and here is where the Gentile distinction of religious/secular proves to be utterly inapplicable to this people. A Jew is a Jew, and whatever it is that makes a Jew, it is not religion. This is recognized by the Talmud and also by the so-called secular "Law of Return" of the Jewish state. In that "secular" state, *Shabbat* is truly a day of rest as no Sunday is in any land of what was once Christendom. In the Diaspora, where the subtle linguistic and other forces of the pervasive Christian culture have left their mark, Jews themselves are tempted to use the distinction of religious/secular, but in the state of Israel, even a Christian is hard pressed to apply it. Jewishness is a unity, and the Jews are one people.

The solidarity of all Jews in the one people Israel is a theme oft reiterated in Diaspora demonstrations in support of the state of Israel. At all times, but especially in moments of danger, Jews acknowledge this unity without distinction between "religious" and "nonreligious," between Diaspora Jew and Israeli, between Orthodox, Conservative, Reconstructionist, and Reform. The Jew who stands with his fellow Jew in the service of the Jewish people, or the Jew who stands with others, Jews and Gentiles, in the service of their fellow human beings, is doing the work cut out for the people Israel, no matter what other differences there may be between them. Israel as one whole people Israel is the central Jewish concept that makes distinctions of religiousness utterly irrelevant.

In this central part of Israel's witness to the possibility of cooperation with each other in cooperation with God's call to his people, there is to be detected the reality corresponding to the vision of the last days of Dietrich Bonhoeffer. Bonhoeffer had not learned to look with attention to the witness of living Israel, but he had begun to learn to read the Scriptures as far more than a preparation for the Apostolic Writings. To support his vision of what he called a "religionless Christianity," he could have found a living model in Israel's worldly holiness.

The Gentile church is called to attend to Israel's witness of worldly holiness and learn from it not to worry so much about its denominational distinctions. The people Israel stands as a sign of a lived oneness, holiness, and catholicity which the church has sought to learn only from the apostles. It should recall where the apostles learned of this. Indeed, Israel's embodied, worldly holiness should encourage the church not to worry too much about "faith," about "being Christian," even about being "born again." For God has called the Gentile church to be to the people Israel what Diaspora Jewry is to the Jewish state.

Consider the proportion: The Gentile church is to the Jewish people as the Diaspora is to the Jewish state. On what level and to what extent will this proportion hold? On one level, it is clearly false, for the Jew of the Diaspora and the Israeli are both Jews. On the level of theological dependence and support, however, and so as a guide to understanding the church's calling in relation to that of Israel, it has possibilities.

Let us look first at the second half, the relationship between Diaspora Jewry and the state of Israel. It seems clear by now that the Zionist goal of a total *aliyah* of all the Jewish people does not represent the reality of the Jewish response to the latest developments in its covenant with God. There is every indication that the Diaspora is going to continue — indeed, that the Jewish state depends in part on the support, and therefore on the existence, of world Jewry. That support is only partly financial. It is also political and spiritual. Jews of the Diaspora work and pray for the Jewish state and count its survival and well-being a matter of deepest concern. The support is therefore mutual: the Jewish state supports all Jews in their identity as Jews and in their sense of solidarity as the whole house of Israel. The Jews of the Diaspora do not on the whole feel that they have to join — that is, move to — the Jewish state, but they would be devastated were it to come to harm. The Jewish state makes it possible for many Jews to remain Jews. We can summarize this complex relationship by saying that within the fundamental unity that overarches all differences, the Diaspora supports the Jewish state upon which its own Diaspora existence depends.

We come then to the first half of the proportion, having to do with the relationship between the church and the Jewish people. We have already argued that this is first of all one of theological dependence. It is as painful and difficult to imagine what would become of the church were there no more Jews in the world (as a result of any combination of disasters, total assimilation, or mass conversions) as it is to imagine the effect on the Diaspora of the disappearance of the Jewish state. God may know what he would do under such circumstances, but his revelation to this point offers the church no clue as to how it could carry on. The covenant between God and Israel and between God and the church would surely be up for renegotiation. As it is, however, the church is supported in its existence by the life of the Jewish people as the Diaspora is supported by the Jewish state. A reciprocal support, however, then comes immediately into view. As the Diaspora provides material and political support for the state of Israel, so it would appear that the church is called to provide such help to the life of the whole Jewish people.

In spite of the overwhelming evidence that the church has not provided such support, there are tokens of it running through the whole history of the relationship between the church and the Jewish people. That support appears to be the logical, at least the theological, conclusion to which a Christian theology of the people Israel must arrive. Israel's witness to the possibility of creaturely cooperation with God tends in this direction. The final possibility of human cooperation with God — and this is consistent with all of Israel's witness — would thus take the form of human cooperation, specifically, that of the church with the Jewish people. The shape of this cooperation is therefore the final subject for a Christian theology of the people Israel.

CHAPTER ELEVEN

The Church's Service to Israel

The church, called to be a witness to Christ among all the nations, and having a special relationship to Israel, has the specific mission to the Jewish people of serving them in their task of being a light for the nations. In fulfilling this special mission, the church will be witnessing to Jesus as the one Jew through whom God has brought it to the service of his people, which is the foundation of all its service to their, his, and now its own God and Father.

1. THE CHURCH'S MISSION — AND THE JEWS

i. The church as mission

We come to the final task of a Christian theology of the people Israel: the definition of the church's service to God's elect people, the Jews. This *novum* for theological reflection and church practice presupposes the more startling *novum* of the very existence of the Gentile church. The concept of the church's service to Israel is only possible on the basis of the strange new step taken by God in calling into existence things that were not in a new way, by taking what can only be regarded as a radical new turn in his history with his creation. That new step, grounded in the death and resurrection of the Jew Jesus and initiated with the calling of his apostle to the Gentiles, was to bring Gentiles into the history that he had begun with his people Israel. This step cannot be regarded as the beginning of a new history, as Marcion would have had us believe, but as a new step in the history that began with Abraham, as Paul saw so clearly. The old story was alive and well, but now a strange new chapter was begun: the Gentiles were to be part of the central plot.

Until this point, the plot focused almost exclusively on Israel, with the other nations mostly on the periphery. Other nations, notably Egypt, Assyria, and Babylon, had had important roles to play, but the story was essentially Israel's. In order to keep Israel's history intact, it was apparently necessary to keep this small people apart from the other nations, lest it be swallowed up and assimilated into the surrounding, powerful cultures. An essential part of the reforms initiated by Ezra and carried through by the Sages, Pharisees, and Rabbis, was the development of the oral Torah as a means of preserving the distinctiveness of Israel.

With the beginning of the new step of bringing Gentiles into the story, it was all the more important that Israel's distinctness not be lost. Who could predict the success of this new venture, this experiment of Gentiles *as Gentiles* in the service of the God of Israel? Where was the Gentile church to look to remind it who this God was, launched as it was in the sea of Gentile polytheism and the cultural and religious pluralism of the Roman Empire? For such was the commission of this new entity. It was to go out to "all the nations," the *ethne*, the *goyim*, making disciples from among them (Matt. 28:19). That entailed coming into the closest conversation with the Hellenistic world and its ways, in which listening had to take place as well as speaking, learning as well as teaching. The risk that the church would lose its way in this venture was great. It was clearly in the interests of keeping the covenant on course, that, during the launching of this new enterprise and as it was getting steadied on its course, Israel should concentrate on developing its distinctiveness, precisely for the sake of this mission by Gentiles to other Gentiles in the name of the God of Israel.

With Israel's life firmly anchored in the Torah, then, God could take the risk with the church of sending out a Gentile-staffed mission to the Gentiles, in order that what he had begun with his people could begin to work its way slowly into the lives of all his peoples. That mission was and is the Gentile church. It exists as the outer extention of the covenant between God and his people Israel, laying the claim of God upon all his creatures which he had modeled forth in his covenant with the Jews.

The author of Luke/Acts would appear to have misled us when he put in the mouth of Paul (Acts 13:46), "The word of God has to be declared to you [Jews] first of all; but since you reject it and thus convict yourselves as unworthy of everlasting life, we now turn to the Gentiles." From what we have of Paul's own thoughts on the subject, he could never have said such a thing. The author of these words had a simplistic or unitary view of "the word of God," in contrast to Paul's more dialectical sense of God's work. What "the Jews"—or rather some of them—rejected was the idea that Jews should associate with Gentiles on equal terms in this new enterprise, for they would thereby be putting their Jewishness in jeopardy. Some of them—again we do not know who or how many—did not agree with Paul that the death and resurrection of Jesus was God's signal for opening to Gentiles a life with him outside of Torah fidelity. Paul, unlike the author of Acts, was well-enough trained in Pharisaic theology to know that no one was ever "worthy" of "everlasting life": everlasting life is God's gracious gift. But Paul was also sure that a human rejection of this new turn of events could in no way entail God's rejection of his people. Paul regretted deeply (cf. Rom. 9:1ff) that his fellow Jews did not share his enthusiasm for the new chapter in the story of Israel, in which the Gentiles appeared as co-beneficiaries of the promises to Abraham, but it is clear (2 Cor. 1:20—all God's promises find their "yes" in him, *not* their "fulfillment," as the *NAB* would have it) that he saw this chapter as a confirmation of all of the story up to this point. Paul was no party to the displacement theory of Acts. What he did share with the author of Acts was the conviction that the church exists as the mission of the God of Israel to the nations of the world.

ii. *The fate of the mission*

The history of that mission is simply the history of the church. It would not be until the nineteenth century, when the church had become thoroughly confused about its own origin, identity, and purpose, that the theologically impossible idea would surface that there should be "missionary societies," as if the church could itself be other than that. For several centuries the story of the church was the story of the penetration of the Bible and the biblical awareness of the God of Abraham, Isaac, and Jacob into the world of the Roman Empire, although not without some reciprocal penetration of that empire and its culture into the church. The risk involved in this mission was everywhere and at all times evident, although seldom seen at the time. The Hellenization, not to speak of the Byzantinization, of the church was the almost unavoidable price of the Christianization of the Hellenistic and Byzantine worlds. It was well for the future of the covenant that the Rabbis labored hard to "build a fence around the Torah" and keep Israel true to its covenant.

As the empire came to an end in all but name, the mission reached up to the north and there took such a hold that out of Ireland came a new stream of the mission, reaching down into Teutonic lands and building the base for a new "Holy Roman Empire" that was the foundation for Europe. With the expansion of European power around the globe, "the cross followed the sword," and the phrase reveals how much the church had paid for the mission which was its identity. It was now "European Christianity" that was spread around the globe, not without its roots in Israel's covenant, but also not aware of itself as the Gentile mission of the God of Israel. It had long since drunk too deeply at the wells of Rome and Byzantium to have been able to distinguish between the sweep of God's claim and its own presumptions to universality.

Mixed as the picture has been, however, the church's history is the history of God's Gentile mission to the nations. The church *is* that mission, and there is no proper understanding of it apart from that task begun with the calling of the apostle to the Gentiles. The great difference between what began with Paul and what was carried out in the following centuries is that Paul was a Jew and knew full well that his calling and sending was directly connected with and confirmatory of God's promises to his people. Paul's successors were Gentiles, and they lacked both Paul's training and also his deep concern for his people Israel. The greatest weakness in the church's expression of its missionary identity was that it forgot the people whose existence provided the base for its work. It became "Western" or "Eastern," "Protestant" or "Catholic," "Asian" or "American" Christianity, no longer *Israel's* Christianity. It had long since lost all sense of wonder before the miracle of its own existence as Gentiles who adored the God of Israel. Indeed, it had engaged in the supreme act of theological forgetfulness to such an extent that it saw itself as the sole reason for Israel having existed. It could therefore make no sense of Israel's present existence. Little wonder, therefore, that it was utterly unprepared in this century to offer resistance to an attempt to eradicate the Jewish people. The mission had gone thoroughly astray.

iii. *The strange modern idea of "mission to the Jews"*

The mission of the God of Israel among the Gentiles was over seventeen and a half centuries old before anyone who was a part of it hit on the strange idea of setting up a special society to carry on a mission to the Jews. It will be worth the time to think through how such an eventuality could ever have arisen. It happened in London, in the year of the Common Era 1809, and was soon being duplicated in other places. Other "missionary societies," focused on other targets, were also coming into being at the time. It was a time of great entrepreneurial enterprise in all areas. The European nations were spreading their empires about the globe, not accidentally to the great benefit of their large trading companies. Why should not the church have done something similar?

In one sense, the missionary activities of these societies was an expression of the commitment of the Christians who set them up and went overseas as their missionaries. These Christians could therefore be seen as the representatives of their churches, doing vicariously, as it were, what the whole church had been called to do. Whatever may be said of the results, surely the intention was of the highest sort. On the other hand, these missionary societies could hardly have arisen had not the church on the whole settled down to a stable existence that laid little emphasis on its calling to "make disciples of all the nations." Had the church assumed that this had already been done at home, so that now it had only to make disciples from among "the heathen" in the recently acquired overseas possessions of their home countries? Insofar as the answer is affirmative, to that extent the appearance of foreign missionary societies must also be judged to have been an expression of self-satisfaction on the part of the western churches.

The founding of these societies reveals something more about the state of the church at the beginning of the nineteenth century, and not only at that time: the dominant conviction among Christians was that the only way any human being could be "saved" was by becoming a Christian. Proof-texts from the Apostolic Writings in support of this conviction were not wanting. For example, there was Romans 10:9: "For if you confess with your lips that Jesus is Lord and believe in your heart that God raised him from the dead, you will be saved," followed four versus later by a quotation from Joel 2:32: "Everyone who calls on the name of the Lord will be saved," both serving the purpose best when read out of context and with the assumption that each positive claim about who would be saved entailed a negative one about those who would not. The same hermeneutics produced stronger proof-texts from the Gospel of John, and with more justification, since that Gospel goes out of its way to spell out the negative side of its positive assertions. "God so loved the world," begins its best-known verse (3:16), but the negative side of this appears two verses later: "He who believes in him is not condemned; he who does not believe is condemned already." Add to this the Johannine saying attributed to Jesus, "No one comes to the Father but by me" (14:7), and the case seemed complete. The saying of Cyprian (the third-century bishop of Carthage), that there is no salvation outside the church (again, taken out of context), also counted, especially for those wanting some support in the tradition for biblical proof-texts. On these foundations, missionary societies came into existence in order to "save" from eternal damnation the unfortunate heathen not blessed by birth in a Christian nation.

Since the fourth volume of this theology of the Jewish-Christian reality will be devoted to the relations of not only the church, but also the Jewish people, to other religions and convictions, I shall not further pursue in this place the subject of the church's missionary efforts among Muslims, Hindus, Buddhists, and others to convert them to Christianity, nor explore whether another view of God's presence and purpose in the histories of these other peoples, than that which informed those efforts, might not be possible. Here, too, Israel will have something to teach the church. At this point, we must stick to our subject.

More striking and strange than the church's assumption of the exclusive universality of its message and purpose was the incredible idea that the Jewish people, the Israel of God, fell within the scope of its mission to the *Gentiles*! What else is to be concluded from the founding of a special mission to the Jews within the context of the missionary movements of the nineteenth century? Israel had to be seen as a nation "like all the others." Forgotten had to be the fact that the church was called to be a mission of the God of Israel. That Jesus lived and died a Jew, that all his disciples and apostles were Jews, that "salvation is from the Jews" (Jn. 4:22), was ignored. Having so fully forgotten who the Jewish people were, it was inevitable that the church should lose its own sense of identity. Such would have to have been the case for it to have invented the theologically impossible notion of a "mission to the Jews." The full extent of the apostasy involved was not seen at the time. In the years 1933 to 1945 it became painfully clear.

iv. The incoherence of "mission to the Jews"

What have been the consequences of this "mission to the Jews?" It was of course a striking sign, for any who could read it, that the church had forgotten where it came from, who it was and why it was here, and so had lost its last shreds of credibility. The nations, the Gentiles, knew well enough in their own way who the Jews were, but who knew what the church was — and who cared? Having lost its center in its elected tie to Israel, the church increasingly came apart around the periphery. As for "converts," the numbers were small. That was hardly surprising. To whom or what should the Jew convert? Did not he or she already know the one God, the God of Israel? The most that the Jew could do was to *turn back*, or turn again, repent, to that God. The most the church could offer was an unfitting Gentile way for the Jew to do that, in contrast to the way that God had given his people. In short, the church could only reach the Jew who had lost his Jewishness. The church may have "won" a number of assimilated Jews, but probably no more than the Jews "won" converts from among ex-Christians.

Except in the case of mass, forced "conversions," there have never been many Jews who have joined the church, and that is just as well. Too often the apostate who joined the church in the past turned out to be the worst sort of anti-Jewish force in the church, stirring up pogroms with all sorts of libels based on a presumed knowledge of Jewish beliefs and practices. It has, however, been even more of a blessing for the church than it has for Israel that its various attempts at converting Jews have been so singularly unsuccessful. Every such effort is in effect an attempt to rid the world of Jews, and where would the church be if it were to succeed in such an undertaking? Of course the church is mission, nothing but mission, but it is the mission of the God of Israel. A God of Israel who had lost his Israel, the God of the covenant who had lost the covenant partner, could hardly be the God who had called together a Gentile church in fulfillment of a part of his promise to Abraham and in confirmation of all his promises to his people Israel. A church without an Israel could hardly confirm Israel and God's promises to it. It could only be a sign of the failure of the covenant and so of the failure of God. It would be living a stark contradiction.

There are former Jews who have joined the church, just as there are those who have been baptized who have become Jews. This has been the case almost certainly since the first century of the Common Era. Whatever the reasons that might be given in either case, these persons may be looked upon as evidence of the intimate theological relationship (however unpleasant the actual historical relationship) between the church and the Jewish people. They surely could not be regarded as "converts," since on either side they could only have known the God of Israel. As in the case of the apostle to the Gentiles, it would be more proper to speak of them as having received a calling to serve God in a new way, and God's call can come in many and diverse ways. A "mission to the Jews," as it has been conceived since the beginning of the nineteenth century, however, seems hardly a likely candidate for one of these ways. Instead of pursuing such a self-contradictory and ultimately self-defeating project, it would be better for the church to think through again the meaning of its special relationship to the people Israel. Only on the basis of that relationship can it discover and carry out its proper mission to the Jews.

2. THE PROPER MISSION OF THE CHURCH TO THE JEWISH PEOPLE

i. *The proper setting*

The special relationship that is the foundation for rethinking the church's mission to the Jews is one that exists between the church and the Jewish people — the people Israel, not individual Jews. The church may properly approach the Gentiles around it as individuals; it may only relate to the individual Jew always as one of his or her people. To put it another way, the church is obliged by the special relationship that exists between it and Israel to relate to Jews in a manner exactly opposite to that of the Enlightenment slogan, "Everything to the Jew as an individual; nothing to the Jews as a people." The reason is simple: the church's relationship to the Jews depends on and is defined by the covenant between God and Israel, and that covenant was made by God with Israel as a people.

The church, as we have said, is defined by its mission. In all that it is and does, it lives in this sending. Its calling is to penetrate and diffuse itself among the nations with its message and worship of the God of Israel. Its relationship to the Jews will therefore also be that of a mission, unavoidably set in the context of its having been sent to the nations. In this sense, then, the church will also have a mission to the Jews, although what that mission is has yet to be defined. We must not let the connotations of the term "mission," given to it by the nineteenth century, determine its use. The church has been redefining the term in recent decades as a result of much fresh thinking about God's relation to and its own reason for being in his world. It is therefore to be expected that as Israel has a special relationship to the church, unlike that of any other people, so a special redefinition will be necessary here. If one sets the theology and practice of the nineteenth century to one side for a moment, the word "mission" appears open to many possible interpretations. One need think only of the variety of patterns which emerge under the heading of a diplomatic mission, such as those of nation-states. The nature and task of a diplomatic mission depends entirely on the relationship between the countries concerned. So it will be with the church's mission to the Jews.

The first determination of that mission is that it will be concerned with the Jews "as a people," not with the individual Jew "as an individual." Of course the individual Christian will enter into all sorts of relationships with individual Jews, but that can only count as part of the church's mission to the Jews when the individual Jew is seen and treated as one of the people Israel. To do otherwise would be to deny the election by God of his people, which would be to undermine as well the foundation of the church. If the church would be faithful to God and his calling, it will relate to the Jews as an elect people and to the individual Jew as one of this people. This follows from the proper setting of the church's mission, which is the relationship with

Israel out of which it was born and in which it has been set by God.

ii. *The burden of the past*

The setting for the church's mission to the Jews is profoundly marked by the past. Almost nineteen centuries of that past have with rare exception seen nothing but an attitude on the part of the church of scorn, disdain, and often hatred toward Jews, both individually and collectively. The record is uncomfortably consistent. The church's mission to the Jews can only be reconsidered and set on its proper course by a church that acknowledges to itself, to God, and to the Jewish people that it needs to be forgiven. The burden of the past is too great to overcome in any other way. The church has no right to count on that forgiveness. It can only "bring forth fruits worthy of repentance" (Matt. 3:8). The *NAB* offers a free translation of this admonition of John the Baptist that fits well: "Give some evidence that you mean to reform." In the last analysis, the Jews and God, not the church, must be the judges of the credibility of whatever the church offers as evidence of a serious intent to reform.

The Jews and God must be the judges in this matter, because they are the ones who have been hurt. At one level the church has done great harm to itself by taking the world's side against the Jews, indeed by leading the world in anti-Jewishness. How could it not harm itself when it was attacking its own foundations? The harm to the church was a loss of credibility and a perversion of its witness. It succeeded in making the cross a symbol of oppressive might, hatred, and persecution. Its own Holy Week was turned into a week of fear and bloodshed. The church now has to live with these hard facts. For the Jews, however, the harm was not just to the soul. They felt the hurt in the flesh. Jews died at the hands of Christians throughout the length and breadth of Christendom. No mission to the Jews can conceivably be undertaken that forgets this past, unless and until the Jews themselves ask that it be forgotten. As for God, who ever suffers with his people, what must have been his hurt to see his

Gentile church killing his people Israel! It is hard to conceive how his wisdom and purpose in beginning that Gentile enterprise could have been called into question more fundamentally.

Adding insult to injury, the church made an anti-Jewish symbol out of the sign around which Jewish hope is gathered, the Messiah. With a hardhearted, unspeakable lack of sensitivity to Israel's hopes of redemption for an unredeemed world, the church presumed to tell Jews that Israel's Messiah had already come. It did this while it was giving Jews the most convincing evidence imaginable that what it said could not possibly be true. This too is part of the setting for rethinking the mission of the church to the Jewish people.

The church would be misunderstanding the meaning of *teshuvah, metanoia*, repentance or turning back, if it thought it should begin by saying to the Jews that it is sorry for this past. Turning back is an act of the whole person. In this matter, turning back would mean a return of the church to the cooperative relationship with Israel for which it was called into being. If the church is indeed sorry for its past, it will begin by acting toward Jews in a new way which reflects and is consistent with its theological dependence on the Israel of God: it will take up the role of the servant of the servants of God. When it has given evidence which is credible to Jewish eyes that it is really on the way to reform, only then will its words of repentance begin to be credible in Jewish ears, and until it can speak credible words to Israel, there is no point in its even contemplating asking forgiveness of the God of Israel.

iii. The necessity of a special mission

The church's relationship to the Jewish people is fundamental. The church exists both as an extension of the work which God had begun with his people, and as a confirmation of that work. It is living proof of the fruitfulness of the covenant and therefore of the election of the Jewish people. There would be no church were not the covenant between Israel and God alive and effective in the world. With no other people or group in the world does the church have such a relationship. It follows from this that the mission of the church to the Jewish people will be unlike any mission which it owes to any other people. The church must have a mission to the Jews, as it has a mission to all people, but its mission to the Jews can only be special. It will be *sui generis*, as its relationship to Israel is *sui generis*.

Every mission of the church is a form of service, because it is sent in the name of and on behalf of him who came to serve (Mk. 10:45; Phil. 2:5-7). The church owes to every nation the gift it has received from Israel by the Spirit of God: the knowledge and service of God. The church has been and is ever anew being called to join its voice and heart and hands to those of Israel in the praise of the God of Abraham, Isaac, and Jacob and the practice of his righteousness. Its calling is to go to the nations and offer this same opportunity to praise and serve God. It has no other reason to exist. It lives in this service which it owes to the nations of God's creation.

It is immediately clear, however, that the church could not possibly owe this same service to Israel, for Israel was already engaged in this service of God before the church began. It was from Israel that the church learned of it, and it took up this service from the beginning alongside of and as an extention of what Israel was already doing. Its service to the nations is itself a confirmation of the service already undertaken and still being exercised by the Jewish people. As the church is indebted to Israel in a unique way, so its service to Israel can only be unique.

Certainly the individual Christian owes to the individual Jew everything that he or she owes to every other human being. This debt includes peace, love, justice, and mercy. The Jew is also one of God's creatures made in the image of God. It should go without saying that the Christian owes to the Jew all that is owed to fellow human creatures by one who has been called into life out of death by the Creator. More explicitly, the Christian owes to the Jews everything that could be owed to the brothers and sisters of the Jew Jesus. Jesus made it clear that the judgment of God hangs on whether his disciples visit and relieve the hardships of the least of his brother and sister Jews (Matt. 25:40–46).

Beyond this, however, there is the special service which the church — and the individual Christian as a member of the church — owes to the Jewish people, and to the individual Jew as a member of that people. It is the special mission of the church to the Jewish people. We may define it as the duty to serve Israel as Israel. This definition appears to be pleonastic, but its elaboration will show that it is only apparently so.

iv. The service of Israel as Israel

Israel might be served by the church, or by anyone else, as a group of individual human beings, with all the needs of any other group of human beings for material and psychological support. The Jewish people might be served by the church, or by anyone else, as the bearers of one of the world's major living religious traditions, needing perhaps the protection of its right to practice its own religion. These would not be negligible services, and the church might well perform them, as others might too. They would not yet be, however, the service that the church owes to Israel, which is to serve it *as Israel*.

What makes Israel to be Israel is the covenant — and therefore ultimately its election — and nothing else. What makes Israel special for the church is that election, and nothing else. The election of Israel is the foundation on which the church's election stands, and consequently the mission of Israel defines the proper mission of the church to Israel. To serve Israel as Israel will therefore mean to serve it as God's elect witness in the world. This service can only consist of helping Israel to be what it is in the covenant by God's election and so to help it perform its mission. It will consist in helping Israel to be Israel, to be itself as it is defined by its election.

At first sight this seems an impossible task for the church, for surely Israel itself, and only Israel, can be itself as the people of God. That is precisely what the covenant is about and for just this end Israel was given the Torah, written and oral. True as this is, however, there is more to be said. Israel lives its election in the context of the unredeemed world. That context is often far from supportive of Israel, as we discussed under the headings of its conflict with the nations and its inner conflicts. The Jewish people, in their land and in the Diaspora, can always use the help of friends, if they are friends of Israel as Israel. The friendship of the Enlightenment was a false friendship. The mission of the church to the Jewish people is to offer true friendship, one that derives from and is premised on an acknowledgment of Israel's election.

Since the mission of the church to serve Israel as Israel is grounded in the election of Israel and the church's derivative election, its foundation may also be expressed Christologically, as when the apostle to the Gentiles said, "Christ became a servant to the Jewish people" (literally, "the circumcised") (Rom. 15:8). We have touched on this service in noting the apostolic witness to the mission of Jesus to seek out the lost sheep of the house of Israel and bring them home to the faithful service of their God. His servanthood having been devoted to helping Israel be true to its calling, the church of Christ can have no other task. In serving Israel as Israel, therefore, the church centers itself in the heart of its very identity in Jesus Christ. It takes up his service and lives its election in Christ as the fruit of "God's faithfulness, therein confirming the promises given to the fathers, and, as Gentiles, glorifying God for his mercy" (cf. Rom. 15:8–9). This may not be all that the church is called to do, but if this were missing, all of its mission would be lacking its center. A Christian theology of the people Israel has therefore the duty to define at least the outlines of this service.

3. THE CHURCH AS THE SERVANT OF ISRAEL

i. *The external service*

Jews are different. They are called by God to be different. Indeed, as we have heard, the Rabbis taught that God gave his people his oral in addition to his written Torah in order to underscore their difference from all other peoples. The result is that the Jews never totally fit into their environment. This has almost always given rise to more or less resentment on the part of non-Jews, Gentiles. Israel's self-understanding raises questions, sometimes uncomfortable questions, about the self-understandings of other peoples, and this contributes to the phenomenon of Gentile anti-Jewism. It has always been so and there seems to be no reason that it will not continue.

The Jews therefore need protection, for Israel is a small nation. It is sometimes said that antisemitism helps Jews to remain Jews and to stand by each other. Be that as it may, antisemitism, which is in fact anti-Jewism, has also led to the death of many Jews. In this century it has cost them a third of their people. Jews therefore need protection from anti-Jewish Gentiles. It is for just this reason that Jews have founded and maintained the Anti-Defamation League of B'nai B'rith, usually known simply as the ADL.

The existence of the ADL is a scandal and should be a cause for shame to the church, for it exists because the church has failed to undertake its own mission of being the Anti-Defamation League of the Jewish people. This is the first and minimal external service that the church owes Israel. When one reflects on the special relationship existing between the Gentile church and the Jewish people, this service should be obvious, for the church has been called in such a way as to make it ideally suited for it, and all the more so at the present time when Christians exist in such large numbers in every land of the Diaspora.

The church is suited to be the Jewish people's defenders against slanderers and slayers because it knows what makes Israel to be Israel. It knows of God's election of this people. It knows God's promises to this people and it knows why the Jews are so important to the future of creation, not least to its own future. It therefore understands — or certainly ought to understand, if its theology of the people Israel is in order — why Israel is different and how important it is for the world that Israel maintain its difference. The church is suited to be Israel's ADL because it knows of Israel's election, having been called into existence by the God of Israel.

The church is further suited to be the defender of the Jews from Gentile hostility because it is itself Gentile. It knows Gentile perversity firsthand, as that from which it was called into life by the God of Israel. It knows all too well the nature of Gentile anti-Jewism: it has led the world in this evil enterprise for too many centuries—before being jerked to its senses by God through the events of Jewish history in this century—to plead ignorance! Who is better placed to anticipate the next form of Gentile anti-Jewism than the Gentile church?

The church is therefore perfectly suited to be the Jewish people's ADL. It lacks one essential element: experience. While the church has wandered in confusion, the Jewish people have set up their own ADL and its record of achievement—and not only in defense of Jews, but also of other minorities—is impressive. Before the church can take up this service, therefore, it had best go to school and learn from Jewish experience what has been done and what needs to be done. Israel needs more than a servant of good intentions. It needs a well-trained servant. With the appropriate training, however, the church would be well suited by its election as Gentile servants of the God of Israel to be a mediator and a pleader for Israel's cause and reality in the world.

Part of the service as the ADL of the Jewish people to which the church is called is to help protect the Jewish state. The service owed here is surely not that of a propaganda arm of the Israeli government. It is surely not to argue on behalf of the state of Israel, right or wrong. It is to defend Israel *as Israel*, as part of the vanguard of creation's redemption. Service to the state of Israel is therefore part of the church's service to creation, and in this service the church owes to God the Creator that *facts* be taken seriously. A large part of Israel's relations with the nations of the world is twisted because the facts are not known or are distorted. The church is called to fight the defamation of the Jewish state that is based on distortion of the facts.

One of many examples that could be cited has to do with the Palestinian refugees. The church owes to Israel a clear presentation of the facts of this problem, how it arose and why it has continued. The church should first learn and expose the facts of its origin (not excluding the fight for the village of Deir Yassim, just west of Jerusalem, in which, according to one eyewitness report some 30–35 Arabs were killed; Israel's "friendly" neighbors referred to this at the time as "the massacre of Deir Yassim," using it to spread panic among Palestinian Arabs). Further, it should set these facts within the context of a war launched by all of Israel's neighbors aimed at destroying the new state, and the call of Arab leaders for Palestinian flight, when the new government was pleading with them to stay and help build the new country. The Jewish state may be far from living up to Jewish standards of justice, but its detractors have not been noticeably concerned to set the facts in order. That service is one which the church owes the Jewish people. Indeed, the church as the ADL of the Jewish state should also hold up to the attention of the nations the high standard of justice (which the world first learned from Israel) with which they judge Israel, and it would point out to them how little their own behavior conforms to that standard.

There is a wide area of external service for the church to perform for the people Israel. To this end, every parish and congregation should be raising money and contributing to setting up offices and staffing them, in order to relieve the Jewish people of this task that belongs so properly to the mission of the church. That this is not happening, except at the most modest level and in few places, is a sure sign of the church's confusion about what it is, where it came from and, above all, whose it is. Were the church to engage in its proper service to Israel, it would of course learn that all is not well with the household of Jacob. The fact that it has yet to begin this service, which is its due, reveals how much more is not well with the household of Jesus Christ.

ii. *The internal service*

We come now to a more delicate and subtle side of the church's task to serve Israel as Israel. The external service is designed to allow Israel to *be*, for if it cannot live, it can of course not live as Israel. Indeed, if it must live in fear for its physical existence, that can hardly be expected to leave the Jewish soul and spirit untouched. Here, however, we must consider a more agonizing hindrance to Israel's existence and mission as the Israel of God: Jewish neglect and even denial of its election.

This development, which has become so much more acute since the Enlightenment, would seem at first sight to be a purely Jewish problem, one that can only be dealt with by Jews. What possible service can the church render to the household of Jacob in this matter? Yet the relationship between the church and the Jewish people is more complex than that quick response suggests, for the church has contributed immeasurably to the universalizing, generalizing, and spiritualizing tendency that marked the Enlightenment and which has taken its toll of the Jewish people, as well as of the church. The Enlightenment, it should be remembered, did not happen in a vacuum. It was a development deeply rooted in the culture of the Christendom in which most Jews perforce lived. The church contributed to its universalizing tendency by having scoffed for centuries at the concept of a chosen people and at Jewish particularism. It created an immeasurably large part of the climate that made and makes Hasidic Jews, for example, appear to be total anachronisms. As if the structure of the church, its creeds, and its liturgy were not anachronisms! If they be regarded by thoughtful Christians as blessed anachronisms, why not also the Jews, and the Jews first of all?

If the church has contributed so largely to the making of the so-called "secular" climate that has made it difficult for Jews today to take their election seriously, then it is clearly an important part of the church's mission to the Jews to do all it can to change course so as to help Jews be Jews. Also at this most basic level it has a mission to serve Israel as Israel. This service can be illustrated by considering several specific matters, namely the church's policy with respect to intermarriage between Christians and Jews, and its policy with respect to Jews who become Christians.

Intermarriage with Christians has become a matter of deep concern to the Jewish people, for the obvious reason that most Jews who marry Christians lose their ties with the Jewish people. They become Christians, or in any case they become nonobservant Jews. Moreover, their children are in most cases not brought up as Jews, for they are not brought up in a Jewish family. Jews of course have to realize that all is not well with the household of Jesus Christ and that many so-called Christians have but the most tenacious grasp on an inherited Christianity. The unbelieving baptized are as lost to the church, in effect, as the nonobservant Jews in such a marriage are lost to Israel. Were they both to become either serious Christians or serious Jews, the cause of the God of Israel would be furthered. The only cases in which church policy is relevant are those of marriages between concerned Christians and Jews, whether observant or not.

There is a service of the church that opens at this point. The church can begin to encourage its members who wish to marry Jews to think carefully about what they are doing. There is more than one option, and none is without difficulties. One course would be for the Jewish partner to be baptized, or for the Christian partner to convert formally to Judaism. That would settle how their children were to be raised, but the decision would be a painful one, especially for a Jew seeking baptism, for this clearly runs head-on into the past unhappy relations between the church and the Jewish people. However joyful Christian connotations of baptism may be, for a Jew it cannot but mark a radical break with one's people. On the other hand, for a Christian, the act of conversion would seem to cast doubt on the decisiveness of God's act in Jesus Christ to call Gentiles *as Gentiles* into his service in the church. Either way, this first and obvious option has difficulties.

Another and perhaps better course would be for Christians considering such a marriage to take seriously their own calling as Gentiles in the service of the God of Israel and try to strengthen their partner in living the covenant of the people of God. In this time of new beginnings in the relationship between the church and the Jewish people, such families could help to explore the frontiers of that relationship. Here the difficult decision would concern the upbringing of children. A decision to leave it to the child to decide later is no decision, and it is not, in my judgment, a service to the child. If the wife (or wife-to-be) is Jewish, the case for bringing up the child as a Jew would be supported by the fact that it is already a Jew by the Halakhah. Whether the decision is to raise children as Christians or as Jews, it should be thought through with care and carried out consistently. In working out this difficult matter, the church should at least bring to the attention of its members the consideration that the relative numbers of the church and the Jewish people mean that a "loss" to the church is as nothing when compared to the gain for Israel, and if Israel truly gains, the church cannot lose.

A related matter in which the policy of the church requires reconsideration in the light of the service it owes to Israel, is its attitude concerning Jews who seriously "convert" to Christianity. They would not be the first Jews who heard the word of the God of Israel, perhaps for the first time, or perhaps more powerfully than they had heard him before, in Jesus Christ. But that does not mean that they have no part in the covenant of their people with God. They remain Jews, however irregular their status with their people will be because of past church policy. That status could change, however, if the church were to do all in its power to encourage its Jewish members to remain faithful to Torah, and thus to be among Gentile Christians a living sign of the people on whose election that of the Gentile church depends. Clearly we move into uncharted waters in this matter, but they are uncharted because the church has not taken up its internal service to Israel as Israel.

The case of the Jew who finds it more possible to worship the

God of Israel with the congregation of Jesus Christ than with the congregation of Israel needs attention too, for there are such cases. The church cannot close the door on such Jews, but it cannot make baptism the necessary key to opening the door, for the reason that the church has made of baptism an unambiguous sign for Jews of their departure from their people and a renunciation of the covenant. A church in the service of Israel will share all it has, not excluding the Eucharist, to such Jews *as Jews*, and seek God's forgiveness for having so misused the sacrament of baptism that it has seemed to require such a departure and renunciation on the part of the Jew who desires to worship God in the company of the Gentile church. We shall have to return to this issue in a Christological context in the third volume.

These examples are intended only to stimulate reflection on ways in which the church could begin to give concrete evidence that it takes Israel's election seriously. If it were to undertake such a service, it could possibly help some Jews to take their own election more seriously. That would be the finest fruit of the church's mission to the Jewish people. It could reach especially the lost sheep of the house of Israel, and these are the Jews for whom the church cannot but have a special responsibility. If the church were to make a continuing effort to encourage those lost sheep to return to their own home within the household of Israel, it would be doing the most it could to remind Jews of and recall them to their own mission. Whether effective or not, the church would at least have entered finally into its elected role as the servant of Israel.

iii. *The demeanor of the servant*

A faithful servant will know what is on the mind of the master or mistress and will share that concern. A church faithful to its calling will learn to be sensitive to Jewish concerns and worries, and it will do this not as a superior who knows better, but as a servant. The church's service to Israel can only properly be undertaken as the church finds itself able to accept the role of the servant that God in Christ has determined for it. If Mary may be said to personify the role of her people as the handmaid of the LORD, God's "lady in waiting," the church is called to be the chambermaid in the service of the servant of God. It is in fact a high calling and a singular blessing conferred on no one else. It is the special privilege that God has conferred on the church.

As there is an external as well as an internal service that the church owes to Israel, so there is an appropriate demeanor for the servant as it goes about one or the other task. This is not just a matter of appearance: the church can hardly count as ir-relevant "the *form* of a servant," seeing that it is being con-formed by God to the one who binds it to Israel. But the demeanor of the servant will differ as the nature of its service differs. We shall consider these in order.

In its external service to Israel, the church serves what anyone can see: the Jewish people. Its service will therefore be out in the open and visible to all. It will concern itself with the facts and will undertake its task of being the anti-defamation agent of the Jewish people by being knowledgeable, informed, careful about the evidence. Armed with this knowledge, it will be vociferous, speaking up against every distortion of the truth and every slander of the people of God. Finally, it will be concerned with results, with actually removing external pressures on the Jewish people, especially the sort that put Jews on the defen-sive, for these are hardly the best of conditions in which Israel can find and be itself. Thus the church may try to make it more possible for Israel to be Israel.

For the church's internal service to Israel, a quite different demeanor is required. Here it serves what no one can see about the Jews, their election, and it is appropriate that this service be carried out, if not in secret, at least quietly. Here its service depends less on knowing the facts than on listening attentively to the witness of the Jewish people, past and present. In this work it will not be so outspoken, but it will be no less fervent. Only here the fervor will find its outlet in prayer to God for the health of his people. Its intention will be less centered on results and more on developing a supportive compassion.

4. THE CHURCH'S WITNESS TO JESUS CHRIST IN SERVING ISRAEL

i. Jesus and Israel

We return in this different context to a matter we have already had to consider, the relationship between Jesus and his people. Here we must do so in order to show that there is not only no conflict between the church's service to Israel and its witness to Jesus Christ, but that that service is one of the most fundamental forms of its witness to him. We reverse the order of the terms, however, putting "Jesus" first, in contrast to the order of the title of Chapter Eight, because we have to show here how the church, with its primary focus on Jesus Christ, does not shift that focus by serving Israel, the Jewish people. Building on our earlier reflections, we may be concise here.

The commission and task of the Gentile disciples of him who was sent to the lost sheep of the house of Israel is to follow him and to continue his work. The church in the past, lacking an adequate theology of the people Israel, has turned immediately to Christ's work among the Gentiles, ignoring that this was not his own priority. Of course the church is to go to the Gentiles, as it has been commanded, but its first obligation is to follow Christ, and his first work was for his own people, and especially for their lost sheep. Indeed, according to the Matthean testimony (10:6), Jesus' first commission to his disciples was to go themselves only to those lost sheep. The church is therefore re-presenting Jesus in his primary work when it exerts itself to draw the lost sheep of the house of Israel back into their own home to serve the God of Israel in their covenant with him.

To bear witness to Jesus is to point to him as he was and is. To bear witness to Jesus is to present him as he was and is, both as the Word of God incarnate, and as God's Word so incarnate. The term "incarnate," however, directs us into history, Jesus' history, the creaturely circumstances of his birth, life, and death. Those circumstances included much that is shared by all human beings, but their fundamental feature was the context of Israel. If Jesus is comprehensible at all, it is as a Jew, nourished on Israel's Scriptures, brought up in and faithful to God's Torah, devoted to the covenant of his people with God and therefore understanding himself as one sent to serve his people's faithfulness to God. In seeking to draw Jews to Jesus in a manner that took them away from fidelity to Torah, the church has denied Jesus. In order to witness to him as the way in which God chose his Word to be incarnate for the Gentiles, Gentiles have no alternative but to serve Israel as Israel.

A word of warning is needed here, coming as it does directly from the apostolic testimony to the teaching of Jesus himself. The church that would truly serve Jesus as his disciples will serve Israel for its own sake and God's, without a thought of any indirect service to Christ. The ones on the right hand in the parable of the Judgment (Matt. 25:34–40) served Christ's Jewish brothers and sisters with no thought of doing anything else. They are the ones whom Jesus pronounced blessed of his Father.

ii. Israel, Jesus, and the Gentile church

In the church's self-understanding, Jesus is the one who in fact binds it to the people Israel, their covenant and so their God. He is the one who links its life to that of the Jewish people. As his service to Israel was a demonstration of "the truthfulness (or trustworthiness) of God by confirming the promises to the fathers" (Rom. 15:8) which included also bringing the Gentiles to "glorify God" (v. 9), so the church, by serving Israel in its Master's footsteps, demonstrates the efficacy of Christ. As the church serves the Jewish people, it shows that it really has been brought close to the covenant by Christ. It therefore becomes itself a living testimony to the trustworthiness of the God of Israel in fulfilling in Christ his promise that Abraham would become the father of many Gentiles.

The church's service to Israel also constitutes its highest praise of Christ. It demonstrates that Jesus did indeed become a light for the Gentiles, for there they are in the name of the God of Israel, serving his people for his sake. At the same time, with their service they also demonstrate the other half of the prophecy of Simeon (Lk. 2:32), that Jesus would bring glory to (or would be the glory of) God's people Israel. There is, consequently, no way in which the church can make a fuller and deeper witness to Jesus Christ than by serving Israel as Israel.

It would be nice if we could find support for this conclusion not only in the affirmations of Paul (Rom. 15:8, 9) and Luke (2:32), but also from the author of the so-called letter to the Ephesians, whoever he may have been. That writer saw in Christ the effective act of God's peace, who had "broken down the dividing wall of hostility" between Israel and the Gentiles, so that both might "have access in one Spirit to the Father," with the Gentiles now becoming "fellow citizens with the saints and members of the household of God" (Eph. 2:14, 18, 19). He saw this, however, only within the confines of the Christian community. He gives no sign of having seen that the reconciliation between Jew and Gentile which he saw there had any bearing on the relations of that community to the people of God. (On this see Osten-Sacken, *Grundzüge*, 100ff, and especially 102.)

When the church serves Israel as Israel, then it becomes a living witness to the efficacy of Christ as God's great act of reconciliation, whereby the hostility between Jews and Gentiles is overcome. The author of Ephesians apparently thought he saw evidence of that in his own time, but he was looking only within the church. Whatever reconcilation was taking place there, however, had no correspondence with what was happening outside. That church of "reconciliation" was itself becoming increasingly hostile to the Jewish people. The text of Ephesians must therefore stand as a sad reminder that the witness made by reconciliation among Christians within the church is a poor substitute for its living witness to God's act in Christ for the reconciliation between his church and his people Israel.

iii. God the Father of Israel, Jesus, and the Gentile church

In serving the Jewish people, the church bears witness to the God and Father of Israel. If the church were to take up its calling to serve Israel both externally and internally, becoming known as the defender of the Jewish people and concerned for the health of the house of Jacob, even the secular observer would have to ponder this. One "religion" serving another? One religious organization looking out for the interests of another, rather than concerning itself primarily with its own preservation? That in itself would make the church's service to Israel noticeable. Beyond this, however, it would make far clearer than is now the case that when the church speaks of God, it speaks not of its own personal "religious preference," but of the God and Father of Israel, the God of Abraham, Isaac, and Jacob.

The apostolic witness was surely to the God and Father of Israel, but the church has heard and repeated this in such a way as to make it possible for some within it to think that it witnessed to another in its worship of the God and Father of Jesus Christ. Jesus, however, knew and served no other God than that of Israel. The one he called Father was he whom Israel called and still calls Father. We may conclude that the church's talk will not by itself overcome this misunderstanding. No amount of theological purification will lay the ghost of Marcion, which haunts all that the church says, until the church turns around and takes on the role of a servant in the cause of Israel's well-being.

Once that role is filled and that task assumed, it will start to become clear to the church and then to other Gentiles, yes and even to the Jews themselves (who have had such compelling reasons to doubt it), that it is indeed the beloved and elect church of that same God. For the sake of its witness to the unity of God, the church owes its service to Israel. In the role of the servant of the Jewish people, the church can bear a more nearly unambiguous witness to the oneness of the God and Father of Israel, Jesus, and the Gentile church.

5. CHRIST—SERVANT OF THE JEWISH PEOPLE

i. Romans 15:8–9

"For I tell you that Christ became a servant to the Jewish people [literally, the circumcised] to show God's truthfulness, in order to confirm the promises given to the fathers, and in order that the Gentiles might glorify God for his mercy" (Rom. 15:8, 9). We have discussed the apostolic witness to the service that Jesus performed, or sought to perform, for his people, in gathering its lost sheep back into the house of Israel. But as Christ lives, so his service continues. We are therefore confronted with further questions about this service. We have to ask not only what Jesus has done for his people; we should also ask what he is doing now, and what he may yet do, as a servant of the Jewish people.

Before beginning, however, it would be well to dwell for a moment on this assertion of Paul; and we note first that the apostle to the Gentiles stressed that this was an assertion. He wanted his Gentile readers in Rome to see in Christ himself how they were to conduct themselves with respect to the Jewish people. The context of these verses is an exhortation to "welcome one another," the grounds for which is the assertion that Christ has welcomed you. Indeed, the passage continues, coming to the verses under review, Christ became a servant of Israel in order that you (the Gentiles) might be welcomed. That means, welcomed into the realm of the knowledge of God and God's mercy where Israel is to be found. How could the Gentiles have been welcomed into this realm were not Christ of and for Israel? Only as Israel can Jesus be God's way of inviting the Gentiles into the promises and mercy of the God of Israel.

A few more details of these verses warrant attention. "Christ was made a servant of the Jewish people." Paul used the word "Christ" as a proper name, as usual (interchangeable with "Jesus" or combined with it as "Jesus Christ"). He was concerned that his Gentile converts confess Jesus as Lord. There is no trace of his wanting them to confess Jesus "as the Christ." Such a concern could only be based on that "other gospel" that Paul thought was no gospel at all. Christ was made, became, appeared in history, happened as a servant; the verb encompasses the totality of his existence. The word for servant is *diakonos*, which occurs nowhere in the Septuagint, from which Paul usually quotes Scripture. The Septuagint translated the Hebrew word for servant, *ebed*, with the Greek word *doulos*, and Paul followed suit. A *diakonos* was one who served at table, but it had a broader usage as well. It is not clear that the choice of this terms has special significance. Paul used the term "the circumcised" frequently for the Jewish people, especially when contrasting them with the Gentiles.

(*Th. W. z. N.T.*, II, 88, in the entry on *diakonos*, remarks on this verse, that it "of course only [!] means, that (Christ's) work was applicable first of all to the people Israel." The author of that remark evidently had in mind the "work," which applied to the Gentiles, of bringing them out of darkness into light, utterly ignoring the Gospels' witness to the work of Jesus specifically for his people, so different from what he has accomplished for his Gentile followers. When Paul is read as if he were a Gentile, the priority of Israel, so characteristic for a Jew, and the difference between Jew and Gentile, always seem to evaporate).

Christ's being the servant to his people "shows," or was on behalf of, "the truthfulness of God, in order to confirm," or thereby confirming, "the promises to the fathers." This repeats the theme of 2 Cor. 1:20, that what happened in Christ was a confirmation of the promises, especially the promise to the father of fathers, Abraham, that he would be the father of many Gentiles, which Paul had developed earlier in Romans (3:21ff, and Chapter 4). "Confirm" is better than "fulfill." The verb means to ratify, validate, strengthen, not at all to displace or bring to an end.

Paul's assertion was that it could come about that the Gentiles could be welcomed into the relationship with God that Israel enjoys, because Christ became a servant of Israel. Christ could welcome them, that is to say, because he could represent Israel to the Gentiles, and he could do this because he so faithfully served his people as to make their cause his own. Christ's service to Israel is therefore the foundation of the Gentile church.

It follows from this, however, that the Gentile church can continue to exist because Christ continues to be a servant of his people. Paul's assertion therefore leads us to ask about the continuing service of Christ to the Jewish people, a question to which a Christian theology of the people Israel must address itself.

ii. Promised redeemer?

In support of his assertion, Paul quoted (15:12) a verse from Isaiah (11:10, following exactly the Septuagint, itself a rather loose, not to say inaccurate, translation of the Hebrew), selected out of a long and beautiful passage of hope for the coming Davidic successor, whose reign would be one of righteousness in a totally renewed creation. Nothing that the author of this passage had hoped for had come to pass, except the one thing mentioned in the verse Paul cited: one had risen to rule the Gentiles and to be their hope. That had happened, but nothing else. Is that why Paul cited only this verse from the longer passage? It is noteworthy that Paul consistently kept all talk of Christ as redeemer in the future tense. He was a good enough Jew to know what sort of world he lived in. Would that the church had followed his example! Instead, the church tended to read Paul as if he had quoted the whole passage from Isaiah, and as if he could simply have called Christ the promised redeemer, with no qualification. In fact, Paul was more reserved than that.

What sort of service was it that Christ gave to Israel in becoming the means whereby many Gentiles came to the knowledge and service of the God of Israel? The answer to that question could only be given by the Jewish people. The question for them would run, in effect: Is it any comfort to you that because of you, others have been comforted? Is it any consolation to you that one part of your reason for existence has begun to be a fact in the world, a fact which has changed reality for the better for millions of human beings? Paul's answer, at a very early stage of this development, was yes. Not many of his fellow Jews agreed with him at the time. The question, however, is still open.

iii. *What Jesus Christ has not done for his people*

The question about Christ's service to his people is open only to the extent that it is moved out of the past and into the present. The question is more liable to be raised by Christians in the past tense: What has Jesus done for his people? If this is to remain a question about the past, the answer has to be largely negative, precisely in order to force the church to raise the question anew about the present and the future. Putting it in the past tense is an understandable if misguided tendency of Christians. It is understandable because they are Gentiles and for them the great event is indeed behind them: they have been brought from pagan darkness into the light of the God of Israel. This has already happened, and so great a change is this for the situation of Gentiles that they understandably wax eloquent on what Christ has already done for them. But the question is also misguided, for it asks not about Gentiles but about Israel, the Jewish people, who were walking in the light of the Torah of the God of Israel before ever the church was born, and who have walked by that light ever since. Important as is the work that God has accomplished for the Gentiles in Christ, it is a witness of Israel to which the church should attend that God's greater work of redemption, not only for Israel and the church but for his whole creation, is still outstanding.

Israel has therefore to remind the church of what Christ has not accomplished for his people. He has not redeemed Israel. He has not brought his people into that renewed creation of which Isaiah sang. He has by no means brought with him the age which Israel has awaited in messianic hope. He cannot therefore be Israel's Messiah. And perhaps a Christian theology of the people Israel should add that he did not in his lifetime, and he has not since his resurrection, called his people Israel away from their life of fidelity to Torah, as their covenanted service to God, in order to enter the Gentile church. They are and remain, after all, his own people, the Jewish people, the people Israel.

iv. What Jesus Christ may now be doing for his people

In his brief career in Galilee and in and around Jerusalem, Jesus labored to the end that Israel be more truly Israel. In his far longer career as Lord of his church, he may now have just begun to succeed, after centuries of failure, to set his Gentile church into the path of service that he began. Gentiles cut his own service short; it would be fitting that Gentiles be used by him to start it up again.

The hesitant, groping steps that the church has been taking over the past couple of decades may be the harbingers — more than that they cannot be — that Christ may be drawing his church to turn around. He cannot make it turn around; it will have to turn itself around, for there is no passive for *teshuvah*. But he can draw it, coax it, long for it to turn around and begin helping his people be what God has called them to be. It may therefore come to pass in the mercy of God that his people Israel, and the Gentile church with its international and multinational composition, may become mutually supportive partners. They would thus become fitting partners with God for the renewal of creation.

With God all things are possible, Jesus is reported to have said (Mk. 10:27). If that is true, then with God nothing is necessary. Therefore no more can be said than that Christ *may* be beginning to move his Gentile church into the service of his people. This may be what Christ is doing now for his people. It remains to be seen.

It is fitting, having begun this volume with a criticism of Karl Barth's definition of theology, that we come at the end to recall some words of his which still need to be heard, addressed in 1966 to the members of the Vatican's Secretariat for Christain Unity: "There exist today many good relations between the Roman Catholic Church and many Protestant Churches, between the Secretariat for Christian Unity and the World Council of Churches; the number of ecumenical study groups and working groups is growing rapidly. The ecumenical movement is clearly driven by the Spirit of the Lord. But we should not forget that there is finally only one genuinely great ecumenical question: our relations with the Jewish people." (*Freiburger Rundbriefe*, 27, 1976, cited in *Handreichung*, 39, 102, *Evangelische Kirche im Rheinland.*)

v. *What Jesus Christ may yet do for his people*

The question about today has turned into a question about tomorrow. Israel no less than the church is living in a time of crisis, both in the sense of a time of tension and decision, and in the sense of divine judgment. Whither Judaism? Whither the Jewish people? Whither the Jewish body and the Jewish soul? Whither, finally, the Jewish state? These are heavy questions, for they ask about the next chapter in the story that began with the call of Abram. Any who care about that story can only ask these questions in an agony of uncertainty, knowing full well that Israel has no choice but to work out its own next steps in fear and trembling, for God is at work in its life for the sake of his creation.

The Gentile church cannot but care about Israel's story, seeing that its own is a dependent part of it, and so it can stand apart from Israel's next steps only at the peril of being cast adrift from its own moorings. Today is a time of crisis for Israel, for never has it faced a less charted future. If it is a time of crisis for Israel, then it is also one for the church. In Israel's need, will it stand and perhaps suffer alone, or will it have the body of the servant of the Jewish people, the body of Christ, to stand with it before the world and before God? The question of what Christ may yet do for his people is one that he turns back to the church.

The question about Christ's service to his people, therefore, raises the fundamental question for the church of how it understands and relates to him. That subject falls outside of, even if it must presuppose, a Christian theology of the people Israel. It will therefore be taken up in the third volume, which will be devoted to an articulation of a Christology for the Jewish-Christian reality.

Glossary

Aggadah   Narrative or interpretive exegesis; generally, everything in the *Talmud* that is not *Halakhah*.

Coram deo   Before or in the presence of God.

En Sof   Term in Jewish mysticism for "the infinite"; the utterly unknowable Godhead.

Galut   Exile; the condition of being in exile.

Gemara   Part of the *Talmud* which elaborates and comments on the *Mishnah*.

Halakhah   "Going," "walking;" rabbinic decisions or judgments concerning conduct or behavior.

Halakhic   Pertaining to *Halakhah*.

Kavvanah   Inner directedness; profound intention

Mishnah   The original codification of the oral Torah, completed by the early third century of the *Common Era*.

Mitzvah   A commandment.

Mitzvot   Plural of *Mitzvah*.

Olam haba   The world that is to come, usually distinguished from and conceived as following the Messianic Age; the future.

Shekhinah   The divine presence.

Shema   "Hear (O Israel, ...);" The quasi-credal recitation of Deuteronomy 6:4 or 6:4–9.

Talmud   The collection of the oral Torah, in either the Palestinian or the fuller Babylonian version, completed by about 500 *C.E.*

Tanakh   An acronym for *Torah, Neviim, Khetuvim* (Torah, Prophets, Writings): the Hebrew Scriptures.

Tannaim   The Rabbis whose teachings and decisions make up the *Mishnah*.

Teshuvah   To return, to turn back (to God).

Tikkun   A kabbalist term for restitution or restoration (of the brokenness of creation).

Tsimtsum   A kabbalist term for divine contraction.

Ubi et quando visum est deo   "Where and when God pleases."

Yetzer ha-ra   The evil inclination (in human beings).

References to the Scriptures

References to the Apostolic Writings

References to Rabbinic Writings

Index to Names